ETERNALLY YOURS

ETERNALLY YOURS

(Alim LiTerufah)
The Collected Letters of Reb Noson of Breslov
Volume 2

translated by
Yaakov Gabel

edited by
Moshe Schorr

Published by
BRESLOV RESEARCH INSTITUTE
Jerusalem/New York

Copyright © Breslov Research Institute 1993
ISBN 0-930213-47-5

First Edition

No part of this publication may be translated,
reproduced, stored in any retrieval system or transmitted,
in any form or by any means,
electronic, mechanical, photocopying, recording or otherwise,
without prior permission in writing from the publishers.

For further information:
Breslov Research Institute
POB 5370
Jerusalem, Israel

or:
Breslov Research Institute
POB 587
Monsey, NY 10952-0587

This book is dedicated
to the memory of

Rabbi Zvi Aryeh Benzion Rosenfeld
ben Reb Yisrael Abba z'l

who devoted his life
to disseminating the teachings of

Rebbe Nachman of Breslov

Meyer and Roxanne Assoulin

Table of Contents

Letters of 5595 (1834-5) 3

Letters of 5596 (1835-6) 163

Letters of 5597 (1836-7) 239

Letters of 5598 (1837-8) 291

Letters of 5599 (1838) 339

Appendix A: Biographical Sketches 347

Appendix B: Rebbe Nachman's Lessons 361

Guide to the Book

Eternally yours is the collected letters of Reb Noson of Breslov (1780-1844). The letters provide a vivid and intimate portrayal of Reb Noson's life. They also give the reader a chance to see for himself how it is possible to truly *live* Rebbe Nachman's teachings.

History: The letters have been arranged chronologically. At the beginning of each year we have presented a short historical review of what was then taking place in Reb Noson's life. This Volume covers the years, 5595-5599 (1834-1838) which are known in Breslov circles as "The Years of Oppression." During this period, the Breslover Chassidim, especially Reb Noson, endured incredible hardships, as will be seen in our text.

Notes: Editor's notes by the compiler, Reb Nachman of Tcherin, and publisher's notes appear at several places within the text. These help to clarify certain incidents mentioned in the letters.

Breslov teachings: Summaries of Rebbe Nachman's lessons and stories referred to by Reb Noson in our text are found in Appendix A.

Biographical Sketches: Numerous individuals are mentioned in the letters in relation to various events in Reb Noson's life. Readers wishing some background on these personalities may consult Appendix B, "Biographical Sketches," which gives brief information about those known to us.

Sources: Woven into Reb Noson's poetic style are numerous quotes from Scripture, Talmud and Rebbe Nachman's teachings. However, referencing all these quotes would have interfered with the flow of the text and so only certain sources, particularly those from Breslov teachings, have been included. In addition, not all of Reb Noson's words could be translated. Honorary titles and the like, although beautiful in the Hebrew original, were deemed too redundant in the English.

Eternally Yours

Letters from 5595 (1834-35)

The year in review

In the years leading up to 1834, the Breslover Chassidim faced steady, ominous antagonism of some of the other chassidic groups in the Ukraine. Principal among the opposition were the Savraner Chassidim, headed by Reb Moshe Zvi of Savran (1779?-1838). The contributing factors to the strife, exacerbated by the slander and jealousies of reckless hotheads, are enumerated in *Through Fire and Water*, Part VI.

Early in 5595 (fall of 1834), the conflict exploded into a full-scale battle. Encouraged by their own false impressions that their battle was "for the sake of Heaven," bands of ignorant chassidim began a progressive campaign of oppression against the Breslover Chassidim which began with a financial boycott and escalated to physical beatings and other cruelties intended to coerce them into renouncing Reb Noson and Breslover Chassidut. The suffering was so intense that some succumbed and left Reb Noson, others were forced to flee their homes and still others were subjected to daily torment and other forms of brutality.

Reb Noson himself was in grave danger and suffered terribly. He became a target of public humiliation and even had stones thrown at him by hostile youths and older men as well. His enemies raged with such evil passion that an attempt was made on his life, with the hired murderers killing another Noson who lived in Breslov. On Shabbat Chanukah, 5595, during *shalosh se'udot* (the Third Meal), he gave a discourse to his followers including guests from out of town, as well as from Breslov. His detractors saw this as a golden opportunity and informed the authorities that he was leading a seditious group. His house was surrounded by the police. Many of his followers were arrested and nearly all his writings were confiscated.

That night Reb Noson, in fear of his life, fled Breslov eastwards to the Tcherin area, where he remained most of the winter. Before Purim he traveled to Uman, staying there until Rosh Chodesh Nisan (April, 1835), when he received notice that it was safe to return home. But even in Uman he was subjected to ridicule and attempts to harm him physically.

Upon his return to Breslov before Pesach, he found that his enemies had "suggested" to the government the requisition of part of his home where they temporarily set up a boot factory for the platoon of soldiers who were in Breslov. After Pesach, seeing that their attempts to be rid of Reb Noson were not succeeding, they hired false witnesses and Reb Noson was denounced as a revolutionary against the government. Reb Noson was placed under arrest, jailed during that summer and subsequently exiled from Breslov to his birth-town of nearby Nemirov (about nine miles from Breslov). That same summer his travel permits were suspended and he was ordered to remain in Nemirov until his case was reviewed by the High Court in Kaminetz.

*

This is a general review of the incidents of the year 5595 (1834-1835). The Hebrew word for strife is *machloket* which is used in our English text. In Breslov writings, the years are referred to as *Yemey HaTlaot*, "The Years of Oppression." At each letter where Reb Noson refers to an incident that took place, we will describe the circumstances with enough detail to understand what was then taking place. For full details, the reader is referred to Reb Noson's biography,

Through Fire and Water, sections VI-VII. Brief outlines of the lives of several of the principal people involved in the strife and mentioned in our text appears in Appendix A, Biographical Sketches.

* * *

The following historical review of this period was written by the compiler of *Alim LiTerufah* and its translation presented here (prior to letter #160 in the text).

Generations to come should know that during this year there was a very great *machloket* (strife). It started between Rosh HaShanah and Yom Kippur and continued throughout the year. It remained in full force throughout 5596 (1835-1836), as will be evident to anyone who reads the following letters, and carried on until 5598 (summer of 1838), when the slanderers, who insidiously shot their arrows at innocent people, met ignominious and unnatural deaths.

Among these slanderers was the respected man-of-standing, Moshe [Chenkes] from the town of Sherevitz, who returned evil for good. In his early years he was childless and extremely poor. But he held vigil at the doors of our master, teacher and Rebbe [Nachman], of sainted memory, hoping to arouse his pity and secure his help. The Rebbe had pity on him and promised him that he would be very wealthy and have children. So it was.

The entire story is too long to relate here. But many years after the passing of our master, teacher and Rebbe [Nachman], of blessed memory, Moshe became filled with resentment and jealousy until he actually turned into an enemy and persecutor. He was the father-in-law of the grandson of Rebbe Nachman, of blessed memory, Reb Avraham Dov, son of Adil, and he forced him, because of the *machloket*, to divorce his daughter. It is a very long tale, but the essence of it is that he repaid evil for good and turned into a pursuer. He persecuted our teacher and rav, Reb Noson, all through the years 5595-5598 (1834-1838). He incited enemies against him, had Reb

Noson imprisoned and afterwards had him exiled to Nemirov from his home in Breslov.

There too he incited enemies against him on several occasions, until before Shavuot, 5598, when our teacher Reb Noson was in Breslov taking council with his friends there about how he could return to his home in Breslov. He had no home of his own in Nemirov and, among many other hardships, he was forced to live there in rented quarters. When Moshe found out that Reb Noson wanted to return home, he stood in the middle of the street and said, "He wants to move back here?! As long as I'm alive, he's not going to live here! All I have to do is to go to the governor!" (That is to say, "I'll inform on him to the authorities.") And so he did. He went straight from the street to visit this official.

When he arrived, the governor was with a Jew who was ordered to wait outside. There he indeed heard [Moshe] talking about Reb Noson to the official. Suddenly [Moshe] fell to the ground unconscious. There was a tremendous outcry and the official ran outside screaming, because he couldn't revive him. They poured whiskey, perfumes and the like on the fallen man, but nothing helped. The official shouted that they should take a cart and transport him to his home. Not finding a cart, they took a large carriage used for carrying refuse and manure from the street and from horses and laid him down in this. The Jew who had previously been with the governor, along with a number of gentiles, brought him to his house. There was a huge commotion. Just half an hour before, they had seen him strong and in good health and now he was dead! But their shouting did nothing. He lay there unable to speak, sweating profusely from his belly, and after about 24 hours he died.

Subsequently, many opponents and enemies regretted what they had done and became friends. They even took pains to bring Reb Noson to his home in Breslov. In 5599 (September, 1838) between Yom

Kippur and Sukkot, Reb Noson left Nemirov and returned to Breslov. With that, the *machloket* died down.

"From our youth many have tormented us, but they have not overcome us. God has not abandoned us to their hands." The fire of the Torah and of the holy fear that he [Reb Noson] worked to instill in us so that we would fear the Master of All will never be extinguished. As the Rebbe himself said, "My fire will burn until the Mashiach!" I have stated all this so that the person who reads the following letters carefully will be able to understand and interpret them correctly (*Alim LiTerufah* #160).

153

With thanks to God, Friday, Erev Shabbat, the Ten Days of Repentance, 5595.

I arrived yesterday evening and found your letter. It uplifted me tremendously, but I am still terribly pained that you have not yet recuperated. [Reb Yitzchak became ill a few weeks before Rosh HaShanah and was still sick nearly three weeks later.] I hope to God that you will soon have relief. "He does not stay at odds forever," but He afflicts and then He heals. For God's sake, fortify yourself! Push yourself to get rid of your downheartedness any way you can! May the Master of Compassion have mercy on you and may He cheer you with His salvation. May you quickly recover your strength and may everything turn into good — and may you be sealed for a good, long and peaceful life. There is a lot going on here right now. It is also time for prayers and the carrier of this letter is in a rush. Please write me on Sunday too, God willing, and also after that, because I wait all day just to hear good news from you. May God have compassion on us and let us hear gladness and joy from you soon.

The words of your father, praying for you.

Noson of Breslov

I gave two gold coins as a redemption for you to our friend and teacher, Reb Yudel, may his light shine.

154

With thanks to God, Erev Yom Kippur, 5595.

My dear, beloved son.

There are tears in my eyes as I write and I think about your anguish at not being able to be with us this past Rosh HaShanah. You can be absolutely sure, though, that this too is really for the best. God's ways are very very exalted and His thoughts are extremely deep. Just now God had the carrier of this letter, my friend Reb Isaac, may his light shine, present himself at my house. This was one of God's wonders too, as he will tell you. Please, my dear son, be sure to write me about how you are right after Yom Kippur. May the Master of Compassion forgive your sins; may He cure your illness and may you recover completely. Our Rabbis said (Nedarim 41a), "A person doesn't recover from illness until all his sins have been forgiven." How much more does this apply to you, who have also gone through Rosh HaShanah and Yom Kippur! Without a doubt, all your sins have been forgiven and you can walk in God's ways from now on! May you fortify yourself in devotion and Torah any way you can, and rejoice and be happy over God's salvation. May you be sealed for a good long life and for peace.

The words of your father, praying for you.

Noson of Breslov

155

I exult in God's salvation that He has helped you this far — as you wrote three times in your last letter. May God continue to be with you and give you a full recovery, physically and spiritually. Begin anew with new determination to walk in the ways of God and to draw nearer to Him through Torah, prayer and good deeds for many long, good years to come. Amen. May it be His will.

> The words of you father, happy over your salvation
> and hoping to hear all good from you always.
>
> *Noson of Breslov*

Greetings to all our companions with a great love, particularly to my friend, Reb Shimon.

156

[On the eve of Simchat Torah, Barukh Dayan and his friends, opponents of Reb Noson, had a drinking party to "celebrate" the festival. Already drunk on their way to synagogue, they passed the Breslover synagogue and began hurling insults at Reb Noson and his followers. Reb Noson urged his followers to remain silent in the face of the insults but several of his chassidim could not contain themselves and they went out to protest. A fist fight developed and the police had to be called to stop the brawl.]

Wednesday night, Bereishit, 5595.

My beloved son.

I received your letter now, in the dark of night, and I was very happy. I cannot write you much right now though, because the messenger came as I was composing Torah [insights] and I really have to write them down immediately. You will also profit from this though, with God's help, when in the coming days you will be able to see them through God's great mercy.

You have already heard about the suffering and abuse we have had the last few days. Still though, His compassion on us is strong and with His amazing power of salvation I was happier these days [of Sukkot] than in past years. Also on the day after the last day of Sukkot, God, in His marvels, arranged that Reb Shmuel Tzoref finished the Torah scroll he was writing and gave me the honor of carrying it into the synagogue. Praise God, we rejoiced that evening both outside the synagogue and within, and we joyfully danced a great deal. This too was by God's hand, because all our rejoicing is through God's salvation and enormous miracles; because rejoicing in God is our strength!

And how you uplifted me, my son, when you wrote that you roused yourself to rise at midnight because of the abuse we received [see *The Sweetest Hour*]. This is the way! This is proper for us, that we should break our hearts as a result of this! But more than this we need to overcome everything and rouse ourselves to be joyful almost the whole day over His great kindness — that we have been saved from being among the *mitnagdim* who oppose such a point of truth. Had God not helped us, God forbid, *we* might also have been with them. Thank God, Who separated us from them and Who has illuminated for us pure truth! So may He be with us that we can fulfill the Rebbe's holy words and

Letter #157

apply his awesome practices and holy advice! For they are the councils of God and they will stand forever.

The words of your father, praying for you and hoping to see you happy.

Noson of Breslov

157

[Reb Noson had some renovations done to his house in the late summer. One addition was an extension for a sukkah.]

With thanks to God, Monday, Rosh Chodesh Cheshvan, 5595, Breslov.

My dear, beloved son.

Blessed is He Who is constantly doing new things! A person who pays attention can see the amazing, new things that the Creator, may His Name be blessed, is doing constantly, every day, "Who in His good is constantly renewing the Creation every day." How many new things originate every day! How many wondrous things are created anew! A few of them we can see. Many are hidden from us or occur in other towns! God alone performs great wonders all the time! And all to reveal His Divinity and His Great Blessed Name to the world's inhabitants and so that His Name should be talked about throughout the world!

My dear son, whom I love heart and soul, what can I tell you about everything that has happened this month according to the miniscule comprehension that our minds can grasp? There was Rosh HaShanah and the Ten Days of Repentance,

Yom Kippur and the four days between Yom Kippur and Sukkot. And there was Sukkot and Hoshana Rabbah, Shemini Atzeret and Simchat Torah and the days following. It was the month of *Eitanim*, of mighty deeds: the month that is mighty and strong with its many mitzvot (Rosh HaShanah 11a). This is for the Holy People Israel as a whole. But what was done with each individual, and particularly with me, is absolutely inconceivable and inexplicable.

Be sure to speak a lot with the deliverer of this letter, Reb Nachman [Tulchiner], may his light shine. [He was with Reb Noson most of the time from Rosh HaShanah until after Sukkot and knew all the details of the escalating conflict.] Perhaps he will tell you, according to what our minds can comprehend, all the kindnesses and wonders that God did with us during these days. It always seemed like just *then* it was impossible to be happy, impossible to utter a single word, especially with the great conflict and uproar of these days which so tried to upset and distract us.

But His lovingkindness toward us is great and God's truth is forever, so that I was able to speak many amazing new Torah ideas that enliven souls forever. I also rejoiced and danced a great deal, with God's help. More than in other years! Joy in God is our fortress! And then today I was able to write down a new prayer, as you will see for yourself, since I am sending it to you with the deliverer of this letter. May your eyes see it, your heart be stirred and your soul rejoice! Look carefully at the wonders of God! It has been many years since I've been worthy of a new prayer and you have a great share it in! Because you had a share in the new sukkah that through His great kindness I sat in this

Sukkot. You'll hear a few amazing things on the subject of a new sukkah from the deliverer of this letter: because a sukkah has to be new and there are authorities that invalidate an old one (*Orach Chaim* 636; Reb Noson's insight referred to is extant, lost when confiscated by the authorities after Shabbat Chanukah; see below, Letter #169). A new sukkah is the concept of a new prayer (cf. *Likutey Moharan* I, 48). Everything began anew *this* year when I merited to have a new sukkah! Thank God Who gave you the privilege of having a share in this, and it was the largest share of all, at that.

Now accept my *mazal tov*! May it be His will that your newborn daughter will be a source of good fortune, blessing, happiness and joy for you! May she become a God-fearing woman from whom good righteous generations will come forth which will magnify His Blessed Name and increase Torah and prayer among the Jewish People. Thus may the new holy practice of making prayers out of Torah lessons spread, and draw all of Israel closer to God. Everything else is vanity, as is written (Proverbs 31:30), "Charm is a lie and beauty is vanity, but a God-fearing woman will be praised." This verse refers to prayer, as is known (*Likutey Moharan* I, 14:8) and the ultimate prayer is one created from a Torah lesson (*Likutey Moharan* II, 25).

There is a lot to be said on this subject, but would that we were able to put this into practice. To relate the story of what has happened during these times up to today is beyond our comprehension, but each person according to what is in his own heart can vaguely see and understand from it the greatness of the Blessed Creator and the greatness of what we are doing. Happy are we! Happy are we! That we are the ones to be called in the name of our holy Rebbe, of sainted memory! I don't have time to write any more. But this letter also is one of God's miracles and acts of kindness.

May God strengthen your heart and bring your soul to joy! May you truly walk in His holy ways and may your feet remain strong! May you be among the people talked about in the verse, "Those who hope in God will renew their strength. They will raise up their wings like eagles. They will run and not tire. They will walk and not weary" (Isaiah 40:31). May your feet run to serve God and may they not tire!

> The words of your father, always waiting for salvation.
>
> *Noson of Breslov*

Greetings to all our comrades with great love to each and every one of them. Everything I wrote here was meant for them too! You should show them this letter along with the new prayer. May God help us to add more new prayers as a group, and everyone of us for himself, until He looks down from Heaven and sees us, and makes us worthy of returning to Him in truth forever.

158

With thanks to God, Wednesday, Noach, 5595, Breslov.

My dear, beloved son.

I received your letter now along with the pen. It is time now for the Afternoon Prayers. You are receiving sealed up here

Letter #159

another two prayers which will certainly arouse your soul. And you need them all. They talk about things which relate to you: about being rescued from fevers, God save us, not eating a lot and about perfecting the mind. The second one talks about giving a lot of charity and about finding worthy poor people to give to in order to have a rectification through this. You need all of this and I know that your thoughts yearn for these *tikkunim*. May God soon allow you to receive them. (The prayers are based on Likutey Moharan I, 263-264 and found in Likutey Tefilot I, 151-152).

Look at the great power of desire! All the prayers which were now born and came forth from God through amazing miracles, only did so because of your good desires and yearnings! There is still hope that all of us will realize everything that we ask for in our prayers, because "God is great and extremely exalted. His Greatness cannot be fathomed" (Psalms 145:3). It is very late in the day and I absolutely cannot go on. May God allow me through the power of these prayers to pray Minchah with concentration.

> The words of your father, waiting to see you in life, health and joy.
>
> *Noson of Breslov*

159

Thursday night, Erev Shabbat, Noach, 5595, Breslov.

My beloved nephew and dear friend, our learned teacher, Reb Yitzchak Isaac, may his light shine.

It is after midnight and God just put the idea into my mind

to write you, so I won't be remiss and I'll write right away. I really don't know what to write you though. My nephew, I'm upset about you. I brought you up, and my intention was to raise you to everlasting greatness and eternal life. From the time you entered my home, this was my only concern. And now, how distant you have grown from me! You distance yourself further each day and who knows what the future will bring [Reb Noson was referring to the suffering and torment that the Breslover Chassidim were enduring. His nephew was seriously affected by this opposition but later returned to Reb Noson.]

In the past week I have sent three new prayers to my son, may he live. Open your eyes! Open your heart! Look at them honestly and sincerely, and you will be able to understand the truth of what we are doing! Who would have thought that I would need to strengthen *your* belief in our holy, awesome and exalted efforts!? But I heard from your own mouth that what really kept you from coming for Rosh HaShanah was a lack of belief. Is it possible that after all you've heard from me and after everything you've seen in his holy books... After you've already roused yourself many times in your youth with many good points, is it possible that you are still undecided, God forbid?

My son and student, think about this now very very carefully. This is no light matter. Your life depends on it! I don't have time to write a lot so this comment will have to do. Strengthen yourself to come here for Shabbat soon! Maybe, just maybe, I will be able to talk from the "point in my heart" and arouse you anew (see *Likutey Moharan* I, 34). But regardless of that, every single minute that you spend here, every single word that you hear from us will be of true eternal benefit to you. For God is with us! To rouse the hearts of the Children of Israel and to direct them on the path which our ancestors have always walked — no-one in the world is doing this now except us, with God's help, with the heritage that was left us by our awesome exalted master, teacher and Rebbe, of sainted memory.

If the "truth is cast to the ground" right now — and it is forbidden to reveal these words to anyone who is not with us, lest he oppose us even more, God forbid — it *is* nonetheless the truth. Because there is only one truth, and words of truth will endure forever.

Pay careful attention to my words and think about them very well. I have done what I had to do by trying to awaken you just now. Do what you think is best. May the Master of Compassion take you on the straight path and may He constantly bring you back to the point of absolute truth, so that all your efforts are not for nothing. Take pity on yourself! Do whatever you have to do in order to hold on to us, so that there will be hope for your future and you will escape with your life.

> The words of your uncle, writing from the heart, and advising you for your eternal good and for that of your children and your children's children for generations to come eternally.
>
> *Noson of Breslov*

I received your pen and started writing with it. While I'm not entirely happy with it, I do need it very much. It even has a share in the writing of this letter, because I began the letter with it. So I fulfilled the verse (Ecclesiastes 10:10), "If the iron is dull and its edge is not sharpened, he will need to exert himself more..." See Rashi's explanation there and understand it well, especially since the quill was made of iron. Take careful notice of how we find every single thing in the Torah and stir ourselves to God through everything in the world!

And greetings to my dear, beloved friend, Reb Shimshon, may his light shine. As I was writing to my nephew, I remembered you, my dear friend. You are closer to me than a brother. My love for you is boundless, just like a son or a brother! So I just couldn't restrain myself now either, from reminding you (Proverbs 6:9), "How long will you lie there, lazy man?! When will you get up and start your life again" —by coming close to us as you once were, or even closer?! All the delights of our holy treasure houses are before you, stashed away in his holy books! It is impossible to imagine all the new insights that we discover every day! Because the Rebbe is a flowing spring that gushes constantly, every minute, every day. Here is the book *Likutey Eitzot* [Advice] for you to look at until [text is missing] which just came out. I also recently sent some new prayers. You've already seen the old ones.

I know that you are strong in your belief, with God's help, and that the truth *is* glowing a little in your mind. So that even if there are still many coverings and veils and several barriers, the truth is that, given even the small glow of truth that shines in your heart, you ought to be skipping over mountains to run to a source of truth such as this! Even if it were (Deuteronomy 30:13), "across the sea," for this it would be fitting for you to cross it! How much more so when it is really not far from you at all!

I have so much to say, but the page is short and there isn't enough time, because the holiness of Shabbat is rapidly approaching. We must always think of the day that is entirely Shabbat (*Kohelet Rabbah* 1:36). This is why I wrote you all this. But I can't spend all my time on you alone. If you want to listen, what I have said here is enough, because I have hewn your ears by pointing this out to you. You do what you think is best. Choose life, so that you and you children will live!

Noson, as above

160

With God's help, Sunday, Lekh Lekha, 5595, Breslov.

My dear, beloved son.

I received your letter now with the three prayers. I won't write a lot now, since you will be here by tomorrow, God willing. Reb Isaac, my nephew, came here for Shabbat. It was really the hand of God that the previous night I prepared a letter for him, as he will tell you. I also included a note for Reb Shimshon. Therefore be sure to get the letter from Reb Isaac and give it to Reb Shimshon to read. Get it back from him though afterwards and return it to Reb Isaac, because I told Reb Isaac to save it.

I just now received a letter from my friend Reb Naftali in Uman. He wanted me to explain fully to him the source of this whole *machloket*. I already wrote him a letter right after Yom Tov, but now he asks me to explain it in detail. I wrote him that it is rooted in the sin of the First Man (Adam), and in our many sins and transgressions. May God have mercy on us and turn everything into good!

Reb Naftali and our comrades also asked to know how you are doing and about your health. I intend to answer them right away, so I don't have time to write you at length right now. May God strengthen your heart for Torah, prayer and good deeds, for many good years to come.

The words of your father, hoping to see you happy.

Noson of Breslov

161

Monday, Chayey Sarah, 5595, Breslov.

Greetings to my beloved son, our teacher, Reb Yitzchak, may his light shine.

I received a letter from you just now, in addition to the one I got on Sunday. What you wrote there about patience really inspired me! Thank God, Who has helped us until now, that the Rebbe's awesome words are beginning to shine in you and to affect you positively! Even if it *is* still only in a very small and limited way, I was nonetheless extremely happy about this first great sprouting of salvation.

Because this is exactly what the Rebbe wanted. His whole wish and goal was that you should live his teachings *in practice* and fulfill them according to their simple meaning. He wanted people to understand what was implied in his words and to constantly glean advice for themselves. Whatever is happening with a person at any time: day or night; when he lies down, or

Letter #161

when he gets up; when he is walking on the way; young, middle-aged or old, from his beginning to his end; in personal matters, in domestic matters, in his behavior toward his wife, his children, those close to him and those distant from him, with his friends and with his enemies, God forbid — there is absolutely nothing about which we cannot find sound advice and direction for ourselves in the Rebbe's words. And this applies whether a person is down, God forbid, or up: on every level and in every place that a person can reach in his life.

Someone who understands this to some extent, fine. One who doesn't understand, or even understands a little — when he reaches a point where he cannot understand, he must always believe beyond a shadow of doubt that whatever is happening with him, and with the entire world, and everything that he hears people talking about, that it is all there within the Rebbe's lessons, stories and holy conversations. Through this belief a person will be able, according to his own mind and his own spiritual level, to find what he needs in the Rebbe's books. His thoughts are very very deep indeed and anyone can encourage himself with them for eternal life, forever and ever! Happy are we who have merited this!

Today's letter also afforded me some pleasure and comfort from the great pain that I have over the *machloket*. For I see that you are taking in a little of what I said to you about how we have to really rouse ourselves, and try to use the *machloket* to actually come closer! What greater mustering of inner strength could there be!!

Be strong, my son, be strong! Encourage and help each

other! Tell each other (Isaiah 41:6), "Man will help his friend and say to his brother 'Be strong'!" Carry out the teaching, "Receive from one another!" Each thing that happens to us at any time, both as a group and as individuals, even down to the smallest detail, is far from insignificant!

Be sure to remember everything we have already gone through, and also what is happening right now, so you will be able to relate them to future generations, "that children yet to be born may know." Because, as it appears, they too are going to experience enormous opposition, and it will give them strength and comfort to hear and to know that we already went through it all many times: how they constantly rose up against us..., God forbid, and how each time God rescued us! For in every generation the story of what happened with us will be told, even when Mashiah comes — let him come quickly in our times!

The whole thing is just unprecedented: that such revealed truth, in the form of original Torah teachings such as these, should be obscured, disgraced and thrown to the ground in this way! But this is precisely the reason for it! Just because it *is* such truth and just because these teachings *are* so totally original, people disgrace and obscure them so much. But the word of our God will endure forever. The truth is its own testimony. He Who has started will finish, as is brought in the Midrash on the verse, "'And bestow kindness on my master, Avraham.' You started something, now finish it!" (*Bereishit Rabbah* 60:2). In other words, he [Eliezer] said to the Blessed Holy One, "Master of the Universe! You started to do miracles for Avraham, now finish what You began!" Fortify your hearts and be strong! Don't be afraid of them, because God is with us! I don't have time to write any more.

The words of your father, who loves you truly and eternally.

Noson of Breslov

Extend loving greetings to all our comrades. They'll understand by themselves that all these words were meant for them too. Not just for you. "But for those who are here with us now and for those who are not!" (*Rabbi Nachman's Wisdom* pp.344-5) Anyone who desires life needs to know everything I just said!

162

With thanks to God, Sunday night, Toldot, 5595, Breslov.

My dear, beloved son.

I received your letter just now. I have some news for you. Thank God, I am preparing to travel to Uman, God willing, on Tuesday, the first day of Rosh Chodesh Kislev, and I just hired the carriage. From the day all this upset began last Yom Tov, I have been longing to go. Now our distinguished friend Reb Naftali, may his light shine, has stirred me to undertake the trip, when he wrote and told me that the [Savraner] Rav there spoke out against us, saying things against the *kloyz* in particular that he really ought not to have said. [Savran was a city about forty-five miles south of Uman. This placed the Savraner Rav in close proximity to a center of Breslover Chassidut, where his influence could be very effective. Therefore,] Reb Naftali very much wants me to come and, though it is a tremendous burden for me to go there right now, I really must. May God have mercy on me and guide us in paths of righteousness for His Name's sake. May He let me walk on the true path in every single movement I make and may we be able to accomplish there the eternal good that we must. May God in His great lovingkindness grant us relief in this world too. Those who hate us will see and be ashamed! I do not have time to go on any more. May God give me a safe trip.

    The words of your father.

Noson of Breslov

Warm greetings to all our comrades!

    Thank God, last Shabbat we danced very much, and I too danced a little, with God's help. I spoke on the lesson "And you will be a kingdom of priests for Me" (Likutey Moharan I, 34), about the three holy points: how a person has to receive from the tzaddik, from his friend and from within himself. In this way he nullifies his disgraced and shattered heart, which is the site of holy love. Happy are the ears that hear words such as these! Happy are we! Happy are we! Happy are we! to have been privileged with every one of these utterances, not to mention every one of these lessons, which ascend to the loftiest heights and reach down to the infinite depths, inspiring and binding our souls and the souls of all Israel to their Root! Who can express the mighty works of God and His enormous miracles and acts of kindness which we have experienced in this destitute generation?! Happy are we!

163

With thanks to God, Sunday night, Vayishlach, 5595, Breslov.

My dear, beloved son.

I received your letter in the study hall between Minchah and Maariv. I read it right away. You really revived my spirits at this time, especially with the letter from Lemberg. God's deeds are great and His thoughts are very deep. We really have no understanding at all. We just have to give thanks for the past, for every single "expansion," every bit of relief, that God in His mercy gives to us in our difficulties. For so great is the darkness and distress on every side — with such a *machloket*, with such humiliation, with our livelihood *so* strained (and most important with our *spiritual* livelihood so strained) — that it is impossible to pray any prayer properly.

Nonetheless God is constantly with us and He alone is performing great wonders! He illumines our minds all the time and constantly shows us the glimmer of the sprouting of salvation. What can I say? What can I say? It is this that enables us to wait constantly for *complete* salvation. For our God has already done so much and "His miracles and thoughts are for us."

Our friend, Reb Nachman from Tulchin, may his light shine, has already told you about my safe arrival home, thank God. You will hear more about this and you will understand God's wonders! I don't have time to write any more now. Be sure to send me iron pens soon and it will count as a great merit for you. My mind is still unsettled from the difficulty of the journey so I'll keep it short and say goodbye.

The words of your father, who is praying for you.

Noson of Breslov

Greetings and great salvation to all our comrades. Fortify your hearts and be strong! There is only one truth and there is no way in the world to destroy it! As it is written (Proverbs 12:19), "Words of truth will always endure" and God's truth is forever!

164

[Compiler's note: This is the letter which our teacher, Reb Noson, himself wrote to the Savraner Rebbe in order to calm the controversy and save his life and the lives of his followers, and to rescue them from the life-threatening attacks to which they were subjected. However, he was not successful. His words didn't penetrate the Savraner's heart because of all the slander and calumny that he had heard. "Were it not for God Who helped us and answered our cries from persecution...." "Blessed is God Who did not give us as prey to their teeth."

Reb Noson's letter enumerates many of the abuses — physical and emotional — heaped upon the Breslover Chassidim, giving the reader a rough idea of the suffering endured.]

With God's help, Wednesday night, Vayishlach, 5595, Breslov.

From afar I call in peace, from the moss on the wall to the towering cedar of Lebanon; the holy, renowned Rav, whose name, may its light shine, is known throughout the Jewish People; the mighty pillar, the great hammer, the holy man of God; holy is said of him, his fittest praise is silence: Rabbi Moshe Zvi, may his light shine.

I know it is not customary for the lowly to give initial greetings to the great. But for the sake of peace, whose enormous value our Rabbis of blessed memory praised so highly relating that God says, "Let My Name be erased in the water [of the *sotah* (wanton woman)] for the sake of peace" (Sukkah 53b), along with many other similar statements, I have decided to overstep the bounds of convention. I write this letter with great trepidation. For who knows if my words will enter his pure heart? For "a covenant has been made for slander to be accepted" to the extent that our Sages teach that [even] King David accepted slander (Shabbat 56a). But I must do my part, no matter what. So I am sending these words in order to save my life and the lives of the good people who depend on me. You, my master, whose wisdom is like that of one of God's angels which know all that takes place in the world, will understand that these words come from my heart in sincerity and truth.

My mind is really too unclear to compose a letter fit to be sent to one of the generation's greatest men, because of the great controversy and suffering which attack me from all sides. "Waters surround me. They threaten my life." But who could remain silent at a time such as this?! I shudder to think of it, but from what we hear here about statements which his learned honor has made, it appears that he has lent support to the people who are nurturing this *machloket*. Most of them, as his wisdom knows in his heart, have attacked you as well, my exalted, honorable and scholarly lord.

Now let my lord please remember "[the laws of] the redeeming of innocent people" and do not allow innocent Jewish blood to be spilled. Because they are spilling our blood already with the greatest indignations, the like of which has never been heard. They pelt us with stones and dirt, and pity neither children nor elders. "If God had not helped us, they would have swallowed us alive!" So now let my lord turn his pure heart to do what he has done so well in the past and mediate a peace in Israel, a peace between fellow men. While conceding something to the guilty party is often unavoidable, a wise man knows the value of a compromise. How many thousands of times more valuable is it and how much more is a person who has it in his power to make peace *obligated* to do so, when he sees a *machloket* of these proportions which involves a danger to life and a *chillul Hashem* (a desecration of God's Holy Name)?!

For they have gone ahead and are tearing up the holy books that our master, teacher and holy Rebbe, of sainted memory, composed. They tread on them with their feet and throw them into garbage dumps and unclean places. Has such a thing ever been heard? Has anything like this ever been seen? And they never think to open the book to see what is written there, and whether or not it deserves such abuse.

And our companions who take shelter in his holy shadow and study his holy books which have already circulated throughout the Jewish People to the ends of the earth, and we have been informed that they have already been reprinted in distant places — when they see the generation's impudent people so shamelessly disgracing the books, they are forced to remain silent and bite their tongues. But the opponents aren't satisfied with this and they slander without restraint, going so far as to raise their hands and strike our poor persecuted comrades. Then our comrades can no longer restrain themselves and they meet these attacks with all their might. For they are embittered men and, having been persecuted to the breaking point, their counter-attacks are that much stronger, as the wise man said, "No-one is braver than a desperate man." So that the quarreling and fighting have intensified and have broken out on many occasions in many different towns.

Would it be conceivable to feed the fire, God forbid, of a *machloket* such as this and to enflame it even further? In his heart my master knows that we are firmly committed to the point of truth and that it is impossible to shake us from him, of blessed memory, and from his holy books, God forbid. For we know in our souls the truth of his holy words which are founded and stand upon the pediment of truth which we received from our Rabbis of blessed memory, in the Talmud, the Codes and in all the holy *mussar* literature composed by the holy tzaddikim who followed them, may their merit protect us. The entire House of Israel has seen this; at least anyone who wanted the truth and looked at them [Rebbe Nachman's teachings] honestly and sincerely. How is it possible to deny words of truth such as these?! If people do not wish to look at them, no-one is going to force them. Those who wish to will listen, and those who don't will refrain.

But what gives anyone the right to feed a fire, God forbid, which has already been burning now for many years? It is well known that I, poor destitute man that I am, have already put my life on the line and have given myself over completely, soul, body and money, for the truth. God knows it is true that I spoke extensively with the great leaders and holy men of Israel, the tzaddikim, the foundations of the world, may their merit protect us, even after I drew close to our master, teacher and illustrious Rebbe, the holy Rav MoHaRaN [Moreinu HaRav Rebbe Nachman] of sainted memory. All of them welcomed me with great love and warmth. This was especially so of our teacher, the holy and awesome Rav [Levi Yitzchak] of Berditchev, and after him the holy Rav [Avraham Ber] of Chmelnik and the holy Rav Shalom of Probisht, all of sainted memory, along with other great leaders [Rabbi Zusia of Anipoli and Rabbi Mordekhai of Krementz among others]. Before I drew close to our master, teacher and illustrious Rebbe of sainted memory, I was sitting in the dust at their feet. Afterwards, when they saw how I had changed for the better and was, with God's help, giving myself over with greater devotion to Torah and prayer, their love for me only increased, and all of them had me give him, of blessed memory, their good wishes.

Today I am well over fifty years old [Reb Noson was fifty-five then] and have endured much. "All Your breakers and waves have gone over me." I have been involved with his holy books now for over thirty-two years. I have had the merit of printing them many times, with the approbations of the Great Men of Israel, famous and brilliant writers themselves, and these books have been dispersed throughout the Jewish People, especially in Lithuania, Reissen, Greater Poland and in the Land of Israel. In all these places people praise them and say that they are indeed awesome words of truth which open doors to all who come knocking in *teshuvah* and that they direct people on the straight path.

Letter #164

Only in our region is there so much *machloket*, because of the foolishness that left the mouth of his great adversary [Rabbi Aryeh Leib of Shpola, 1725-1812], whom I totally and absolutely reject and do not want to discuss. You, my master, know too that it was not correct to oppose him [Rebbe Nachman], of blessed memory, and that he only increased *machloket* in Israel. So much so, that even if the greatest of the great wanted to set things right, I don't know if he could. For I know that what he has spoiled will remain so for generations until our righteous teacher comes and reveals the truth. At the very least though, the *machloket* must not be exacerbated.

Please, my master, who loves the Jewish People and who works for their rectification, forgive me if my pen has written anything which affronts his great honor. Give me the benefit of the doubt. I am writing amidst great trials and pain, with a sincerely broken and downcast heart, downcast very much indeed. I am overwrought in the extreme. "God! How much longer will this go on!?" My spirit has been torn apart within me. What can I say? What can I say? What can I say to justify myself? God has found my sin. He is just and I have done wrong. But (*Vayikra Rabbah* 27:5), "'God looks after the persecuted,' even if the righteous are chasing the guilty." And this is certainly the case in this *machloket*, when their accusations are totally unjustified. For it is revealed and known before Him Who spoke and the world came into being, that our master, teacher and Rebbe guides us on the straight path with his holy books, the path our ancestors have always traveled.

Now, I bow down and prostrate myself. I beg my master a

thousand times! Please let him take to his good heart all my words, which I have spoken in rightness and truth. Let him not brush them aside. And if something has affronted his honor, God forbid, let him not count it against me. I have not spoken out of rebellion or treachery, God forbid. It is just that our suffering and persecution are overwhelming, and "a person is not blamed for what he does in his anguish." Do not listen to the slanderers who are whispering in your ear, but rather let the righteous man adhere to his accustomed way and rescue the oppressed from the hands of the oppressor. Let him mediate peace in Israel!

God, Who knows each person's heart, knows that I very much wish I were able to go to his holy house and speak with his scholarly honor there face to face, and explain myself to him. But a mountain stands between me, the poor man, and his exalted honor. I have so many troubles coming at me from every direction that he would not have enough time to talk to me. For in order to explain fully and save myself, I would need his scholarly honor to speak with me many hours a day over many days. This is not possible, when he is so busy with matters of Heaven and of the community. In addition, I, poor man that I am, would be unable to remain there long, because many people come there who gnash their teeth at me and with whom it is impossible to sit together and discuss anything. So I could certainly not stay there over a period of days as my master, with his clear understanding, will realize.

It is really for this reason I have refrained thus far from coming to see you. Now in particular, it is impossible for me to pass from my home to the home of his holiness, because I am afraid of my opponents, and especially of those shameless ones among them to whom my blood is considered "permitted." All these things form a great wall keeping me from his exalted honor. I even have doubts about sending this letter to his great, learned honor, but I could not restrain myself.

In every move that I make, I give over my mind and my heart to God and I will do what He wants. Though there are many things I would like to say, I will keep this letter short, so as not to burden the tzaddik with a lot of words. May he flourish, as both he and I, this trod-upon doorstep, would wish. I stretch forth my hands, seeking peace and truth.

Noson, son of Reb Naftali Hertz, of Breslov

165

With thanks to God, Thursday night, Erev Shabbat, Vayishlach, 5595, Breslov.

My dear, beloved son.

I received your letter from the carrier of this letter, our friend Reb Nachman of Tulchin, along with the pens and the one silver ruble from our friend Reb Shimshon, may his light shine. When Reb Nachman arrived at my upper room, our comrades were with me and I was talking with them about the *machloket* that has recently flared up again. In the middle of this discussion he walked in. I saw his letter and heard what he had to say. [The *machloket* was especially fierce in Tulchin which is about nine miles from Breslov. Reb Yitzchak, Reb Noson's son, lived there as did Reb Nachman Tulchiner, Reb Shimshon, Reb Noson's nephew mentioned earlier, along with several other Breslover Chassidim. See *Through Fire and Water*, pp.399-401.]

It may have been appropriate to burst out crying over such pain and suffering, but instead, marshaling my strength, I overcame it and kept myself happy. Joy in God is our fortress! The most important thing of all is to fortify yourself and be joyful! Only during a certain specific hour every day my soul will undoubtedly cry privately over persecution such as this.

Now, my son, my heart and my soul, and all our dear comrades, attend closely to everything we have talked about. Because God has supplied us with the treatment before the blow in the form of the gems of wisdom, the holy words, that you have heard from me and from the holy books. They have the power to inspire every single one of you even now! We see that the reawakening of this *machloket* has also reawakened most of our comrades. They are all saying that our opponents, through the *machloket*, have roused them from their slumber.

My sons, do not be sad or angry! God is with us! Do not be afraid of them! As for his question about whether or not to pray in the *kloyz*: I have told the carrier of this letter to pass on that I incline towards your not going there this Shabbat and I think it might be best for you to choose a new place to pray in town where our comrades pray. I have spoken more about this with the carrier of this letter.

Chatzot, midnight, has arrived and it is Erev Shabbat. Besides, as you can understand for yourself, I have a lot to talk over and get straight between me and my Creator. Maybe I will be able to express myself fluently to Him and really pray that

Letter #166   37

He take pity on our disgrace. So I must keep it short. You are receiving a copy of the letter that I prepared to the Rav this morning before dawn (see Letter 164 above). There too you will see the wonders of God: how He put the idea in my mind today to write that letter. Advise me as to how you think I should proceed with it. You will hear more from the carrier of this letter.

> The words of your father, so persecuted, who flees every time to God. He strengthens me in His great mercy and saves me with joy. It is in Him that my heart rejoices.
>
> Noson of Breslov

166

[Publisher's note: Reb Yitzchak's wife, Chanah, was from a family who opposed the Breslover Chassidim. Prior to the outbreak of hostilities, the enmity remained dormant but in the beginning of the Years of Oppression she fought fiercely against Reb Yitzchak. This letter and the next refer to some of Reb Yitzchak's difficulties stemming from his wife and from the opponents in Tulchin. This letter also relates the murder of Reb Noson Apteker, who was erroneously killed instead of Reb Noson by hired assassins.]

With thanks to God, Sunday night, Vayeishev, 5595, Breslov.

My dear, beloved son.

I received your letter tonight. I was sleeping when the messenger came and awakened me and I read the letter carefully. What can I respond, my dear, beloved son? It is good to thank God for every single "expansion," every bit of relief, that God in His enormous mercy gives us "from within the pain itself," and particularly for what you wrote about your situation at home, from which I understand that God has helped you. This is the most important thing, and you needn't worry at all any more. The main impediment, that can really be called an impediment, is in this area alone. And it is necessary to break this too for the truth, the *takhlit*. Regarding anybody who doesn't break it and swerves from truth in the direction of falsehood through his wife's influence, as is happening now with many, God save us, it is written (Bava Metzia 59a), "A man who follows his wife's advice, falls into Gehennom." His life in This World is extremely bitter as well, because it is certainly impossible to do *exactly* what she says. So he ends up "bald on both sides," God save us, as we know.

Therefore a man must use his intelligence to overcome this, and not follow his wife's advice in spiritual matters. Only in worldly matters is it appropriate to listen to her, as is explained in that same Gemara on this subject (ibid. 59a), "How can you say 'A man who follows his wife's advice falls into Gehennom,' when we have learned, 'If your wife is short, lean over to her,' i.e. listen to her advice?" The answer given is that the first statement refers to spiritual matters, while the second is talking about worldly ones. Thank God, we have already faced much suffering and many impediments and God has helped us to break them and not be influenced by them. Ultimately, through His kindness, *they* came around to our way of thinking, as is written (Proverbs 16:7), "When God is pleased with a person's actions, even his enemies will make peace with him." Since God has saved you somewhat in this, you need not look again at all the humiliation, even in the slightest. It is all a great favor.

In my opinion it would be good for you to select a place to pray with the people in the *bet midrash* (study hall) of the new city. It does not look as if the *mitnagdim* have any power there to act against our comrades. Why go into a place when you may be humiliated? What honor will you gain if you pray in the *kloyz*? You already have humiliation anyway, since they are talking about this, which in itself is a great embarrassment. May He Who sees the disgrace of the shamed have pity on our humiliation, have mercy on us and save us.

As for what you asked about, it is presently night-time and it is impossible to investigate. May God have pity on the weeping and screams of Israel, and on the cries, bitterer than death, that are heard through the streets. Woe to our souls for what we have caused by our sins, to see bitter sorrow like this in our generation! Woe and bitterness to the opponents and *mitnagdim*, when they can now speak arrogantly against truly righteous and God-fearing men, who cleave to the true tzaddik who sweetens the world's bitterness and in whose hands rests the continued existence of the world! What can we say!? How can we justify ourselves?! The tears drop from my heart and eyes, as I have to answer you about this. I just heard out of the darkness of night a loud, bitter cry: "Woe! Woe and bitterness! Wailing on every street! A bald spot [ripped out from grief] on every head!" Who could hear this and not weep? At least we have this to comfort ourselves in our destitution, that we do not oppose the point of truth. With this alone we have the energy to console ourselves, and even now to make ourselves joyful and turn all the groans and sighs into joy.

I am sure you have heard about the bizarre, terrifying event that took place here last Friday night, how everyone in the home of Reb Noson, son of Reb Zvi Apteker, was killed. On Shabbat morning, during the time of Morning Prayers, this Reb Noson, his wife, his brother Reb Aharon Moshe and the maid were all found murdered in their house. Only two children were still alive. The older one, a girl aged four or five, is now lying in bed, bruised and beaten from the murderers' cruel blows, and the younger one is still a nursing infant. The victims were just buried today. May their deaths be an atonement for the Jewish people and may their souls have eternal life. The murderers have not been found yet. Just one gentile has been caught.

I do not have time to go on any more. It is just like prior to the miracle of Chanukah, when the Jews had enormous suffering on every side. That's exactly how it is now! On one side, there is what we just told you — we were anguished at what we heard; on the other side, a *machloket* such as this, with such abuse and hatred. Above all is the great enemy within the person himself that arises against him constantly every day, and every moment launches a new attack. The Rabbis, of blessed memory, teach that this is what is referred to in the verse (Psalms 37:32), "The evil man waits for the righteous, seeking to slay him. But God will not abandon him to his hand." The Rabbis said too that the verse, "He rescues the poor man from the one who is stronger" is also talking about this.

The truth is that all these sufferings, God save us, fuel each other. But "God's kindnesses never run out. They are new every morning" (Lamentations 3:23). Rashi explains on this verse that lovingkindness is created anew every morning. And through this we have the energy to look, hope, wait and yearn constantly for His salvation. For He has finished and He will finish everything for the good. "For You, God, are eternally exalted" and He always has the upper hand. It is written, "God's right hand is exalted. God's right hand does mighty deeds." These are the mighty deeds of the tzaddikim, i.e. the righteous people who are attatched to them. They will return to us, not we to them! As the Rebbe of blessed memory said, "I *have* finished and I *will* finish!" (see Tzaddik #115, #126, #322). We have seen a little of it with our own eyes! His mercy has helped us until now and His kindness will not abandon us. So He will continue to save us with His miracles, kindnesses and great acts of salvation! Because the truth endures!

> The words of your father, teacher, friend and student, who truly loves you. Dust trampled under the feet of all.
>
> *Noson of Breslov*

Greetings to all our comrades with a great and mighty love! All these things were said to them too! My beloved son, give this letter to all those who are bound by the chains of our true love to read. Maybe all of them, or some of them, as a result of my words, will wake up and think about their eternal purpose. This is my reward for all my labor. Everything else is vanity, as is written (Psalms 49:17), "Do not be afraid if a man grows rich and the honor of his house increases." We have to remember and take at face value the words of our ancestors and Rabbis, of blessed memory, when they said (*Avot* 6:9), "When a person dies, his silver and gold, gems and pearls do not accompany him; only the Torah he studied and his good deeds." But now, in these generations, a person must look and search in the books of our master, teacher and Rebbe, and among his students, and among his students' students, for true advice on how to escape all the twistedness and confusion of This World, which so flusters and twists the heart. May the King of the World bless them.

Noson, the same

167

With thanks to God, Wednesday night, Vayeishev, 5595, Breslov.

I received your letter just now. You can understand yourself the pain I had. But I didn't let the pain overwhelm me, because I knew that this was going to happen. That is why I thought that you ought not start going there last Shabbat. Then you would not have been disgraced like that. But this is also for the best. Please remember, my dear son, the great kindness that God did for you by allowing you to stay alive and to recover. Instead of mortal danger, you got as a punishment this humiliation, which atones for sins exactly like death. So this is certainly a great kindness from God.

It would be appropriate for you to speak with your wife and ask her what she wants. Are you going to stop being my son,

Letter #167

God forbid, or not come to see me, God forbid? Didn't she know beforehand that you were my son and what that meant? But if you must suffer from this, then it's all for the good. You already know that the world is full of suffering and that "happy is he who suffers for the sake of the Torah"! Most men suffer from their wives over mundane things! I hope to God that through your determination to attain the truth, with God's help, you will win her over and she will come back to you, to fulfill (Proverbs 16:7), "When God is pleased with a person's actions, even his enemies will make peace with him". "We do not know what to do, but our eyes look to You." We have no-one to lean on but our Father in Heaven.

As for what you wrote about how people are saying that, God forbid, they will obey him when he gives the order to set fire to the study hall in the new city, this they cannot do. It seems to me that, with God's help, our comrades are strong there. Since our opponents know this, they will not start up there, realizing that they cannot succeed. "God has not decreed that the name of Israel should be obliterated" and in our hardship He sent us relief. He will surely leave you a place to pray, with God's help. He has helped us already, and may He continue to help us and save us more and more from now on. May everything turn into great good, that we may be worthy through this of awakening from our slumber! Everything that is presently happening to us is intended to arouse us from our sleep, to begin to renew ourselves to walk in His holy ways and come close to Him so that we will return to God from wherever we are!

Just a short while ago I decided to send the letter to the Rav [of Savran, see Letter #164]. I immediately sealed it. You are receiving it enclosed here and should send it on to him. I did what I had to do to save myself. May God do what is good and turn his heart to look at the real truth. The Lord, our God, is Truth and in His enormous mercy He has helped us to this point. We trust in Him alone that He will not abandon or neglect us now either. His miracles and thoughts are for us.

The words of your father, waiting expectantly for salvation.

Noson of Breslov

168

[Publisher's note: This letter alludes to the police activity around Reb Noson's house on Shabbat Chanukah, the arrest of his followers and the confiscation of his writings. This precipitated Reb Noson's flight for safety eastward to the Tcherin area (Kremenchug, Medevedevka, etc.), and the reader will notice the different cities Reb Noson writes from in succeeding letters.]

With thanks to God, Sunday night, Mikeitz, Chanukah, 5595, Breslov.

My dear son.

You have already heard about our troubles — and yours, I have no doubt that you're aware of. But it is also impossible to relate or explain the miraculous "expansions" within the straits themselves that God has performed for us, and for me especially, during these days. Even what I can perceive myself I cannot express, let alone what is beyond my perception. God's intention is undoubtedly to give us great good and awesome salvation!

Letter #168

And His primary intent is to awaken and rouse us, and the whole world, from sleep, so that we should wake up in the morning the way that they said (*Orach Chaim* 1:1), "Rise mightily in the morning like a lion... Arise the morning star!" I have explained in an exceedingly beautiful discourse that the essential meaning of this dictum is that we go with the teaching of *Azamra!*, "I will sing to God with what I have left!" (see *Likutey Halakhot, Hashkamat HaBoker* 1).

This Shabbat we spoke at length on the lesson "In suffering He gave me relief" (*Likutey Moharan* I, 195) and about how Chanukah embodies this teaching. It is very closely related to everything that is happening with us now. We are waiting constantly to leave the straits completely and to come into great "expansion." Our enemies will see and be ashamed! The carrier of this letter, as he will tell you, is very pressured, so I cannot continue.

The words of your father, full of great joy and happiness, especially in a time of trouble and pain, God save us, because of the great, amazing and infinitely awesome kindness that God did with me and with all Israel by bringing us near to a holy, awesome light such as this! This is impossible to express. It is "for each person according to his own heart's understanding." It is Chanukah now. Who knows how deep the mystery of Chanukah runs? I well know, with God's help, that it shows those who dwell below and those who dwell on high what they need to be shown. I really cannot continue.

The words of one waiting constantly for God's salvation.

Noson of Breslov

[Publisher's note: In Breslov, Reb Noson had a very close friend and follower, Reb Shmuel Weinberg, who had some influence with the government. Thanks to Reb Shmuel's tireless efforts, Reb Noson's followers were released a few days after their arrest. He also worked to release Reb Noson's writings which took longer and he was mostly successful. One volume of his writings, known in Breslov circles as krakh khaf (the 20th volume) was never recovered. It contained Reb Noson's original discourses of Likutey Halakhot on Yoreh Deah. After completing a certain amount of discourses Reb Noson had them bound and this was the 20th volume. The letter also refers to the results of the incredible pressures faced by the Breslover Chassidim and some of the unfortunate results.]

169

With thanks to God, Friday before dawn, Va'eira, 5595, Kremenchug.

My dear, beloved son.

You revived me with with the news that, thank God, through His lovingkindness and miracles, the books have been returned. I have been pining away about this until now. I arrived here at nightfall from Tcherin, tired and weary, hoping that maybe I would find a letter here from you. And by the kindness of God, before entering the house I received your letter from Reb Efraim, may he live, who had got it yesterday. I read it immediately.

I am surprised at you, my dear son, for not telling me right at the beginning of the letter about the great salvation that we had. Instead I had to read much of the letter and hear about our great pain and disgrace, God have mercy, all the while longing to hear this report. Not until the second page did I find the heartwarming good news. How great are God's kindnesses and

Letter #169

wonders! What can we return to God for all the kindnesses He has done for us!?

As for all the humiliation that you wrote of: while I am pained by it all, it really is insignificant. Our lives are like a passing shadow and the time rushes by. Soon it will all be gone and forgotten. Happy will be the one who held his ground! Who continued to dwell in the shade of the Rebbe's holiness and to work with his holy books! One who did the opposite, God forbid, will certainly be ashamed of himself and feel great remorse in This World and the Next. Humiliations such as these have already occurred in past generations, when the Baal Shem Tov, of blessed memory, shone his holy light in the world. I too and all our comrades went through all this. If the humiliations now are greater in some respects, this is only in proportion to the consequence of what we are doing! (see *Likutey Moharan* I 66:4).

Look and you will see miracles! Even now, God steers a straight course with His anger, and the barriers and humiliation which deter a person, God forbid, all come carefully measured to the one on whom they have been decreed. Everything is precisely calculated. Even if we do not know the exact reason for everything, it is still beyond question that God is just in everything He does. For His thoughts are very deep.

The entire world is full of trials every day. Surely Reb Itzik, the son of Reb Avraham Dov, ought to have stood up to the test and let himself be purified by what happened to him. He acted foolishly at the beginning doing what he did, at a time when a wise person would have remained silent. Then he added to his mistake by subsequently separating himself from us; as he himself knows in his heart from the point of truth. I am sure that at any rate he will not be a *mitnaged*. And if he gained only *this* from all the times he traveled [to us], good enough!

Extend greetings to every one of our comrades. It seems to me that any one of them who has a real brain in his head will fortify himself on his own and will fulfill (Isaiah 26:20), "Hide for a moment until the fury passes." For God will certainly not abandon us. He will show us a good sign and our enemies will see and be ashamed! They will come back to us, and not we to them! The words of the Rebbe, of blessed memory, will undoubtedly come true, when he said, "I *have* finished and I *will* finish' (see *Tzaddik* #115, 126, and 322).

I wrote you a letter from Tcherin and sent it to Tulchin. I told you there that I had sent you from Uman a number of letters for Breslov and to you specifically. [Reb Yitzchak was the postmaster in Tulchin and could control the flow of mail to and from Reb Noson without interference from his opponents.] I am very surprised that not a single one of them reached you and I am pained about this. But the salvation that you told me about is more important than anything and my hope is in God that everything will turn out well. As for your own situation, you already heard my response above: the world is full of tests of all kinds every day. But we already have for all of them a strong foundation, which is firm and endures forever. This is the tzaddik, "foundation of the world," the undivided foundation. Every one of us in whatever happens to him has *him* to lean on. For we did not come to This World to eat, drink and satisfy our cravings, God forbid. Nor did we come here for money and imaginary status of This World! We came here to suffer toil and struggle in order to know our Creator and Maker, may His Name be blessed, in accordance with the Torah that Moses placed before the Children of Israel, and with the direction that the true tzaddikim give us in every generation! We must suffer bitterness again and again, and afterwards God in His kindness helps, as we have already seen many times. This is the verse (Isaiah 38:17), "For the sake of peace I have great bitterness," as explained in his holy books (*Likutey Moharan* I, 27:7).

The way it appears now, you needn't send another letter here, because it is unlikely that I will be here long. From now on, be sure to send me a letter with every post to Uman and let me know precisely everything that is going on there, so I will know what to do. That way, when I get to Uman shortly, God willing, I will find your letters waiting for me and they will inspire me, with God's help. It looks as if I will be in Uman, God willing, two or three weeks from now. May God in His good will direct me on the true path. In every move I make I rely on Him.

At present, every place I come to I greatly inspire all our comrades there. Here as well, they received me with great love and eagerness. They joyfully came out to welcome me, more than ever before. Never have they received me with the love and joy that they did now! But the suffering that I have had thus far from the traveling itself is beyond description. The roads here are in terrible condition and the horses are weak. For a man getting on in years as I am, my ability to endure the difficulties of travel is just about finished.

Even so, though, there have been an endless number of

"expansions" to alleviate the hardships. If only God will give me the opportunity to tell you everything, so that you will understand the miracle of God's supervision — how He in His goodness is constantly renewing the world every day, and contracts Himself from His Absolute Infinity down into every act, word and thought of every person according to the place and time, and gives him hints (Likutey Moharan I, 54:2). *Gevalt!* Why are we silent after we have heard things such as this?! About every single word of them, we must say a thousand times, "If we had come to the world only to hear this, it would have been enough!" And they are ripping up and desecrating these books! Woe to them! And woe to their souls! May the Master of Compassion return them to the truth. May He return us to truly fulfill the Rebbe's holy words, spoken with truth. And they [God's hints] happen on a general level, on an individual level — with every person at every time — and it is carried down to the smallest details every moment of every day.

What can I say to you, my dear son, and to all our faithful comrades? Pay close attention to what is done with a person in this passing world, this fleeting shadow. Everyone knows that This World is complete vanity, vanity of vanities. And if they aren't able to right their deeds, and even commit wrongs, as every single one does in this place of vanity and as they themselves know (may God pardon them and return them to the truth!), they are further impelled to go against the point of truth who was worthy of leaving the vain wind of This World *completely* and who did not want to leave any vanity in This World at all (as explained in *Rabbi Nachman's Stories*, Story #13, The Fourth Day).

Letter #170

Ashreinu! Happy are we! How good is our portion! That our souls have escaped *this* like a bird from a trap! Thank God, the Merciful One, Who has rescued us from this! May He go on to rescue us from all the vanities of This World and to engage all our lives in Torah, prayer and good deeds. Amen.

As it appears, I will not stay here long. I have only been here a short time, so I cannot tell you what is happening here now. In addition, it is now time for the Morning Prayers. May God send forth His mercy and allow me to pray with great concentration, to acknowledge this day's complete renewal of Creation and to fulfill, "to speak of His lovingkindness in the morning."

The words of your father, hoping to see you soon, with God's help,

Noson of Breslov

Greetings to all our companions with much love.

170

With thanks to God, Wednesday night, Beshalach, 5595, Krakov.

Greetings to my honored, beloved son, Reb Yitzchak, may he live.

I already wrote you that I reached Kremenchug on Thursday night, Parashat Va'eira. There I found your letters telling me that the holy books had been returned, thank God, and this greatly encouraged me. On Friday, the following day, I sent you my letter and until yesterday I was in Kremenchug. All that time I did not receive a single letter, neither from

Breslov nor from Uman, and I do not know what to think. It must be that during a time of suffering such as this, God have mercy, we need to have this pain as well.

But my consolation amidst my destitution is that, by God's kindness and enormous miracles, they succeeded in getting out the books. What can I give back to God?! How good is the lot of Reb Shmuel Weinberg that he was able to have a redemption of captives such as this accomplished through his agency! *Ashreihem!* Happy are all those who took part in this! Happy are all those who gave money for this redemption of souls and of the holy Torah! Woe to them and woe to the souls of these informants with their false charges! They have rebelled and sinned against the honor of God, the honor of the holy Torah, the honor of the Baal Shem Tov, of blessed memory, and his holy students, and the honor of our master, teacher and Rebbe, of blessed memory, all of whose holy books were impounded as a result of their treachery! May God pay back the evildoer according to his evil. And in His great lovingkindness let Him have compassion on us poor, persecuted paupers. May He quickly save us for the sake of His great and holy Name in which we hail. For His great Name is found in the name of the true tzaddik, as explained in the lesson "In the beginning — in the sight of all Israel" (Likutey Moharan II 67), which I spoke about last Shabbat Chanukah and to which I added a few finishing touches here.

I was already prepared to go today. But God in His compassion arranged that I should be extremely busy and so ended up traveling past the post office with Reb Efraim, may his light shine. Reb Efraim went in and there he found two of your letters! One was written on Sunday, *Bo*, and the other on Thursday, *Bo*. I was quite overwhelmed by God's enormous lovingkindness and I quickly went to Reb Efraim's house. I read each letter carefully through twice. I do not have to tell you how your letters affected me. Distress and comfort! Weeping and song! You can grasp only a little of this, but not all of it. At the time I was extremely preoccupied with crossing the Dnieper River and preparing to spend the night.

It is two or three hours after dark and I just arrived here in Krakov. I am writing this letter immediately upon my arrival and I am extremely busy and preoccupied with a number of things, your letters in particular. People are also coming here to welcome me. Still I have postponed everything and am making myself write you immediately whatever response God puts under my pen.

Your letters encouraged me enormously, even though you told me how intense the *machloket* still is, may God have mercy. Nonetheless my hope is in God that the whole thing will turn into good, especially since we see His tremendous miracles and kindness within all the suffering, God save us. For God is still with us and near us, and right by our side, as you wrote, that our comrades in Uman have seen the beginnings of salvation in a number of areas. We see in this the greatness of God's deeds! How deep are His thoughts! And we see the great power of the holy elder, the elder of elders, whose power is still with us. Even to ripe old age it will never abandon us....

As for encouraging you, you already wrote to me, thank God, that you are, as you should be, adamant in the truth. I was really pleased by what you said in your letter that you inspire yourself with the various things that you've heard from me. In my opinion God has provided us with the treatment in advance of the blow with the many holy conversations that I have been having with you for many years now, and with all the holy lessons and stories, and the holy prayers which God gave me the merit of composing. These contain more than enough to inspire yourself even during troubled times such as these. So much so, that you ought to be dancing now every day over the greatness of God's salvation and enormous miracles in that He saved us from being opponents to a point of truth such as this. What can I say? What can I say? With what can we come to meet God after all the good He has given us?!

At present I am suffering because I have not yet received a single letter from Breslov. In addition, I have yet to get my visa. My mind is really not clear at all right now. Fortify yourself and be strong! For God is with you! There is reward for your work! And there is good reason to be hopeful about our end! If you look closely at one holy lesson out of his holy books, you will be able to comfort yourself for all the troubles that come upon us! Salvation is in God's hands! May He rescue us from them in the Rebbe's great merit! I have much to say, but time just does not permit it.

> The words of your father, hoping to see you soon in
> life, peace and joy.
>
> *Noson of Breslov*

Send greetings to all the inhabitants of Breslov who have

risen to help us! May God be with them! May He repay what they have done and give them great reward. May they merit every good in This World and the Next eternally. Amen.

Through all the suffering and turmoil that I have gone through, and that we all have gone through as a group and individually, especially throughout the enormous distress and fear that we have experienced this year from Rosh HaShanah until today as a result of the tremendous awakening of the *machloket* and of those who hate us — through it all I only encourage myself with what the Rebbe, of blessed memory, said on the verse, "The evil man waits for the righteous, seeking to slay him. But God will not abandon him to his hand." Look up what he wrote there (see Likutey Moharan I, 114 and 208). But *they* [the wicked] conceal [the righteous] so much that a person can't even breathe, God forbid! "But God will not abandon him to his hand," which we see for ourselves.

We have to believe that the *machloket* is undoubtedly very good for every single one of us. However, in that which they desire, to uproot everything altogether, they will not be successful. Anyone who really wants to be a good Jew, the way that our master, teacher and Rebbe, of blessed memory, taught us, to live with true, simple purity and sincerity in accordance with the Torah that our teacher Moses commanded us and that our Rabbis, of blessed memory, passed down to us — without a doubt no barrier in the world can stop him! For the rule already stands: a person is never faced with a barrier that he cannot break. So that if you need to pray alone, well, so did many of the pious of earlier times. They did not want to be disturbed in their prayers by praying with the community. I already wrote you that you should fulfill (Isaiah 26:20), "Hide for a moment until the fury passes." You can rest assured that not so long from now you will be able to pray in whatever study hall you want. This sort of thing *has* to happen to all the tzaddikim and to all the good Jews attached to them, because "at first they have suffering and in the end — contentment."

I have no time to continue.

Noson, as above

171

With God's help, Motzay-Shabbat Shirah, 5595, Tcherin.

Greetings to my beloved brothers and companions, my kind and faithful friends; my teachers, my Rabbis, my friends and my students; my children and grandchildren, may they live: may you all enjoy blessing, life, peace and all good in This World and the Next, eternally. Amen, may it be His will.

Listen to me and God will listen to you. I just recently received all your letters: my friend Reb Shmuel Weinberg's with the visa [Reb Noson's travel permit], my friend Reb Avraham Ber's, may he live, and the greetings from Reb Yosef, the son-in-law of Reb Zalman. They are all full of loud and bitter screams and cries over the enormous persecution that we, and especially I, are suffering at the hands of those who groundlessly hate. In return for my love, they hate me. But "I am all prayer." Amidst the enormous sufferings, though, we have had miraculous and awesome shows of salvation and relief. For, thanks to the living God, through His great kindness, we were able to recover the books! What can I give back to God for all the good He has done for me?! We should be making a huge "Purim" over this, because it was no small miracle! (see *Chayey Adam, Megillah* #41; a person should make a mini-Purim when a miracle occurs to him or his family). *Ashrekha,* my friend Reb Shmuel! Happy are you that the miracle was performed through your agency! *Ashreikhem!* Happy are you, my brothers and friends, and anyone who had a part in rescuing these souls and the holy Torah!

> [Editor's note: The incident referred to here is the following: On Shabbat Chanukah of this year, Parashat Mikeitz, at the Third Meal, just after our teacher Reb Noson, of blessed memory, began to give a Torah lesson, his slanderous enemies incited the governor of the city against him and the governor surrounded his house with soldiers. The house was packed full at the time with good Jews who had come to hear his holy words. The governor incarcerated a number of people and confiscated many books, both printed ones such as copies of the Talmud, the Codes, etc., and some of Reb Noson's own manuscripts. Our teacher, of blessed memory, was in enormous danger at that time, and the Monday after Shabbat Chanukah the governor wanted to take him into custody. Our teacher, of blessed memory, was thus forced to flee secretly to Uman, and from there to Tcherin, as related. You will find reference to this episode at the beginning of The Laws of Dagim 5 in Likutey Halakhot, Yoreh Deah where he wrote that it was composed during "the uproar and flight." He is referring there to his flight to Tcherin. God subsequently had compassion, and that same week immediately following Shabbat Chanukah all those who were incarcerated were released. The books, however, were in great danger until Shabbat Shirah. With God's help, [Reb Shmuel Weinberg] succeeded in freeing them too and nothing was lost except one volume from Likutey Halakhot, Yoreh Deah, from the middle of the Laws of Shechitah 5. You will notice in the printed edition of Likutey Halakhot, Yoreh Deah that Discourse #5 of each section is missing up to the Laws of Dagim. It was lost at this time, along with our teacher of blessed memory's manuscript of Likutey Eitzot (Advice).]

Any efforts that anyone has made, physical, financial or

both, will all be counted in his favor on high. Every step taken, every word, every movement, every *prutah* (small coin) that was expended for this effort until the desired outcome was achieved — their righteousness will endure forever, for them and their children for generations to come. The visa that you sent was also immensely encouraging. I have been yearning to see this from the day I separated from you. God arranged things that I would stay in Krakov until that Wednesday and so I received it there, though I was already set to travel here. It was all with God's amazing providence, as I will tell you, God willing, when I arrive safely home.

Thank God, I arrived here safely for Shabbat, as I said, and, thank God, everything here is all right. In all these districts, no-one makes disparaging remarks, there is not even the slightest mention of the *machloket* raging in our area. You hear nothing about it at all. From what I hear, there is no talk of it in Zlatipolia and its environs either. The real *machloket* is in our area, because it is there that his holy words have started to enter the hearts of a number of *kasherim*, good Jews. As a result, there is a great deal of antagonism.

I have so much to say to you, but I do not know where to start. I have already talked to you so very much about how you need to break down barriers and how the entire world stands up against anyone who wants to come near us and to hail in his great name, of blessed memory. Every one of our comrades, young and old alike, has already suffered enormous sorrow, bitterness and pain from the very beginning, right up till today.

Many were deterred by it, God save us. But the ones who stood their ground — *ashreihem!* Happy are they and their portion!

You, men of Breslov, have not even begun to taste sorrow, bitterness and barriers! But what can I do, my brothers and friends? Every one has to face many barriers and trials right into old age. Happy will be the one who stands up to them, as you can see from the case of Moshe Chenkes! [see "The year in review"]. Everybody, even the *mitnagdim,* wonder at him and laugh at the way he has slipped and fallen "like an ox snared in a net"! May God have mercy on him. May He put him on his feet and bring him quickly back to the truth. At the moment, though, his pain is real, and it is many many times greater than all of ours. Woe to his old age, the loss of each day in all that he does! [i.e. engaging in the *machloket*]. There have always been such cases, as our Rabbis, of blessed memory, said on the Mishnah (see *Avot* 2:5), "'Do not believe in yourself until the day of your death', because... [Yochanan the High Priest served eighty years in his position and in the end he became an agnostic!]."

In more recent years, as is well known, the same thing has also happened with the Rav of Balfor, who waned at the end of his life [he succumbed to a test and after failing he abandoned religion]. With what can I come before God, after all the good He has bestowed upon me, that I have been able to escape this?! May He not abandon me even in my old age, so that until my soul leaves me I will speak of [His] Might among true Breslover Chassidim, who are attached and close to his holy name, of blessed memory! For the Tester of hearts knows that our holy Rebbe, of blessed memory, guides us on the straight, true path in purity and simplicity, with amazing wisdom and with advice of great depth to adamantly hold our ground always and to fulfill all the words of the Written and Oral Torah, as explained in his holy books. For he speaks in them about all the commandments, all the character traits and all the pathways of holiness in a way awesome in its truth. I will not go on about this now. What can I say? As you know, I have already spoken at length about how the entire world is full of suffering and pain. For "man was born to suffer." His days are short and full of pain, as I have already spoken about extensively.

Through all the places I have traveled here, there is not a word about our controversy. Nonetheless, everyone is full of pain, troubles, suffering and worry and is under stress about their livelihood — *mitnagdim* and our comrades alike. What do all the poor and destitute do in towns where they do not distribute flour, where there is no allocation at all? They are all still there and alive. Who would think that after all the talks I have had with you, that their cutting off the flour allocation from the poor would constitute any test at all?! I am quite sure that anyone with even a small amount of intelligence is, without a doubt, adamantly holding his ground and for him it is no test at all. There may be some fools who have lost their minds... May God have mercy on them and bring them back to the truth.

[Publisher's note: The reference is to the community leaders in Breslov, headed by Moshe Chenkes, using financial pressures against the Breslover Chassidim to desert Reb Noson. Those who received a charity allowance for flour and other basic necessities were in jeopardy of losing their allocation. The next paragraph speaks about the demand of the enemies of the Breslover Chassidim to dismiss them as teachers, ritual slaughterers and other providers of communal services.]

Letter #171

As for the situation of the teachers: you already know that the Rebbe did not want a single one of his followers to work as a teacher [see *Tzaddik* #465; *Crossing the Narrow Bridge*, pp.251-253]. Our friends Reb Yudel from Dashev and Reb Shmuel Isaac, of blessed memory, as well as many other comrades, suffered extreme poverty in their youth and no-one in their towns helped them at all. But they survived, thank God. The same for me, poor man that I am. I gave up my livelihood when I drew near to the Rebbe, and, thank God, I have lost absolutely nothing because of it, not even in This World.

With regard to your worrying and suffering over my pain and the way they are boasting and frightening me: the truth is that you *do* need to suffer with me and pray and cry out to God very much that He rescue me from my enemies and pursuers. You must employ every strategy and all your strength, body, soul and money, to enable me to dwell safely in Breslov. But still, judging from your letters, you are becoming *overly* upset over this and you are completely ignoring the tremendous acts of salvation, the miracles and the wonders that He has already done with me and with you! This is especially true of the enormous miracles, wonders and favors that God has done with us during these very days amidst this sweep of pain and sorrow. For we were able to retrieve the books and to rescue those souls from prison!

This is in addition to the other individual miracles and acts of salvation that God has done for me personally during these days that I have been traveling. Practically every day I have encountered trouble and danger on the road and God has helped me every time. "The poor man called and God heard him." My hope rests on His great kindness that I will surely live, God willing, in Breslov, and they will not be able to do a thing to me. There is no need to worry too much about the rock-throwing. They have windows too. If people start breaking windows, there will not be a window left in Breslov. But in truth, the Czar's law has jurisdiction in such cases. Our Rabbis, of blessed memory, already said (*Avot* 3:2), "Were it not for fear of the government, people would swallow one another alive." These evil stone-throwers really do want, God forbid, to destroy Breslov which is the exact opposite of stones, as is written (Ezekiel 36:26), "I will remove the heart of stone from your flesh and I will give you a '*LeV BaSaR*' [BReSLoV], a heart of flesh." They and their like will perish, and Breslov will not be destroyed, God forbid! The word of our God will stand forever and this verse will be fulfilled, "I will remove the heart of stone from your flesh...." Hear this and understand that God is right there with us, especially since the Rebbe, of blessed memory, said to me explicitly, "God is right there with you. He's right next to you. Do not be afraid!"

I think that I will soon travel home. I may be in Uman next Shabbat and I will confer there briefly with our comrades. When I get there, I want to find letters from all of you. If one of our comrades from Breslov can go there himself, even better. That way, I will be able to hear precisely everything that has happened there from then until now. Salvation is in God's hands. May He soon bring me safely home. "I will trust the God of my salvation and will not be afraid." I trust in His kindness that I will not become "drunk," God forbid, from all the "waters" that I drink every day. "The slanderer accuses his victim of the fault that he has himself." I have said enough for the wise to understand.

The truth is that we feel the suffering of Israel more acutely about whom it is said, "She is drunk and not from wine" (Isaiah 51:21) and "They reel and stagger like a drunkard" (Psalms 107:27). But how great are the kindnesses of God Who has given us the merit to fulfill, to some extent, the following verse, "And they cried out to God in their pain." On Whom else can we lean but our Father in Heaven?

You want to see miracles right away, but you know already that the Rebbe did not practice this. I have already spoken about this extensively. He reveals Godliness in the world only through the awesome Torah lessons that he revealed. And even if we did see many awesome wonders from him during his life, and even more after his passing, still, it is not his way to punish immediately. Because (Proverbs 17:26), "even for a tzaddik to punish, it is not good." When it is absolutely necessary to weed out the thorns from the vineyard and there is no other way, then he clears them out in their proper time. And he has already weeded out a lot. God will help, and now as well the Rebbe will weed out and do away with them, as is necessary, if they do not repent. No matter what, though, of this I am sure: that, with God's help, He will certainly rescue me and all our comrades from them. Just as His kindness has not abandoned us thus far and He helped us to retrieve the books, so will He continue to help us so that I can live in peace and quiet in Breslov. God is with me, I will not be afraid. What can man do to me?

But you still have to do *your* part and employ every strategy you can, particularly the petitions for which you are gathering signatures. Keep on with this determinedly and God will help you finish it! "God will finish for me." And you, my friend, Reb Shmuel Weinberg, my loyal friend, do not be afraid because you stuck your neck out for me. *Ashrekha!* Happy are you that you were worthy to do this! My son, Reb Yitzchak, may he live, already wrote me how you publicly sanctified God's name. I am surprised at you, my brother, that you are feeling frightened about this! On the contrary, you should constantly be joyful that you had the privilege of doing this! I cannot go on about this in writing.

Thank God, that He provided the treatment in advance of the blow in that we were able to speak so much about the greatness of our holy master, teacher and Rebbe, of blessed memory, and about his incredibly holy Torah lessons, conversations and holy stories. All these give every single one of you good reason to hold firm and not to look at or to be afraid of anything! You just need to employ whatever strategy is required in this situation and to cry out very much to God every day. Then strengthen yourself adamantly in the belief that they will not be able to defeat the Rebbe, of blessed memory, as is written (Jeremiah 1:19), "They will fight against you and will not prevail." All this commotion is just to awaken me and you, to study Torah and pray more, especially private prayer with our

Letter #171

Creator. We need this kind of prayer now most of all. Everyone should express himself before God concerning himself, me and the whole group. May God Who hears the prayers of every mouth hear this and have compassion and save me quickly for the sake of His Great Name in which we hail. I do not have time to write any more.

The words of your true and eternal friend.

Noson of Breslov

Greetings to my modest wife, Dishel, may she live, to her sons, may they live, to my daughter Chanah Tsirel, may she live, to my son-in-law and learned friend Reb Barukh, may he live, and to his daughter [Esther Shaindel, named after Reb Noson's first wife], may she live. So they are throwing stones at her too? May God make us worthy, and may generations of God-fearing men and men of truth come forth from her. This is everything to us.

[Compiler's note: The incident involving the little girl [Esther Shaindel] is as follows: that year, they [Reb Noson's enemies] had a practice of throwing rocks at the house of our teacher, Reb Noson, and the situation had become life-threatening. Towards nightfall [his family] would immediately close the shutters, even while a little daylight still remained. On one occasion they forgot to close one of the windows in a small room called the alker in which his daughter Chanah Tsirel was sitting with her daughter, an infant of six months who was lying in a cradle. The cradle was hung in front of the window and the baby's mother was sitting by her side. At one point, the baby began to cry the way infants do and her mother lifted her from the cradle. She had not even completely removed the baby all the way out of the cradle, when a huge rock came crashing through the window and landed right in the cradle. If the little girl had been in the crib it certainly would have killed her, because the rock was very large. It was only by a miracle that she narrowly escaped death.

The reader will now understand the greeting that he gives to his daughter Chanah Tsirel and to her daughter. He will also understand the intensity of the persecution and danger that he faced throughout his holy life. His will was literally like iron to have endured all this. But it never entered his mind to become discouraged and slack, God forbid, in his devotions which he practiced all his days. He only drew himself closer and closer to God. He studied, taught, worked and encouraged others to strive for the betterment of the community; and he did it all with enormous energy and enthusiasm. This was what he did publicly, what we ourselves saw. Beside this are all his inner, hidden achievements which would be impossible to express verbally or to describe in writing. But as a person peering through a small hole, though he only sees a little, may infer much more, so a person with wisdom and intelligence was able to understand what a tiny fraction of the whole picture these hidden acheivements must have been, when he looked at Reb Noson's shining visage or when he spoke with him face to face. For his face would literally burn like a torch, as he became completely lost and absorbed in Torah and prayer. Many, many times tears would stream from his eyes through his great cleaving to God. Everyone who heard him would feel such a tremendous awe and fear and humility that they would hide their faces from the great fear, awe and shame that fell upon them. What can we say? What can we say? Woe for the catastrophe that has befallen us! For the blow we have suffered! May God comfort us soon! Amen.]

Greetings to my son, David Zvi, may he live, and to my stepson, Shmelke, may he live. Don't worry! God is with us! God willing, everything will turn out well! Many Jews have already gone through suffering such as this and they were saved. In the end, our enemies will suffer a great defeat and God will have compassion on us in the great merit of the Rebbe, of blessed memory. We will have a place to live yet. And right there in Breslov! With God's help, our enemies will see and be ashamed!

The words of your father, praying for you.

Noson, as above

Letter #171

Greetings to my beloved and learned son, Reb Shachneh, may his light shine.

My beloved son! I am a little irritated that you have not sent me a single letter thus far. You did not even add on greetings at the end of someone else's letter, such as Reb Yosef, the son-in-law of Reb Zalman. You have acted foolishly, my dear son. And you still have not started to take time every day from your busy schedule to think about your end and your ultimate purpose! You see what happens in This World, and many of your years have already passed! Our days are like a passing shadow. If not now, when? What good is all your worrying about your livelihood going to do you? What would really help you is if you would steal and snatch an hour to cry out to God over your physical *and* spiritual livelihood. This would certainly help you in This World and the Next! The same applies to snatching fixed times for Torah study, as our master, teacher and Rebbe, of blessed memory, wrote about the Rabbis' dictum (Shabbat 31a), " Did you fix (i.e. "steal") sessions for Torah study?" (see *Likutey Moharan* I, 284).

My dear, beloved son! I feel terrible for you, because I know the good in your heart. But your worrying and anxiety so preoccupy you, and you keep putting things off until tomorrow. When are you going to do something for your *eternal* house? God should give you a long life, but all our days will never be enough to accomplish and rectify what we must in This World. For "the day is short and there is much work to do. You do not have to complete it, but you are not free to sit idle either." Just do everything that it is in your power to do. Particularly with all the holy conversations we have had, you ought to be drawing inspiration, encouragement and advice every day that will enable you to snatch all the true, eternal good that you can each day! Be sure, in any case, to write me a letter and send it to me in Uman immediately. Tell me in detail about my wife, and my son and daughter, may they live. Tell me how each one is doing and about everything that is going on there. I trust God that this is all for the good. For a person must know and believe that everything that happens to him is for the good (see *Likutey Moharan* I, 4).

The words of your father, hoping to see you soon.

Noson, as above

Publisher's note: Reb Avraham Dov [or Ber] was Rebbe Nachman's grandson and was married to Moshe Chenkes' daughter, Miriam Raitze. At the outbreak of hostilities, Moshe Chenkes pressed for a divorce for his daughter, which was given. The divorce was so bitter that Moshe demanded that the talit, which is customarily given to the groom on the wedding day (which had taken place four years earlier!) be returned. As we will see in later letters, Reb Avraham Ber married the daughter of Reb Ber of Tcherin, one of Rebbe Nachman's earlier followers and a staunch supporter of Reb Noson.]

Greetings to my very dear friend, our great and illustrious teacher, Reb Avraham Dov [Ber], may his light shine.

My friend, Reb Avraham Dov, may he live! I received your letters in Uman and in Kremenchug and they really encouraged me! Even though you reported a lot of troubles to me, I applaud you for your letter, and especially for all the effort you have expended on my behalf. On this merit, may God allow you to spend many good years devoting yourself to Torah and prayer. Amen, may it be His will.

I already wrote above about how I am doing, and the rest you will infer for yourself. Thank God, what I said was right. God will help us, save us and protect us from them, and we will be worthy of returning to God and of truly drawing close to Him. For this is why we were created.

> The words of your true friend, your forebearer's servant, who is ready to serve you, as the Rebbe, of blessed memory, would wish, until the soul leaves me. God, Who is good, will do what is [necessary to] finish everything well for me — for His sake, not for mine. "Do not give honor to us, God, not to us, but give it to Your Name!"
>
> *Noson, as above*

My beloved friend, Reb Chaim, son of Reb Yaakov, the Scribe. I know you have worked very hard in this effort, but I am a little irritated that you have not written me a single letter. Now, be sure that all our comrades sign the letter that you send to Uman. For my soul is bound up with theirs and I expect to hear from each and every one of them. Extend my greetings to all our comrades from the greatest to the least. Be sure to put proper shutters up on my windows from the outside right away. If you cannot collect enough money to do it, borrow in my name and I will pay it back immediately upon my arrival, God willing. Do exactly as I ask and no differently. The rest I have already written.

Noson, as above

172

Tuesday, Mishpatim, 5595, Uman.

My dear, beloved son, and all our faithful, beloved companions who suffer torment and pain, and who submit themselves to the sanctification of God's Name. Peace to you and peace to your souls! Be determined and strong and do not be afraid! For God is with us! He will surely not abandon us for the sake of His Great Name.

Know, my friends, that I arrived here in Uman yesterday, completing the journey safely. I spent last Shabbat in Terhovitza. I was happy and danced a little and our comrades there were happy and danced a lot, with God's help; especially on Motzay-Shabbat, when they danced to an awesome, heartrending melody in a great cry to God, singing repeatedly the verses (Saturday night *zemirot*), "Pure and clean of hands, favor those who spread forth their wings... Redeem Your People from the arrogant, Your flock from the hands of the shearers!" I weep copiously when I recall this. "Be gracious to us, God, be gracious, for we have had our fill of shame!"

I do not know what to write you. I found more than ten letters waiting for me here from Breslov and also from you, my dear son, from Tulchin. The bitter laments they contain, you know better than I, God have mercy. I was already at the Rebbe's holy gravesite yesterday, also in the *mikvah*, and, thank

Letter #172

God, they did not kill me. I did not even get hit with a single rock, God forbid. I was in Zlatipolia as well, where I prayed the Morning Prayers and was in the *mikvah*. I got out of there safely too! [While in the mikvah in Uman, someone tried to take Reb Noson's clothes and destroy them. He was caught in the act and was stopped.] Who can relate God's miracles and great kindnesses that appear within the sorrow itself?! Who can declare His mighty and awesome acts?! For, thank God, we have survived thus far. I trust in God that He will never ever leave or abandon us and that He will save us from our troubles. Our holy and awesome Rebbe, of blessed memory, will certainly finish everything the way he wants to, as he said, "I have finished and I will finish!"

I hope to God that I will soon come to Breslov, but I am staying here a little longer in order to go to the Rebbe's holy gravesite to express myself there before God, and also to give our companions from Breslov a chance to come and meet me, as I already wrote you. If it is possible for you too to come here right away, so much the better.

I do not have time to continue. It is time for the Morning Prayers and I am presently very busy. May God have mercy on me and on all of you, and may He soon have us rejoice in His salvation. Even now, as I tearfully write this letter, I do so amidst joy, that within such a "hiddenness of hiddenness" we are able to know about the point of pure truth, who is our life eternally! For This World is nothing but vanity, and our lives are like a fleeting shadow. Many days and months of this winter have already flown by, with all that it has brought us. And what have our opponents accomplished through their evil? "They conceived evil and gave birth to falsehood" and have added to their own hellfire. A raging hot wind is their inheritance.

But on us, God has had compassion and has rescued us from people who have so fallen into error that they tear up holy, awesome books such as these and desecrate them so, and who inform upon and spill the blood of righteous people such as these! Without a doubt, not a single drop of our blood that they have spilled, or a single Jewish coin that they have had confiscated has been lost. Without a doubt, they are among those who "go down and never come up," while God's lovingkindness will shine upon us. Without a doubt, this is all atonement and forgiveness for our sins. For God knows that we walk with true simplicity the way our Sages, of blessed memory, taught us. We must joyfully accept the past as atonement and we must cry out to God over the future, that He will act for the sake of His Great Name and rescue us from them. May God hear our prayers and our pleas and say "Enough!" to our suffering. May He soon have us rejoicing in His salvation!

Noson of Breslov

Reb Nachman of Tulchin sends his greetings. It really uplifted me to find him here safe! It is all God's salvation and wonders! Every minute of every day I see the Rebbe's holy words: "Amidst suffering You gave me relief" (Likutey Moharan I, 195) and those words are keeping me alive right now.

173

With God's help, Tuesday, Terumah, 5595, Uman.

Warm greetings to my honored and beloved; my dear, learned son, Reb Yitzchak, may his light shine.

I received your letter of last Friday yesterday and I was overjoyed — even amidst pain and suffering such as this. For I see that, thank God, my words are fixed firmly in your heart and that they are inspiring you, even at such a time as this. This is the way! To carefully remember every single word, so that you can stand up to the test, fortify yourself constantly and give your soul new life every time through everything that comes upon a person in his life — especially a person who wants to come close to an amazing, awesome and unique figure such as the Rebbe, who is our life, eternally!

A person has to fix these Torah lessons and holy conversations so deeply in his heart that, after a hundred years, when the time comes to lie in the grave, even there he will give himself life with the Rebbe's holy words! Similarly, at the time of the Revival of the Dead and for all eternity, to fulfill (Proverbs 6:22; see Avot 6:10), "'When you are walking' — in This World, 'she [the Torah] will guide you. When you lie down' — in the grave, 'she will guard you. When you wake up....'"

You know, my brothers and friends, that all the work we do for our livelihoods and all the business we conduct, is not to make a profit in Odessa or Brody, but rather it is only for the sake of the eternal goal, and God knows our true intentions. Thank God, no matter what. And even if you are not what you should be — given the holiness of these conversations and awesome Torah lessons — you have still greatly succeeded and have truly gained very much! *Ashreikhem!* Happy are you, my sons, my brothers and my friends! Now, especially, you can understand a little of the importance of what we are longing to do from the intensity of the many barriers we are encountering, the like of which we have never faced (see *Likutey Moharan* I, 66:4). May God guard us from now on.

Remember well every single word, every single lesson, every single prayer and every single discussion! Remember their amazing depth and the flashes of Godliness and of the greatness of the Creator that they contain! Remember how they radiate with the greatness of the Torah, the mitzvot and the true tzaddikim, and remember the encouragement, inspiration and simple, clear advice that is contained in every single one of them! Remember how, through his incredible pathways, he enables every single Jew, great or small, to carry out what is written in the Torah! He awakens the sleeping, rouses the slumbering, and literally enlivens the dead! He lifts up the souls of Israel from the depths of hell and even lower, reviving them and allowing them to earn eternal life!

Even if you already know all this, each one of you must now review it mentally and verbally by yourself and with your comrade; all this and more, each one according to his understanding. There is no way to explain either in writing or in speech exactly how each person should do this. It depends on the individual person. But what is critical is that each one should do this so that you will be able to strengthen yourselves now as well. For our lives are like a passing shadow, literally like blown dust, and there is no such thing as time. Soon it will all be past and those of us who stand up to the test and endure the purification will joyfully talk about all this! For God will certainly save us and rescue us from their hands. He will not be at odds forever.

You wrote that you are encouraging yourself with the lessons "*Azamra!*" and "In suffering You gave me relief" (*Likutey Moharan* I, 282; *ibid.* I, 195) and, if so, you are right with me! Because most of the vitality I have at any time, I gain through these lessons, and especially now, during this time of great distress. "If our mouths were filled with song like the sea," it would still be impossible to utter even a thousandth of the incredible "expansions," gifts of relief, that appear amidst the suffering every minute of every hour of every day! How great are God's deeds, how profound His thoughts! For most of our holy gathering are more steadfast in the truth than before!

I arrived here on Monday of [Parashat] Mishpatim and God in His compassion arranged it that I immediately met someone to bring the news of my arrival to Teplik. I sent them a letter with him that arrived there last Tuesday night. They all immediately were roused and did not sleep the rest of the night, which they spent talking about my situation. Two carriages left for here on Wednesday, and they arrived Wednesday night. Two more men from Terhovitza came on Thursday, as well as Reb Zalman, the shochet, from the village.

So all of us, along with our comrades who live here, were ready to go today to the Rebbe's gravesite, downcast, anguished and brokenhearted. Then we received two letters: one from you and one from Breslov, from Reb Avraham Dov. There was also another letter from Reb Shmuel Weinberg to his father [Reb Avraham Weinberg of Uman, who was an influential person with the authorities; he is mentioned below]. All of them, as you know, were replete with bitter, bitter cries. We went to the holy gravesite and there we cried out in prayer to God loudly and bitterly crying and weeping very much. The praying there was louder than on Yom Kippur and our plea certainly went up to Heaven. But we still need to pray a great deal and each one of us must talk privately to his Creator very much. For we are in dire straits indeed, and we need great salvation and compassion. Even without this, every person needs much salvation to cure his soul's spiritual wounds and pains, which, as you know, are what a person *really* suffers from and what is *really* to be pitied. All the uproar and trouble has only come in order to awaken us and to rouse us from our sleep, as I have already written you and as you know for yourselves.

The men from Teplik, my friends, Reb Meir and Reb Nachman, the son-in-law of Reb Netanel, were here over Shabbat and stayed here until yesterday. We naturally spoke a great deal and Reb Meir said that he has experienced a real arousal to God as a result of the *machloket*. And it is really true. For, thank God, he has changed for the better in a number of areas, and, thank God, I inspired him with what I said. He and his friends also inspired me a lot. Here we can see the wonders of God. For the Rebbe's candle will never go out! They will perish and a thousand like them, and not one of his holy words will miss its mark. He has

Letter #173

finished and he will finish! He even said, "God is finishing all the time" (see *Tzaddik* #85).

So even now "we must thank the Master of All" that we have merited to be in the Rebbe's portion! "My lots have landed in pleasant places!" We must strengthen ourselves to be happy every day and to turn groaning and sighing into joy! The more troubles, abuse and embarrassments attack us, God save us — while they are no doubt extremely painful and bitter — the more we must strengthen ourselves adamantly and turn groaning and sighing to joy over the fact that we have been worthy of escaping such wickedness! We have been rescued from ripping up holy, awesome books with teachings such as "The Story of Rabbi Eliezer and Rabbi Yehoshua and Chanukah" (*Likutey Moharan* II, 7), "Psalms and repentance" (*ibid.* II, 73), "The Sayings of Rabbah bar bar Chana," "The Recountings," "The Hidden Book," (*Zohar* II, pp.176b-178b), "The Elders of Athens," and the list goes on and on (these teachings are found in *Likutey Moharan* Lessons 1-31). "Like a bird from a trap we have escaped. The trap has been broken and we got away! Help us in the name of God!"

I have decided for a number of reasons, to stay here until after Purim. Therefore, my beloved, my son, may he live, if you can come here next week (may it be for a blessing) it will be very nice. If you can come here for Purim, God willing, we will celebrate and rejoice even more! From what I hear, your job at the post office is also in jeopardy and they are also gnashing their teeth at you. If so, there is nowhere for you to flee to except here. We will cry out to God and take council together. What God wants is what is going to happen.

[Publisher's note: Reb Mordekhai of Tulchin was detained by opponents of Breslover Chassidim who beat him brutally and led him through the town of Tulchin demanding that he stand up publicly in the market and denounce Reb Noson. Reb Mordekhai stood up and said (Esther 3:2), "And Mordekhai will neither bow nor bend!" The community leaders mentioned here were Hirsh Ber and Moshe Landau, as well as Reb Avraham Weinberg, mentioned earlier. Hirsh Ber and Moshe Landau were leaders of the "enlightenment movement" and were on extremely good terms with the Russian Czar. Rebbe Nachman befriended them (or they Rebbe Nachman) before he passed away in Uman in 1810. Opposed to religious teachings as much as Reb Noson was opposed to the heretical teachings of the enlightenment, they nevertheless remained friendly throughout the years. During the Years of Oppression, they offered to intervene with the authorities on behalf of Reb Noson and could have had all their opponents constrained in several ways. Reb Noson refused, as Rebbe Nachman had promised him that he would overcome all his opponents and he also wished to rely solely on prayer. There will be mention of these people further on and Moshe Landau even came to Breslov in the spring to calm down the campaign against Reb Noson.]

Reb Mordekhai, may his light shine, would also do well to come here, for a number of reasons. All his sins were unquestionably forgiven as a result of the great humiliation that he suffered. And he stood up to the test! All of us have certainly obtained much atonement for sins; but the more one suffers, God save us, the greater the reward. Thank God, the community leaders here are with us all the way — thank God. God will save us.

Your idea that you wrote about traveling to Ladizin is pure foolishness and I am surprised you even considered it. But we cannot change the past. We have no-one to lean on but our Father in Heaven. The time for the Morning Prayers has arrived. Last Shabbat I spoke about the teaching, "Conceptions of Godliness can only be obtained... and for this you must have a Rebbe

Letter #173

who is very very great indeed" (*Likutey Moharan* I, 30:2; see *Likutey Halakhot*, *Basar b'Chalav* 5). *Ashreinu!* Happy are we that we have merited to hear all this! This is what comforts us in our destitution. What can we return to God for all the good He has given us?! Rejoice in God! Fortify your hearts mightily, all you who hope in God!

The words of your father, hoping to see you soon in joy.

Noson of Breslov

Greetings to all our comrades and in particular to Reb Shimshon, may his light shine. You will realize that what I said above is intended for all of you as well. Take careful notice of everything that happens to a person in This World. There are troubles and tribulations without number, overall and for each individual. This evil is different from that evil as is written (Ecclesiastes 2:23), "All his days are grief and pain," for man was born to suffer. And the *Shelah* wrote a verse on the same theme, "There is no moment without flaw, no hour without evil, no day, no week, no month, no year." Look it up.

So then hundreds of years ago the world was also full of suffering. For from the day the Holy Temple was destroyed, every day is more cursed than the previous (*Sotah* 48a). It is only the holy Torah that gives us vitality and that allows us to survive, especially when the true tzaddikim, pillars of Torah and prayer, develop new Torah insights! *Ashreinu!* Happy are we that we merited to know about the true tzaddik who was here in our time! The foundation of the world! "Were it not for the salt" that is the light of the true tzaddik, "the world would never be able to endure the bitterness" (see Likutey Moharan 23:3). And God with His miracles revealed all this to us! I cannot go on about this any longer.

Fortify yourselves determinedly! Do not fear them or be intimidated! Do not be afraid of their many chariots and the shouts of those who imbibe their intoxicating wine, their drunken shouts. The Lord, Our God is with you and He will save you. This is the camp of the Holy Ark, the Torah that He in His abundant mercy and lovingkindness revealed to us. These very books, the ones they are ripping up, disgracing and trampling upon so much, are going to save us! From the dust of our destitution and lowliness, they will pick us up and raise us up high! "Through them the world will be saved!" They are our life and the length of our days, in This World and the Next, forever.

Noson, the same

174

With God's help, Wednesday, Tetzaveh, 5595, Uman.

Greetings and great salvation to all my brothers and friends.

I received your letter today during the Morning Prayers, and I also received one last night after the Evening Prayers from Reb Yosef, son-in-law of Reb Zalman. Everyone is expressing "satisfaction, delight and joy." And without a doubt there [actually] is cause for delight and joy, when amidst such a concealment we have merited to know about truth such as this! The greater the uproar and concealment, the greater our joy should

Letter #174

be! For if we had not drawn close *beforehand* to know the absolute truth the way it really is, not only would it be totally impossible for us to do so now, but worse, God forbid, we too would be doing what they are to these holy, amazing books!

How can we ever thank and praise God enough for all the miracles and wonders that He did with us when He rescued us from wickedness such as this, from such hell and perdition?! Anyone with a modicum of true intelligence in his head will know and understand that no suffering in the world is greater than the suffering of someone who tears up and desecrates holy books such as these, who so groundlessly sheds Jewish blood and who keeps so many from Jewish holiness! They want to completely undermine Judaism, God forbid!

Here too there is a *mitnaged* (opponent) whose son started to draw a little near to us and was studying a lot of Talmud and Codes. The scoundrels, who call themselves "chassidim," are now forcibly preventing him from studying Talmud and Codes, saying that it is better that he talk with them! The father of this young man shouted at him, "I am feeding you on the condition that you learn only one page of Talmud a day and no more! *Anyone who studies all day is a Breslover!*"

The bottom line really is that the *mitnagdim* are not just trying to stop people from studying the Rebbe's books. Their real evil intent deep down in their hearts is to abolish the entire Torah from Israel! For you are aware of the ways of the young, in this generation in particular, and the Torah is the only means of salvation. There is no-one who can bring the study and practice of Torah into the world like our Master, teacher and

Rebbe through the holy pathways that he revealed through me and in his holy books! This is why they harass us so intensely, saying, "Come, let's destroy them!" God forbid.

The fact is that if events were to just take their *natural* course, we really do not know how we could stand up against them. Even through praying and crying out to God — though we do engage in this a little, not one of us with his prayer could stand up against an attack such as this, in which Satan himself has girded his loins and is gnashing his teeth at us. All the same, we still have to do our part and cry out, scream and supplicate the best we can. For God hears the prayers of every mouth. What we are really relying on though is the power of the prayers of the elder of elders. For *he* is engaged in the work we are doing of bringing souls truly close to God and it is for *his* holy name that we are called Breslover Chassidim! He has begun, and he will finish, as he said, "I have finished and I will finish!" He spoke many other holy words such as these and now too I believe with total faith that he will undoubtedly finish everything as he wishes to. In the end, our persecutors' memory will be utterly blotted out. Woe to them! Woe to their souls forever!

In the meantime, though, each one of us must go through trials such as these. I believe, however, that even now there is not a single one of us who is faced with a test which he cannot overcome. The greatest barriers are in the mind. But since, thank God, all of you are strong and steadfast in faith and in the truth, I am confident that, with God's lovingkindness, I will not be ashamed of you, nor you of me — not in This World and not in the Next. Each person must apply to himself the teaching,

Letter #174

"Avraham was One," explained at the opening of *Likutey Moharan II*. I inspire myself with this a lot right now. What would I do if all of you, God forbid, were also throwing rocks at me, God forbid? This is what happened to our Father, Avraham. He was "one," alone in the entire world. Thank God that you have been saved from this!

You too, every one of you, must think to himself that, even if he were the only person in the world who knew this truth, he would have to fortify himself to stand up against the entire world! But God does not send a person a test he cannot overcome (*Likutey Moharan* II, 46). Thank God that we have at least the small holy gathering of sincere, good individuals that we do, who do not opt for ideologies of lies, mockery, or for any of the confused pursuits which are so popular now. Rather they walk with sincerity, truth and integrity on the holy path which our ancestors have always traveled. We would never have merited this, were it not for his holy, awesome words of truth which are the deepest of the deep, and honest and pure as can be. *Ashreinu!* Happy are we! How good is our portion that we have merited to hear all this! *Ashreinu!* Happy are we for every single teaching and every single conversation that we heard from the Rebbe, of blessed memory.

God's compassion has helped us until now so that we merited to hear lessons and stories such as these in the midst of the fierce *machloket* that raged in the Rebbe's day like a fire stretching up to the Heavens, as they tried to "swallow him alive," God forbid. But God had pity on His People and we were worthy of having him settle in Breslov where all his holy books were composed. Who can express God's mighty deeds? Who can utter all His praises? "Tzaddikim are greater after their passing than they are in their lifetime" (Chullin 7b), and since the Rebbe's passing, we have seen totally unprecedented wonders and enormous miracles, even more than we did when he was alive! For the Rebbe has given strength to an exhausted, relentlessly persecuted man such as I to write and publish books such as these, to compose and publish prayers such as these and to assemble a gathering such as this for Rosh HaShanah in Uman. The list goes on.

"You have done much, Lord, my God. Your miracles and thoughts are for us. None can compare to You, for they are too many to enumerate or express!" (Psalms 40:6). We were also worthy of building a study hall here and of praying in it several times on Rosh HaShanah. The God Who has girded me with strength and Who has helped me until now — not on my merit or power, but on the Rebbe's great merit and power — He will also help me now to complete the study hall here this summer, God willing, and to soon return safely to my home in Breslov. For even if I *am* a great coward, against this, God has also made me worthy of having a great deal of holy boldness, and He has established my audacity against theirs. Thank God, I am as resolute in my opinion about what I think as a pillar of iron and walls of bronze. With God's help, I am readying myself for them with "gifts, prayer and battle" (cf. Rashi, Genesis 32:9), [for] in His great power, God will help us.

I have already spoken extensively with our friend, the bearer of this letter, Reb Shmuel Weinberg. I am waiting for his

Letter #174

quick response telling me the good report. I hope to God that I can gradually make my way to Breslov safely. It is impossible to understand what the *mitnagdim* hope to accomplish by banishing me from Breslov. Anywhere I go I am going to tell people about the truth of the Rebbe's holy teachings. So the people there will also become Breslover Chassidim, the true *kasherim*, pious, among the Jewish People! In fact, I have considered the possibility that this is precisely God's intention. But it would be a great pity if I become separated from you so suddenly, God forbid. With God's kindness I am confident in the Rebbe's great power and that for his sake God will surely not do this. Rather He will help me with His miracles to return safely to my home in Breslov soon.

Purim is almost here. May God hear our cry tomorrow on the Fast of Esther and may we merit to pour out our hearts like water before Him. Just as He performed awesome deeds during these days in the past, may He likewise bestow His lovingkindness on us and give us eternal salvation. May we be worthy of soon rejoicing in His salvation on the coming holy days of Purim and may the *keren* (glory) of truth rise higher and higher! Let us always be glad and rejoice in His salvation!

Rejoice and be happy, my brothers and friends! Thank God, you merited to be in the Rebbe's holy portion forever! Give thanks for the past that God has allowed you to hold onto the truth through hardship and suffering such as this, and cry out over the future. Make a sincere effort to supplicate and plead earnestly before God, from the very depths of your hearts. Cry out and beg God every day that each one of you will able to hold on to the point of his Judaism, and that we will be worthy of escaping our enemies and pursuers. They will stumble and fall and we will rise up and take heart! May we soon see each other face to face. Let us be happy and rejoice in His salvation!

Noson of Breslov

Greetings to my illustrious friend, Reb Avraham Ber, may he live. Trust God, my beloved son, for He will certainly not abandon you. Everything will turn into good, peace, joy and life! The words of the Rebbe are alive and enduring, when he said, "God is very great, we know nothing of it. God is finishing constantly" (*Rabbi Nachman's Wisdom* #3; *Tzaddik* #85, #126).

I, poor and destitute, so pursued as I am, will walk in simplicity, to believe the Rebbe's holy words simply and straightforwardly and to tell anyone who wants to hear, all the great things that God did with us, returning us to Him and bringing us near to Him and His holy Torah. May God finish for me. "Even when I am old and gray, God, do not abandon me, until I declare Your strength to the generation and Your might to all who are to come. Your righteousness, God, reaches unto the Heavens."

Noson, as above

Warm greetings to my friend whom I love as my own heart and soul, the Rav and great luminary, our teacher Reb Aharon, may his light shine [he was the Rav of Breslov, one of Rebbe Nachman's closest followers and Reb Noson's close friend]. Greetings to his sons, may they live, and to his whole family — greetings and great salvation! I already expressed myself a little above. What should I add? His scholarly honor knows everything. His heart is as my heart, and his soul is as my soul. All of us are one and we take refuge in God. He will not abandon us in our old age. Let our enemies see and be ashamed. When our time comes, after many long years, let our souls be taken from us still among the Rebbe's followers. May we never be ashamed or humiliated.

Noson, as above

175

With God's help, Thursday, the Fast of Esther, 5595, Uman.

My beloved son. My dear son, apple of my eye.

I just now received your letters of Monday, Parashat Tetzaveh, and Friday, Parashat Terumah, when I came back from the holy gravesite with a number of our comrades. We cried out there, weeping before God over what our souls have suffered in the past and in particular over the enormous suffering that we have now from our enemies and from those who groundlessly persecute us and denounce us for seeking good.

The illustrious Reb Matityahu Leib of Bophilya, may his light shine, was in my house at the time. He also fled from his home over the *machloket*. He has been living here for about two weeks now and does not know when he will return home. Reb Heshel from Teplik is also here. While the *machloket* in Teplik is also intense, it is mixed there with a little more kindness, because, thank God, our side is quite strong. I also received a letter yesterday from Breslov with that "good" news about how they searched my house there to see if I had already arrived. I am sure you have already heard about this. In all these things we have no-one to lean on but our Father in Heaven.

You should know, my dear son, that Reb Shmuel Weinberg was here from Friday of Parashat Mishpatim until yesterday, when he set off for home. I spoke with him briefly about how I should proceed. Right now, after all the tumult and with all their railing at me and frightening me, I am still determined to return safely home, God willing, in the near future. For the time being, though, I am waiting for a response from Reb Shmuel Weinberg. Salvation is all in God's hands.

Thousands of pages would not suffice to describe to you what I have suffered. But God's kindness is endless and He gives me the strength to go on enduring hardships, suffering and humiliation such as this. What is more, His kindness is allowing me to even be a little happy that I was able to be in the Rebbe's holy portion which is (Deuteronomy 32:9), "God's portion is His People."

[*Publisher's note: Reb Noson now refers to one of the slanders being used by his opponents to justify the conflict.*]

The *mitnagdim's* mouths should be filled with dirt for slandering us with what is well-known to be a lie, that, God forbid, we do not believe in the Oral Torah! Let their souls leave them! We learn in the Codes and in the four sections of the *Shulchan Arukh* every day! This is one of the holy practices that the Rebbe advised us very strongly to adopt, as is well-known and printed in his holy books (see *Rabbi Nachman's Wisdom* #29, #76, #185).

Who revealed the hidden significance of the Oral Torah the way our Rebbe, of blessed memory, did? It was he who said that "the essential difference between Israel and the nations of the world is the Oral Law and that this is how you can recognize a Jew!" (*Likutey Moharan* II, 28). What can we say? God has found our wrongdoing. But in *this* matter that they are slandering us, we are not culpable in the least! May He pay back evildoers according to their evil! May He quickly subdue and put down all our enemies and pursuers! Let Him take pity on us for the sake of His great Name. My pain is so great that I do not know what to write.

Concerning your traveling here: in most matters, you came to the right conclusion as far as the few thoughts I had on the subject were concerned. You certainly cannot just abandon everything right now, and the Rebbe does not want this either. But I am surprised that you would even consider going to Ladizin, as you wrote in your last letter. May God have pity and compassion on us, save us and protect us, and have events work out for the best

[text missing].

We trust God that in His great kindness He will give us the place and the council that we need in order to escape now with our lives, as He has in the past, through His many miracles. Now especially we need to go with the teaching "Today, if you will listen to His voice!" (*Likutey Moharan* I, 272) which teaches that a person has nothing but the present day. If one looks at things this way, one can endure the hardship and pain that one must for the sake of the Torah and the truth. We also have to adhere to what the Rebbe said about "Avraham was One" (at the opening of *Likutey Moharan II*). This will enable us to endure the abuse.

We must resolve in our minds to remain fast in the truth. No matter what, God forbid, "until I expire I will not give up what I believe in"! Nor should we be looking around waiting for God to immediately perform miracles in this matter. God's ways are extremely wondrous and the power of free will is very great indeed. Nonetheless, I trust God that our enemies will not succeed against us at all. For, no matter what, God will help us and rescue us from them. Ultimately they will perish and be uprooted, and in the end their memory will be excised from the world! God will shine forth His light and His kindness on us and without a doubt all the humiliation, pain and bloodshed that we suffered at their hands will turn out to have been a great and awesome good for us!

We have to remember well what the books teach, and the Rebbe spoke about it further, that one burn in Gehennom is worse than all the suffering in This World (*Rabbi Nachman's Wisdom* #236). He also spoke about the pain that a dead person has lying in the grave and how he lies there listening to the sound of each crawling maggot (*Rabbi Nachman's Wisdom* #84). Surely this is worse than the sound of voices of the *mitnagdim* abusing us! Their words really *do* bite like the pierce of a sword, but the pain of the maggots, Gehennom and so on are much worse than this. If you are unsure whether all this has released you *completely* from the pains of Gehennom, you *can* rest assured that it has released you from most of them!

I trust God that anyone who really stands up to the test now will certainly not see Gehennom at all; especially since at any rate we have been saved from the additional severe punishment of Gehennom which awaits the persecutors and *mitnagdim* who rip up holy books such as these, trample them in mud and filth, and spill so much Jewish blood. They will certainly go down to the very lowest level of Gehennom. Woe to them and woe to their souls! I hope to God that we will be able to rejoice very much during the coming days of Purim [over our having been spared this]; this, in addition to the fact that we were worthy of hearing such awesome, wondrous teachings about Purim and Chanukah, Shabbat and Yom Tov, and the list goes on and on! *Ashreinu!* Happy are we! How good is our portion! No-one in the world can say, "*Ashreinu!*" over his lot the way we can! Thank God, we have already been able to rejoice many times over the Rebbe's holy Torah lessons. This is especially true now that the concealment has spread so extensively. For, as if from a trap, we have escaped! We know about pure truth such as this, that leads Israel with such simplicity and straightness, yet with such magnificent intelligence! Go and see the great might of your Master Who, in order to allow free choice, has so concealed a truth such as this! And our souls He has rescued!

[*Publisher's note: Reb Naftali moved to Uman some time after Rebbe Nachman passed away. When the Breslov kloyz was built, he had an annex built where he lived. This is where Reb Noson stayed during this visit in Uman. Otherwise, he would generally stay with his family.*]

You should know, my son, that even here I have no peace except when I am in the house of Reb Naftali, may his light shine. Even when I go to the *mikvah*, they lie in wait for me.

Thank God, I have escaped them so far. This coming Shabbat, and on Purim too, God willing, I will not eat in Reb Shmuel's house, may his light shine. He just made a wedding for his daughter, may she live, and the groom from Zlatipolia and his teacher are eating with him. My niece Lana was just at my house here at Reb Naftali's, may his light shine, and she appealed to me to please not be angry at her, and she gave money to Reb Naftali to have me eat with him. [They were from Reb Noson's family who lived in Uman.]

In every move that I make, every day, the suffering and humiliations are very great. But the "expansions," the shows of relief, within the suffering are wondrous indeed! For God has had pity on me and arranged things well for me, so that I have a nice private room here with everything I need, thank God: tea, coffee and everything that a person needs to live. People are attending me with great love, Reb Nachman from Tulchin, and others of our comrades. Thank God, I have people to talk to about our holy efforts and, thank God, we go to the holy *tzion* [Rebbe Nachman's gravesite], almost every day. How great are the kindnesses and wonders of God! So we must trust God that He will surely rescue us from them. Then the verse will be fulfilled, "They will fight against you, but will not defeat you" (Jeremiah 1:19). Just fortify yourself, be strong and trust God! He will not abandon you, nor us, and we will be able to talk face to face again soon. Let us be happy and rejoice in His salvation, especially on the coming holy Purim!

> The words of your father and teacher; and the teacher of anyone who wants to hear my words and who is still uncorrupted. Farewell. Do not be afraid,

for God is with you! They and a thousand like them will perish and not one word of the Rebbe's holy teachings with be nullified!

I wrote all this yesterday when I received your letter. It is now Friday, Erev Shabbat, and I was already at the holy gravesite today before daybreak. It was your letter that impelled me to do this, forcing me to go there today and express myself. I took out your letter on purpose to recall what was written there and I was overcome with weeping. Then God helped me and I was able to express myself before Him a little. I also read two letters before God and before the Rebbe and it was certainly impossible to keep from crying. Now too, as I write this, though I am somewhat happy, I am still crying as I remember your pain, because I suffer more over your pain and the pain of our comrades than I suffer from my own pain. Yesterday as well one of our comrades read your letter, and he started weeping too.

May the Master of Compassion see our tears, especially those of the righteous Adil, the Rebbe's daughter, may she live, and may He have compassion on us and save us quickly. I have deep trust that God will certainly save us from their hands, and He will likewise rescue anyone who is strong and stands up to his test. As for those who succumb and who promise to cut themselves off from their root, their life and their eternal hope (even though in their hearts they are with us) — these people I really feel sorry for, because they end up "bald on both sides." For until they say lies about us, their capitulation will not be believed or accepted, and they are unwilling to uproot themselves from the truth as much as *that*, because they are afraid of the Day of Judgment!

The best thing would have been for them to put themselves on the line from the start, and it would have been better for them in This World and the Next. But I certainly judge them favorably and I really do feel for their suffering. All the same, I believe what the Rebbe said, that no-one is given a test or barrier that he cannot overcome (Likutey Moharan II, 46). Most impediments are really in a person's mind, and the present situation is no exception. Think back on even a tiny fraction of what has been spoken between us, of the marvels that we have seen in his holy books and of the flashes of Godliness and of the Rebbe's greatness that I put into you, with God's help. You will then certainly stand up to the test or else you will endeavor to flee beforehand and thus avoid being tested and subjected to abuse, God forbid. This is what Reb Nachman of Tulchin did. He fled from his home and is staying here. Reb Alek of Breslov did likewise. I trust God that they will certainly return safely to their homes, God willing. Nonetheless, you should not flee right away, but only if you see, God forbid, that the situation really demands it. I hope to God though that it will not come to this. You must, however, still long and yearn and try with all your power to come here. Salvation is all in God's hands.

Even though I wrote earlier that you should not expect to see miracles "on demand," the truth is that I see amazing miracles practically every day. For it is not a simple thing that by God's lovingkindness we, and especially I, have escaped

Letter #175

them thus far. "If our mouths were filled will song..!" So similarly I trust God that He will always rescue us from them and that our enemies will not overcome us. Without a doubt God will perform miracles in Heaven and on earth in order to subdue our enemies and rescue us from their hands. Not for our sakes will He do it, but for the sake of the one who is working to plant the vineyard of the House of Israel, to bring fulfillment of the Torah into the world! My meaning in what I wrote above was not to force the issue. One with faith does not rush. But no matter what, He will surely save me and anyone who will stay with us to hail in the Rebbe's name. He will surely rescue us all. Our enemies will not celebrate over us, but rather they who gloat over us will don humiliation and shame. Lovers of our righteousness will exultantly rejoice! I have said enough for those who desire truth.

The words of your true friend forever.

Noson, the same

Your desire for my words is so strong, that I cannot restrain myself from writing a little more to encourage you, and all those who desire truth, on the topic of holy boldness. For right now we require it very very much and must fulfill (*Avot* 5:23), "Be bold like a leopard... to do the will of your Father in Heaven!" "The Torah was given to Israel only because they were bold" (*Beitzah* 25a). The Rebbe also spoke about this very much and it is discussed in his holy books (see *Likutey Moharan* I, 22:11; ibid. I, 147). It is true that at present it is definitely impossible to really face them with boldness and to say what we really want, since now is their hour and, because of our many sins, they are extremely powerful. Nonetheless, even amidst your silence you must still be very bold. The main thing is to be bold at least in your hearts, and not, God forbid, to be embarrassed of yourselves! As the Rebbe said, "What do we have to be ashamed of? The whole world was created for us!" (Tzaddik #112). For even though each person *should* be embarrassed about his own wrongs, as far as our group is concerned, since we are called after the name of the Rebbe, of blessed memory, we have nothing at all to be ashamed of! This is what we have for all our labor! This is our hope and our comfort! This is our salvation in This World and the Next forever! The person who is stronghearted and who is not ashamed in his heart will have God's help to know how to act properly in his boldness against them, so that he can answer them back peacefully, and yet still pierce their hearts. Thus they will fall before him in their hearts. A person must ask God to help him know how to respond to them properly in order to fulfill (Avot 2:19), "Know what to answer a heretic."

176

With God's help, Monday night, Tisa, 5595, Uman.

Warm greetings to my honored friend whom I love as myself, the learned Reb Shmuel Weinberg, may his light shine.

We received your letter on Sunday after the reading of the Megillah and it gave us great pleasure and joy. It was through your letter that God gave us the additional strength we needed to fortify ourselves and rejoice on Purim amidst sorrows such

Letter #176

as these, God save us — especially after what happened to us last Motzay-Shabbat, the first night of Purim, when a group of scoundrels got together and arrayed themselves against our study hall. They destroyed the door, ripped out four windows and broke off the shutters and threw them outside. A few of them have been recovered... They took out the chandeliers and the rest of the smaller lights which had been put away inside the lectern. They destroyed the lectern as well, and removed all these things that night.

We immediately informed the leaders of the city about all this and they were extremely angry at the perpetrators. They all said that we must file a legal complaint with the governor of the city. But we could not do it yesterday and today his father [Reb Shmuel Weinberg's father, Reb Avraham], may his light shine, sent for the scribes. However, the day passed and they never came. We know, of course, that everything we need is always attended by great barriers, but still, tomorrow we will try again, with God's help, to file the complaint. We hope to God that it will all turn out for the best; that this very event will cause them a great downfall, and they will not be able to terrorize us any more. For the moment, though, we are in need of great salvation and mercy. Our many sorrows have surrounded us on all sides and each one of us is afflicted, as well as the group as a whole. You can imagine our great "delight" on Purim morning, when I wept out of heartfelt grief and pain.

But God's kindnesses never cease and He gave me the strength to fortify myself in the holy ways that the Rebbe taught until I turned some of the groaning and sighing into happiness and joy. I went with simplicity and said, "Thank God that *I* didn't break windows in a holy study hall such as this, which is named for our master, teacher and holy Rebbe." Then I set out to tell his father [Reb Avraham Weinberg], may his light shine, what had happened. It was then that I received the aforementioned letters. I was a little afraid to read them. Who could know what was written in them that might, God forbid, taint the joy of Purim for us? But God had compassion on us and the letters contained news about a few acts of salvation. Thus we gained a little strength, through His great kindness and, thank God, we were very happy indeed for many hours on holy Purim day. We danced a great deal, and I too danced a great deal, with God's help. Our joy on Purim now is something altogether new and is a real show of God's salvation for us.

That evening we went to the authorities and, as you can understand yourself, Reb Naftali, may his light shine, and I waited there to speak with them. I have written this account so that you will have a record, and will be able to relate to future generations everything that happened to us this winter, and especially these days of Purim. No doubt, it is all for the best.

I was all set to travel home today or tomorrow but, because of the breach that they made in our study hall, I am forced to stay on here a few more days. It looks as if I will be here until after Shabbat. Be sure, therefore, to write me by post and tell me everything new that has happened since you wrote that last letter. Also write me explicitly about the days of Purim that just passed, and whether or not there was, God forbid, any damage done to my house or to the property of any of our companions. Give me a detailed report on everything.

Also give me an answer regarding that matter that you are worried about: that the young men, Reb Yosef, the son of R.Y., and Leizer, may he live, who came here last Erev Shabbat, told me that the city official Tamashevski and his men came looking for me at the house of Reb Yisrael, the son of Itzy Pitsherer. See if you can find a way to ask the governor whether it was done with his knowledge. If it was not, let him warn Tamashevski and all the minor officials under him to beware of approaching me, God forbid, without his permission and of harassing me, God forbid. You will understand for yourself how to go about this to my advantage. Write me immediately and tell me clearly with what kind of authority they came looking for me. May God have pity on me and on all our companions in our environs. May He rescue us soon from all our troubles and may He speedily bring down our enemies beneath us. May I soon be able to return home safely, at the very least after Shabbat. May we merit having our study hall stand on its site and finishing the building completely this year.

We must do everything we can to receive the protection of the Czar, may his majesty be exalted. The royal law surely does not condone the robberies and murders they are committing against us. Our main hope, though, is only in God. For we have no-one to lean on but our Father in Heaven. So you, from there, and we, from here, must call to God and seek Him out. With weeping and with pleas we will come before Him, like a son before his father, like a slave before his master. Whether "as sons" or "as slaves," we must make an effort to beg and petition God very much "until He looks down and sees us from Heaven." Furthermore, we must strengthen ourselves and bring ourselves to joy every day! This war is not just for one day. Even when God helps us escape them, and I am quite confident in the power of the holy elder that they will *not* defeat us, still, no-one can escape impediments, suffering and battles. May God have compassion, and may it all be with great kindness.

It is therefore essential for each person to do what the Rebbe taught us and to designate an hour or two [a day] to express himself before God. The rest of the day he should be happy. For joy in God is your fortress! In these times it is especially necessary to practice this. As for all this commotion, it is all meant to repel and drive off the person who does not stand up to the test, and to bring even closer those persons whose hearts have been touched with the point of truth, so that they will strengthen themselves to stand up to the test in everything that has come and that will come upon them. They will be further awakened to follow all the Rebbe's holy teachings and to receive advice and inspiration from all his holy words as explained in his holy books, particularly in the way that I clarified and explained them to you in all the conversations and discussions that we had, through His great lovingkindness and enormous miracles. For the words that passed between us were of no small import.

Think carefully and remember well everything that we discussed. The Rebbe already hinted at everything that is happening to us now! Recall how I told you in our discussions beforehand that enormous barriers will inevitably face everyone. Come now and gaze upon the works of God! Who would have believed that Reb Shimshon ben Mordekhai would go through everything that he is presently facing? He was the apple of his father's eye, and his father-in-law's as well. Not a single barrier stood in his way, or in the way of any of the young men in Breslov. I talked with them about this so many times that a few of them were *inclined* to face obstacles. Well, they got what they wanted and more. May God say "Enough!" to their suffering and to ours, and may it all turn into good. May God send salvation and may I return safely to my home next week.

For God's sake, write me a clear response regarding all the above immediately. Do not forget to write the letter to Tcherin that I talked to you about. Do it right away, if you have so far been remiss. Do not delay any longer! Tell me of the welfare of my whole family, as well as that of our comrades. Tell me in particular about the righteous Adil, may she live, and about her son and daughter, may they live. Tell them to be sure to send a letter to Kremenchug at once. Peace, life and great salvation for you and for me, as you and I, your true eternal friend forever, desire.

> Writing tearfully, but also a little joyfully and waiting for God's salvation at all times. I see His miraculous acts of salvation every day, but I await complete and total salvation very very soon.
> *Noson of Breslov*

Greetings to my wife, may she live, to all my family and to my son, Reb Shachneh, may his light shine. I received your letter and was pleased, as I am with all those who have written to me. I thank them for the past and I request for the future that every single one of them will write me in his own hand, according to the truth and good in his heart, until I am able to return safely home.

Noson, as above

Greetings to the house of the righteous Adil [Rebbe Nachman's daughter], may she live, to the house of the Reb [Reb Aharon], may he live, to all our comrades and to my friends, the illustrious Reb Yoel?, the son of R.Y., and Reb Shmuel Zvi, may their lights shine — even though I heard that one of them signed something for the side that is against me. While he certainly acted foolishly, I know that he truly loves me and my affection for him has not waned. God willing, when I return home, we will talk about it. Greetings too to the illustrious Reb Matyeh, may his light shine, and to Reb Litman and his brother Reb Yakil. They too should regret what they did against me. But God is my hope that everything will work out and that our covenant of love and peace will never be annulled.

Noson, as above

Be sure to send this letter with a trustworthy person directly to my son, may he live, in Tulchin. For I do not intend to write him this post and you know that his soul yearns for my words. Therefore be sure do as my son, Reb Yitzchak, wishes in this matter.

Noson, as above

177

[Publisher's note: Written after Reb Noson returned home from Uman, this letter also informs Reb Naftali of the boot factory set up in his home.]

With thanks to God, Friday, Erev Shabbat, Vayikra, 5595, Breslov.

Warm greetings to my honored friend, the learned, illustrious, pious and renowned, Reb Naftali, may his light shine.

On the day that I arrived safely home, I immediately wrote your learned honor a letter and sent it with the carriage driver. You surely received it. On Friday, [Torah reading] Pikudey, Reb Shmuel Weinberg also wrote you a letter, though I did not have time to write you myself. As yet I have not received a single line from you. Is that proper? Please, my dear brother, remember our love!

Write me a letter immediately and give me a full report on everything that is happening there, in particular about our *kloyz*. Has there been any kind of legal action against any of them yet? Or have they at least been frightened? At the very least have they refrained from making another breach into our holy *kloyz*? May God make breach after breach into all those who break into our holy building. May their arms wither. May they fall and never get up. May God awaken His enormous compassion on us, poor and persecuted as we are. May He rescue us from the sword, their mouths, and may He save the poor man from a mighty hand.

As for what is taking place here, I cannot describe it to you in detail. I do not need to tell you how they are gnashing their teeth and continually contemplating evils against us, and against me especially, poor, destitute and relentlessly pursued man that I am, so as to uproot "themselves" from the world, may God have mercy. But so far His mercy and enormous wonders have helped me and rescued a poor soul such as I from the hand of evildoers. Thanks to the Living God, I have been living in my house now for nine days and no-one has yet confronted me, God forbid, to abuse me to my face. Behind my back, though, they abuse me greatly. The influential [Jews] in the town, those scoundrels, and especially Moshe [Chenkes] and P. [Chaim Pais, see below, letter #180], are daily formulating and conferring about their evil plans to inform on me to the authorities, God forbid, on some false charge. May God nullify their designs and spoil their plans.

Upon my arrival, a boot factory was immediately set up in my house. Moshe [Chenkes] himself arranged this with the governor and gave him money for it. They were in my house from Thursday to this past Tuesday, Rosh Chodesh Nisan. In His mercy, God had them removed from my house after that Tuesday. "Blessed is the One Who released me from this as well." My eyes and the eyes of all those who are with us are lifted to God at every moment, waiting for Him to pity us, to ease this strife and to show us a favorable sign. Our enemies will see and be ashamed.

I do not have time to go on any longer, but I repeat my request a second and a third time that you write me a letter immediately and give me a full report, especially about the building of the *kloyz*. May God have compassion and may we be worthy of finishing it this summer. May your learned honor sit in it in peace and quiet engaging in Torah and prayer. May you hear *kaddish, kedushah, barkhu* and Torah reading there every day, each of them at its proper time, without the suffering and disturbances that you are subject to right now. Salvation is in God's hands. As He has helped thus far to build it to this point, may He add to His kindness and enormous miracles and soon finish it completely. May God finish for us. We do not know what we will do, but our eyes are upon You. In spite of it all though, praise God, we were a little joyful last Shabbat, despite the disturbance of the bootmakers, who were working on Shabbat. Nonetheless, "the holiness of Shabbat stands in its place." May the Merciful One let us inherit the day that is entirely Shabbat. Then everybody will see the truth. This is our hope, our life and our joy in This World and the Next, forever.

> The words of your friend, more attached to you than a brother, wishing you well with love, and waiting for your response.
>
> *Noson, son of Reb Naftali Hertz, of blessed memory, of Breslov*

Greetings to all our comrades with a great love! Be strong and determined, for God is with us! Do not be afraid!

Greetings to my honored uncle, my learned, illustrious friend, may his light shine, and to all the illustrious citizens there who support us! May God repay what you have done and give you full reward. For you have saved many Jewish lives. May God add to His kindness and allow you to rescue us from them and overcome them. Then our enemies will fulfill the verse (Proverbs 26:27), "One who digs a pit will fall into it". They are just boasting that they will slander me to the authorities, God forbid. But " falsehood does not endure" and "truth is its own witness." God's plan will stand forever and He will not abandon His righteous ones.

178

With thanks to God, Saturday night, Tzav, 5595, Breslov.
Greetings to my beloved, my dear son, Reb Yitzchak, may his light shine.

Until now, I did not come across a traveler with whom I could send this letter. I received your letter last week through the carrier of this letter, Reb Leible, son-in-law of Reb Reuven. The past is gone, and at the moment I have no news to tell you. But this I can tell you, and you should view it as new every day: by God's kindness and awesome power of salvation, I reached home safely, and, praise God, I have already spent Shabbat here in Breslov. Who can describe God's mighty acts?! Who would believe this news of mine?! Remember well all the enormous fears with which our opponents filled us, until many of our friends and comrades gave up hope, as if it were just not possible for me to return home.

Come now and gaze upon the deeds of God, awesome downright miracles! This no insignificant event! It is one of the awesome, mighty deeds of our master, teacher and greatly exalted Rebbe, of sainted, holy and blessed memory. "Who has

Letter #178

acted and performed this? It is God, Who sees and calls forth the generations from the head, from the very beginning!" (Isaiah 41:4; see *Likutey Moharan* II, 67). While they are still gnashing their teeth at us, at me especially, and want to find, God forbid, some false charge to press against me, I trust God and will not be afraid. What can flesh do to me? God gives me courage and strengthens me with holy boldness, which is drawn from the Torah and Prayer of God (*Likutey Moharan* I, 22), to pay no attention to any fears and to return safely to my home. Praise to my God, He will help me and finish for me for the best. He will rescue us from the sword of their mouths. I hope to God that we will see them getting what they wanted us to get and that the verse will be fulfilled (Proverbs 26:27), "One who digs a pit will fall into it." God will not abandon His People for the sake of His Great Name. For God knows the truth and the truth is one.

Thank God, from the day I arrived here until now, God has helped me and I have spoken a great deal about the holy lessons and conversations of the Rebbe, particularly about the lesson which talks about truth and how it is one. This is the lesson "Rabbi Akiva said, 'When you arrive at the stone of pure marble'" (*Likutey Moharan* I, 51; see *Mayim*). Thank God, we spoke about this a great deal last week. Fortunate is the ear that heard! *Ashreinu!* Happy are we to have merited what we have, to know about a holy, true Rebbe such as this: a Rebbe for This World who teaches us lessons such as these, who conveys to us perceptions and knowledge of Godliness such as these, wonders such as these! He also is a Rebbe for the World to Come. For the essence [of the Rebbe's greatness] we will know there, with God's kindness, each person according to how much he suffered and sacrificed in order to come close to the Rebbe's name and to his holy teachings — his holy teachings which guide a person on the true path, which put into him the will to truly fulfull Moshe's Torah of Truth, Written and Oral, and to follow the ways of our ancestors, the true tzaddikim. Indeed my lots have fallen in pleasant places!

Now, my son, fortify yourself and be strong! Do not be daunted or afraid! For the Lord, our God, goes with us to save us! He will not neglect us or abandon us! The main thing is: do not be ashamed of yourself in front of them. You be as brazen as they are. Do not speak to them about this at all, but rather lead them off into something else. They will understand for themselves that we are laughing at them, with God's help. They will be ashamed and not we! For as far as our holy assembly is concerned we have nothing at all to be ashamed of in front of them! Our master, teacher and Rebbe himself even shouted these words, "What do we have to be ashamed of? The world was created for us!" (*Tzaddik* #112). We must carefully recall these pure, holy words every day now.

I do not have time to go on any longer. Write me a full account of what happened with Reb Shimshon: why he stood up to them in the beginning with holy boldness, and subsequently handed over to them all the books, including the handwritten one that they did not even ask for? Why did he not take pity on himself? He needs this book very much for his eternal goal. Even though, after the fact, it will certainly turn out to have been for the best, he has nonetheless behaved foolishly. I know well that his soul is still bound together with ours; but from this you can get a glimpse of this whole evil drama that takes place here under the sun and how [the Evil One] lies there in ambush to attack a person all the days of his life. And even after he overcomes someone and succeeds in distancing him, he [the Evil One] still pushes ahead and lies there waiting to knock him down again and distance him more and more. What can we say? Thank God that He helped us and saved us from errors and foolishness such as this! What can we give back to God for all the favors He has bestowed on us?! That we merited to be in the Rebbe's holy portion! I have grabbed on to him and I will not let go! Even when I am old and gray, God, do not abandon me.

<blockquote>The words of your father, waiting for salvation.

Noson of Breslov</blockquote>

Warm greetings to all our comrades with a great and mighty love, just as in times gone by. Our covenant of love will never be broken. "Great waters could not extinguish our love. Rivers could not wash it away. Were someone to offer all his wealth [in exchange for this] love, he would be turned away in disdain." Please write me about every single one of them. What has happened with Reb Mordekhai, may his light shine? And Reb Yaakov, the son-in-law of Reb Moshe Chaim Dainah? His brother, Reb Henich, and Reb Itzy, the son of Reb Avraham Dov? Reb Levi Yaakov, and my nephew, Reb Isaac, may their lights shine? I know that even the school teacher from Pinsherye has not severed the bond of love which joins us and that the chains of love are still holding Reb Nachum. If we could only gather together and talk again; not for the sake of honor, God forbid—you see the honor that I have from you and how people humiliate and curse "themselves" to hamper this — but only for the honor of God and His holy Torah, that we will be able to speak about the true, eternal goal!

I am depending on God and on the power of the prayers of the elder of holiness that all the curses will turn into blessings and the verse will be fulfilled, "An undeserved curse will come home to roost." They will curse and you will be blessed. They will wake up and be ashamed, and Your servant will rejoice! Thank God that we have reason to rejoice! More than enough reason! For it is fitting for anyone with a true brain in his head to say about every single word of the Rebbe's holy teachings, "If we had come [to the world] only to hear *this*, it would have been enough!" How much more is this so when two ideas are joined together. How much more so when the discourse spreads out and progresses like a gushing spring, an endlessly flowing river! Who has heard anything such as this?! Who has seen things such as these?!

In particular there are the amazing and awesome combining and recombining of letters [in anagrams and acrostics] which the Rebbe employs in his lessons, the like of which has never been heard! Who can praise them?! Who can extol them?! You yourselves experience a certain remote beauty in these lessons. As for what you do not fathom, you can believe me, inasmuch as God has illumined my eyes to feel part of the splendor and profundity of the Rebbe's Torah lessons, which ascend to the heights of

Letter #179

Infinity and reach down to the lowest depths. But I also see with my mind's eye, and I believe with complete faith, that I have not started to understand a drop in the ocean of his holy teachings. It is impossible to talk about this at all, because it is something that depends on what each person perceives for himself. But due to the great barriers and persecution which are rising up to obscure the truth entirely, God forbid, I could not restrain myself from relating these few words of mine to my beloved friends.

This is enough for those who desire truth and who sincerely think about their ultimate purpose. Upon them my words will trickle like cool water on a weary soul. Fortify yourselves and be strong! Fortify yourselves and be strong! Fortify your hearts and be strong, all you who hope in God!

Noson of Breslov

179

Monday night, Tzav, 5595.

Greetings to my dear son, Reb Yitzchak, may his light shine.

I received your letter today and I am certainly very pained by the many hardships you are suffering. But thank God, I have already spoken with you a great deal about how "man was born to suffer," how "his life is short and full of grief" and how the entire world is replete with anguish and hardships of all kinds. And no-one has anything with which to comfort himself except the little good that he is worthy of grabbing in these few evil days of his. For this purpose alone he was created: to toil and suffer for the Torah and devotion. But if he is not worthy, then he suffers and toils for Gehennom, God forbid. This is what the Tanna cautioned (Yoma 72b), "Please! Do not inherit Gehennom *twice!*"

What can I tell you, my dear son, my soul's beloved? I have already spoken about this so much. Just now, too, I was discussing this with Reb Leible, the son-in-law of Reb Reuven. We have to *keep* talking about it, though, and remember it every day, despite the fact that anyone with a brain in his head knows it, and wise men in particular. Even the sages of the nations of the world speak a great deal about how the world is full of grief and pain and how a person's entire life is distress and woe. Since they do not have anything with which they can truly comfort themselves though, after they finish talking about it they return to their folly, and pursue only money and the vanities of This World.

But "Thank our God Who created us for His honor! He set us apart from those who err. He gave us the Torah of Truth, and planted eternal life is our midst"! With this we can comfort ourselves and make ourselves happy! And even if we are not worthy of fulfilling the Torah as we should, God has already anticipated our ailment and provided us with its cure by allowing us to know about the truth of the exalted holiness of our master, teacher and Rebbe, of blessed and sainted memory! He gives us life and lets us be happy on every level and in every situation in the world, as you know, my son! It is said about *him*, "Were it not for the salt, the world could not stand the bitterness" (Likutey Moharan 23:20). "He will console us for our deeds and our sadness" (Genesis 5:29; cf. Likutey Moharan II, 2:5).

The bearer of this letter is in a hurry, so I cannot write as much as I would like. This will suffice. Remember for yourself everything that goes in conjunction with this and view it as totally new. Give thanks for the past, that He has rescued you and your family. It is all certainly for good. From now on "may God guard you from all evil. May He guard your soul."

The words of your father.

Noson of Breslov

180

With thanks to God, Sunday, Shemini, 5595, Breslov.

Warm greetings to my dear, beloved son, the learned Reb Yitzchak, may he live.

I received your letter just now along with the containers of wine, and the two gold pieces from my friend Reb Yaakov, may his light shine. May God send his daughter a complete recovery. May He likewise send your daughter, may she live, a complete recovery. For "God is good" for all the ailments and for all the aches and pains in the world, as you know (Likutey Moharan I, 14:11). We have no-one to lean on in anything except our Father in Heaven. Particularly in the area of medications, the rule already stands that we should do nothing at all. Whatever treatments people employ are just as likely to do harm and exacerbate the condition as they are to improve it. We must therefore rely only on God, the Free Healer — the True, Trustworthy and Compassionate Healer. He has already helped us in this area very much, and sent us and our children, may they live, cures of all kinds for all sorts of ailments, and with no action or intervention on our part at all, as you know. If we had merited to receive this instruction alone from the Rebbe, it would have been enough! For it is a matter of a person's life. But now is not the time for a long discussion of this.

My dear, beloved son, through all the letters you wrote me this winter to Uman and Kremenchug concerning the many bitter hardships and suffering that we endured this winter, I always found great "expansions" in them, shows of relief, with which to encourage myself. It would be fitting for you to rejoice over this very much during the holy days of the approaching festival. For with your beautiful letters you inspired me, and you really fulfilled with them the mitzvah "honor your father." May God give you good forever and may you live for many long years. May He give long lives to all your offspring, lives filled with fear of Heaven that they will merit to truly walk in God's ways forever.

How much more did you uplift me now! For even if our suffering and humiliation are presently still very, very great and hard to bear, we nonetheless see His salvation and wonders at all times, that He has not altogether abandoned us. I knew all this already and now I am seeing it every day. I already assured you that you would soon be praying in any synagogue you like, and now, thank God, salvation has begun to sprout and they have explicitly agreed to allow you to enter the study hall. It is difficult and bitter to hear that we need to have their agreement on this issue after all the evildoers and sinners that they do not prevent from praying with them; nonetheless, it is really just the other way around. These are God's mighty acts and wonders!

Letter #180

For considering how the antagonism and denunciation against the point of truth has grown so intense that they seek to banish me every day, God forbid, and likewise to banish each and every one of us, God forbid, how great are Your deeds, God! Who can express His mighty acts, His wonders and His salvation?! For, thank God, I have already spent three Shabbatot here and have gone to the *mikvah* every day and, thank God, not a single person has assaulted me! Now they are also allowing you to pray in the study hall! God is our salvation and our hope that it will all turn into good and that they will be subordinate and subjugated to us. They will be ashamed and not we! For God's truth is forever!

Things are so pressured and hectic that I cannot write very much. It is late in the day and I must think about the Afternoon and Evening Prayers, and particularly about the the mitzvah of "destroying the *chametz* [leaven]." May God likewise destroy the Evil Impulse and the "leavening in the dough" from within us. May He also eradicate, destroy, burn and uproot all those who hate and persecute us for no reason; *or* may we be able to destroy the "leaven" from within them, so that they all return to the truth. This is what I would prefer, as God knows my heart.

There is no news here — just that every day they are contriving evil plans for themselves. Chaim Pais, may his name be obliterated, was here for last Shabbat, and today he exclaimed loudly against "himself" to uproot and banish "himself" from the world. May God nullify his designs and spoil his plans, and may everything speedily turn into good. You should know that yesterday, by God's enormous miracles, I was worthy of dancing joyfully at the Shabbat morning meal and, for me, this constitutes a great sprouting of salvation. May God likewise allow all of us, here, where you are, and in every place where our comrades are located, to rejoice very much and in great happiness that, in His compassion, He has helped us survive among evil beasts such as these. May He further bestow His kindness and miracles and allow us to survive forever, and to truly walk in the ways of God, the way our master, teacher and Rebbe taught us. Even when I am old and gray, may He not abandon me, "until I declare Your strength to the generation and Your might to all who are to come."

The words of your father who prays for you.
Noson of Breslov

I forgot to add this at the end of the letter.

In Uman, the *kloyz* is standing on its site. They have not broken in again, God forbid, as they have been frightened. Nonetheless, there has still been no legal action against them. Reb Avraham and Reb Naftali, may their lights shine, as it appears from their letter, have already sent the matter on to Kiev. This Reb Avraham Weinberg sent me three silver rubles on Erev Shabbat. He is a great friend to us. Reb Moshe Fishel [Landau], who is an influential person there, sent a message to the study hall charging them to stop their harassment, and warning them not to do any more damage to the *kloyz*. In the end they will suffer for it, he said. They also called the *dipitat*, i.e. the official in charge of placing soldiers in private homes to be fed and so forth, and they pressured him to remove the soldier that he spitefully placed in the home of our comrade Reb Avraham Yitzchak. They were going to add more! We were terribly pained about this, because he is extremely poor. So this Reb Moshe Fishel pressured him until they were forced against their will to remove the soldier from his home. Thank God Who has helped us thus far.

[In those days it was customary throughout Europe for soldiers to be placed in the homes of citizens when a platoon was passing through a city.]

In Terhovitza the *machloket* is raging very intensely right now. Reb Yitzchak, son-in-law of the *Magid* [Rabbi Yekutiel of Terhovitza, one of Rebbe Nachman's earliest and closest followers], of sainted memory, has fled from his home and one of our comrades has received lethal blows [he never fully recovered and suffered severely from epileptic attacks]. A doctor has gone there to make an inquiry. With God's kindness, this will be a great setback for them [the opponents], but at the moment we need a lot of compassion. Salvation is in God's hands. I am writing all this after the search for *chametz*. May God obliterate the evil from our midst and may He obliterate our enemies and those who oppose the point of truth.

Greetings to all our comrades with a great love, especially to my distinguished friend Reb Yaakov, may his light shine. I received the two gold pieces and I have already blessed you that you should enjoy a complete recovery. I am surprised at you, my friend, that you have been remiss about putting your hand to paper in a letter to me. While it is true that you do not know where to begin, failing to write altogether is no answer. I trust God that our covenant of love will never, ever be broken. "Great waters could not extinguish our love! Rivers could not wash it away!"

Be strong, my son! Be strong and take a good, careful look at yourself. Consider your ways and look very closely at what is happening in the world — at this whole evil drama that is taking place under the sun, particularly in these last generations before the coming of Mashiach, when "Your enemies, God, are scoffing." If you cannot correct the world, you can certainly rescue yourself! Free choice is always granted, and there is no barrier in the world that we cannot break. "Do not give sleep to your eyes!" Flee, as a deer from its pursuer, and consider your ways carefully! Think about how can you rescue your soul from This World's flood of torrential waters! Is it by ripping up our prayers and holy books, God forbid, or by reading them? Remember and clarify in your mind the difference between these two paths, even if the one who rips and the one who reads are otherwise equal. Certainly we have some idea ourselves as to the difference between them. Beyond this we ought to believe that there is no-one who would tear a single page of these books, who would not first commit a great transgression, God save us. And there is no-one who would say one of the prayers or look into one of the books who would not have some very wonderful thought of repentance, as you know. The rest you will know about, if you merit in the future to meet with us and to hold on to the love which binds us together in This World and the Next, eternally.

Noson, the same

181

[Publisher's note: After Pesach (April 25, 1835), several youths entered Reb Noson's synagogue and caused damage. When the Breslover Chassidim attempted to grab the youths, one went to call his father. A fight ensued, a full battle erupted and crowds of people in the town gathered to watch. Four Breslover Chassidim were arrested in the melee. The next two letters refer to this incident.]

With thanks to God, Sunday, Tazria, 5595

My beloved son.

I received your letter just now. Thank God, Reb Chaim and his friends have been out of jail now for about four hours. This morning they sent after that young scoundrel to try to catch him. His mother implored them on his behalf, thereby allowing him to get away, so they put *her* in jail instead. She is still sitting there. The inquiry has been submitted, but there is no clear answer yet. They said they would investigate afterwards. Beyond this there is nothing new to report. It is good to thank God for the past, that in His enormous mercy He has helped us thus far, and to entreat Him very much over the future, that He will bring down our enemies beneath us. As you know, they are still gnashing their teeth. May God destroy the teeth in their mouths! May He subjugate our enemies and break them! May they fall and not get up! Our souls will rejoice in God and celebrate over His salvation! *Ashreinu!* Happy are we to be on the side of truth, the right side! Truly, for this we can really say "*Ashreinu!*" I have no time to go on. It is time for the Afternoon Prayers.

The words of your father, waiting for salvation.

Noson of Breslov

182

[Publisher's note: This letter was written to the Breslover Chassidim in Tcherin. Reb Dov Ber was an early follower of Rebbe Nachman and was quite wealthy. His daughter married Reb Avraham Ber, Rebbe Nachman's grandson.]

With thanks to God, Friday, Torah reading Metzora, 5595, Breslov.

"Warm greetings to those who love God's Torah; they will not stumble." Greetings to my honored friend whom I love as myself, the learned and illustrious Reb Dov Ber, may his light shine, and to his precious honored sons and all their offspring, may they live; and to my honored friend whom I love as myself, the learned and illustrious Reb Zvi Hirsh, may his light shine, and to his precious honored sons and all their offspring, may they live. May they all enjoy blessing, life, peace and all good forever. Amen, may it be His will.

I have already sent you two letters about our great troubles and I am extremely surprised that, as if ignoring me, you have not given me the slightest response. You should know, my brothers and friends, that the controversy has not yet abated in the least. They gnash their teeth at us constantly every day, and they contrive and devise evil plans against every one of us, against me especially, to have me banished from here, God forbid, and from all the towns hereabout, God forbid. May God banish *them* and uproot them! Were it not for God Who has helped us and performed miracles and wonders for us constantly every day! The main instrument has been the judges. For even though our opponents are paying large bribes and we are penniless, God has pity on us and helps us effect more with a little than they can with a lot! Especially since they all know that truth and right are with us. But even for this little, we have a great many expenses, as you will understand for yourselves. On the accusations alone we have already paid out a huge sum! Sometimes there are other expenses too, because to get off without paying anything is simply impossible.

I have been living here in my house now for five weeks and I cannot go outside. If I do, the youths come out and curse and humiliate me with abuse of all sorts. One time they also broke a window in my house, on Chol HaMoed Pesach, and I was forced to send to the the local governor, who incarcerated the youth. Afterwards Moshe [Chenkes] "the turncoat," who has fallen to complete ruin and destruction, along with the other *mitnagdim*, succeeded in getting the youth out, and he subsequently returned to abuse me a great deal.

Last Shabbat, Torah reading Shemini, there was a big upheaval here. Young scoundrels entered our study hall, destroyed the door and abused our comrades. It has already happened many, many times that they come into our study hall and rip up and desecrate our holy books in front of our comrades. This Shabbat some of our comrades stood up against them and a fistfight ensued. One of the youths ran to his father who then came with another man, and they proceeded to beat up our comrades. They also went to the local governor, and they came and took away four of our dear, good companions. They stayed in jail all of Shabbat and Sunday, and there was a tremendous uproar. They also searched my house for Reb Mordekhai of Teplik to see if he has a travel document. But they were not satisfied with this and they subsequently informed on me to this same governor. He then sent investigators with some other goverment officers to look for me, and they wanted to take me to jail, God forbid. Meanwhile men, women and children had surrounded my house and the whole street around it was filled with people. Were I to describe the humiliation and disgrace that I suffered, you would not believe it.

But God still did miracles and wonders. There was no-one willing to go to the governor for me. All the rich citizens and property owners are on their side. Though there are some who side with me in their hearts, they are intimidated by my enemy and by the wealthy people here and are afraid to take any steps to rescue me. Eventually a few paupers and Reb Shmuel Weinberg's wife went to talk to him. At first he closed the door and did not want to admit them. But with God's compassion they pushed and got in, and they pleaded at length with him until his anger subsided a little. Even so, I still had to go to him. There were so many people surrounding my house though that there was no path for me to get through. Finally the officers had to push the crowd away with their sticks and hit them in order to make a path for me to get out. As I was walking amidst such great humiliation, out came that witch Miriam Raitze, may her name be obliterated. She is the daughter of Elka [and Moshe Chenkes] and wife of our friend Reb Avraham Ber, may he live, and she has turned into the most intense *mitnaged* of them all. So out she came and proceeded to insult and abuse me vehemently in public. I subsequently went to see the governor. Because they had appeased him somewhat, he spoke to me a little and let me return home in peace. That shrew also went to the governor and abused me in his presence. This actually worked a little to my benefit though, since the governor and his wife treated her with contempt and disgraced her for being so insolent as to abuse an old man. She left there humiliated.

So you can understand for yourselves the great suffering, upset and humiliation that all of us have had, especially the righteous Adil, may she live. On this occasion, too, we were forced to put out money in order to placate the governor and to keep him from putting me in jail, as he originally said he would. Later on, after Shabbat, we had to file a complaint. On Sunday he released our imprisoned companions, who were found to have wounds, and he ordered the doctor to apply dressings. This too, I do not need to tell you, costs money. Afterwards the *mitnagdim* beat another one of our companions, a poor, destitute man, and we had to file yet another complaint. There has not yet been a single investigation or trial as a result of any complaint, but they *are* nonetheless effective because they serve to frighten them. If it were not for this, they would be killing us in public, God forbid. For, as is known, it is now considered permissible to spill our blood.

Later on that Sunday, all the *mitnagdim* gathered and raised a large sum for wickedness from all their group and sat down to discuss what to do to me. They agreed on their evil plan, and proceeded to bribe the authorities to have the state prosecutor file a complaint against me stating that it has come to his attention that I am a false prophet, what they call *sanogog*, that I hold seditious meetings at my house, and other such treacherous testimony. The prosecutor has already submitted a document to the police to this effect and they wanted the governor and the local area police commander to sign it as well. I do not have to tell you how upset, scared and distressed we were about this. We were all too overwhelmed and dispirited to do anything. But in His mercy, God sent word to our friend Reb Shmuel Weinberg and his wife. They spoke at length with the official and succeeded in preventing him from signing the document. They also spoke briefly with another authority and he withheld his signature as well. Rumor has it that they have not sent the matter to Kaminetz [Kaminetz-Podolsk, the seat of the High Court of the Podolia region at that time], but we do not know anything definite yet. Our hearts, and my heart in particular, are trembling inside us.

Oh, my brothers and friends! Let the Heavens look down and see if there is any pain, any shame and fear, such as ours. In particular, *my* life is constantly hanging in the balance. Blessed is the One Who gives strength to the weary, Who has given me the strength of iron to endure all this. Therefore, my brothers and friends, you can understand for yourselves how critical it is that you send immediately at least the sum that I have written requesting you several times. I do not need to tell you that, considering the trouble we are in, it is really not much at all. And there is no-one coming to help us. All the people with money are against us. All we are left with are poor people and a few property owners, and they also are too afraid of the enemy and the rich to help us. Nonetheless, they have already spent far more than a hundred *kerbel* (rubles) on this business, in addition to what is required to support me, since my enemies have cut off all my sources of livelihood. For besides the fact that they do not give me or any of our companions flour or *maot chitin*, the wheat supplement for Pesach, Moshe, the turncoat, makes it his business to ruin the livelihood and sustenance of every one of us. Many pages would not be enough to describe to you what Moshe and all the *mitnagdim* do to all our comrades every day in connection with their livelihoods. But we are not even looking at *this*. It is just that they are setting out to inform against me, God forbid, with all kinds of false charges and fabrications, God forbid. May God nullify their designs and foil their plans!

So for God's sake, do not hold back any more! Send immediately, without delay, at least the sum I referred to before. No excuses! So that you will not need, God forbid, God forbid, to send many, *many* times more than this. And who knows if *then* it will do any good? Right now there is still hope that we can save ourselves with a minimal expenditure, though it is impossible to get by without paying anything. "The horse may stand ready for the day of battle, but salvation is in the hands of God." I am too busy and overwrought to go on any longer. I have confidence in your benevolence, so that even though it may be difficult for you, you will nonetheless fulfill my request without delay. God forbid that you should delay even one day! For the *mitnagdim* are not silent and the evildoers roar like the stormy sea. It is impossible to describe the great miracles and wonders that God does for us every day to rescue us from them. But He always employs some small vehicle or event; and money can accomplish anything that is needed, as you will understand for yourselves. There is no need to say any more to wise and generous hearts such as yourselves.

For God's sake, do not hold your peace and remain silent! Be sure to pray every day for us, and for me especially, that we be rescued from them! This thing affects all of us! You have no doubt heard what is happening in Terhovitza. We have just recently heard here that an investigator came to Uman in connection with the break-ins at our *kloyz*. Many of our opponents were imprisoned and were forced to pay a lot of money to be granted bail. We do not yet know any details though, or whether all this is actually true. In any case, we still need great salvation if we are to succeed against them in court. God have mercy.

> The words of your true eternal friend, waiting for your answer, for you to fulfill my request at once, and waiting expectantly for God's speedy salvation.
>
> *Noson, the son of Reb Naftali Hertz, of blessed memory, of Breslov*

Greetings to all our comrades with a great love! Especially to my honored, learned friend, Reb Yudel, may his light shine. I do not need to urge *you* to pray for us very much, since I am sure that you are certainly petitioning for us a great deal. May God hear your prayers, and ours.

Adil, may she live, all her children, the Rav [Reb Aharon], may his light shine, and all of our comrades send warm greetings.

183

With thanks to God, Sunday, Kedoshim, 5595.

My dear, beloved son.

I received your letter last week. Reb Efraim, the son of Reb Naftali, and Reb Simchah Barukh [Rebbe Nachman's grandson] came here this past Erev Shabbat. The influential Reb Moshe Landau, an in-law of the Otkaptshik, also came here this past Erev Shabbat and is still here. [Moshe Landau was an in-law to Hirsh Ber, who was the most influential *maskil* in Uman. He wielded great influence and could have literally destroyed Reb Noson's opponents; see *Until the Mashiach*, pp.75-76.] He is eager to help us and wants to meet with me and come to my house. May God have compassion and may it all be for good. As of now, God has helped us very much. But I had a scare this past Erev Shabbat, when I suffered bitterness and fright the likes of which I do not think I have felt since this *machloket* started to rage.

My friends outside informed me that my enemies were intending to banish "themselves" [i.e. Reb Noson himself] from here *on Shabbat!* I cannot describe to you all that transpired that day in this regard. They literally killed me and revived me many times that one day. Blessed is He Who gives strength to the weary that I endured all this. God helped me, and in pure simplicity I fortified myself with the fact that I was saved from opposing truth such as this and that I also merited to write down the Rebbe's holy, awesome books of truth. Just then the people I mentioned arrived, and this too inspired me very much. Then I believed and saw with my mind's eye that this was from God.

I saw that it was truly miraculous! How great are God's works! How very deep are His thoughts!

Reb Nachman of Teplik also came with Reb Efraim for Shabbat. Thank God, we had a beautiful Shabbat and they also danced a little. It is good to thank God for having helped us thus far! They had already gone [before Shabbat] to speak with the lord governor and the city officials, and they all swore great oaths that nothing would happen to me. It appears, thank God, they were telling the truth. But what we were really afraid of was the police, whom the informers wanted to incite against us without the sanction of the *garadanshik*, who is somewhat unwell. And the police were going to do it! But through God's mercy they changed their minds, because they were afraid of the castigation of their superiors, were they to get caught up in a scandal such as this. There were also people from the outside who talked to them and told them they should not do such a thing. But the evildoers, our enemies, intended the worst and God foiled their plan! So may He foil them, destroy them, uproot, break and bring them down beneath us; and may the truth be revealed in the world! Be strong, my son! Bring yourself to joy over God's salvation and pray to Him concerning the future!

The words of your father.

Noson of Breslov

184

With thanks to God, Sunday, Kedoshim, 5595.

My dear, beloved son.

I received your letter now, and just this morning I sent you a letter with Reb Motil. I have no doubt that you heard from Reb Motil as well about the scare they gave me last Erev Shabbat. May God have mercy on me and let it atone for my sins and turn out to be a great benefit. At the moment, the matter has quietened down. Thank God Who has helped us thus far. The influential Reb Moshe Landau from Uman was at my house today too. I do not have to tell you that he serves our interests and is a thorn in the side of the *mitnagdim*. "May they grind their teeth and may their hearts melt within them!" "God rescues the pauper from the man stronger than he!" May God pity us and grant us complete salvation soon, so that we will never again be frightened! Let our enemies see and be ashamed! May this month of Iyar see the fulfillment of the verse, *"Oyvai Yashuvu Yeivoshu Roga* — My enemies will come back and at once be ashamed!" (Psalms 6:11) [The initial letters for the name of the month IYOR; see *Likutey Moharan* I, 177].

I am surprised at you, my dear son, that you did not say anything about our friend Reb Nachman Tulchiner. Please let me know soon how he is doing. May God send full recovery to your son, and to my son, Nachman, may he live. He too was weak this past week. It appears to be related to a severe flu, God save us. He is still a little weak and he sat in his house at the beginning of the term. May He Who creates cures send them complete recovery along with the other sick of Israel [text missing].

A person can see constantly on every side that there is no such thing as "This World" at all, as our master, teacher, and Rebbe said (Likutey Moharan II, 119). We have absolutely nothing except when God helps us prevail and grab any and all good that we can. Thank God, one can see every day wondrous "expansions," shows of relief, amidst the suffering. The sprouting of the seeds of salvation are visible at all times. But we still need prayer and great outpourings of supplications that God will take pity on us and say "Enough!" to our suffering; that He will come back to us, pity us, rescue us and save us from our enemies and from those who pursue us without cause.

You should know, my dear son, that all our comrades accepted upon themselves to fast this Monday, Thursday and the following Monday. It would be appropriate for all of you to participate with us. Maybe God will answer us and have pity on His great honor. Maybe He will act for the sake of His Name and put down our enemies beneath us, so that they will no longer abuse us and the holy, awesome books. Truth will sprout from the ground, and "Give truth to Jacob" will be fulfilled. If not now, when?

My heart wails for every single one [of our comrades]! My insides tremble! About our times is it said concerning the young (Lamentations 4:1), "The stones of holiness are poured out into the streets," and there is no-one to gather them home! Even somebody who *wants* to flee and escape to a house where they cultivate Torah and prayer, is chased and persecuted in all kinds of ways. Who knows what will be in the future? For the Evil One has spread himself out far and wide, inside and out.

Letter #184

Outside, the sword and the fire of the *machloket* wreak destruction, God save us. At home physical desires, bad thoughts and confusion, financial problems and domestic disputes rise up. There is hardship and pain on every side. Upon whom can we lean? On our Father in Heaven. My comfort amidst my destitution is that at least we know about the truth of the true tzaddik and of his holy teachings, that give life and revive every single person, no matter where he is. *This* is what they are gnashing their teeth at and trying to distance people from, God forbid!

But God's lovingkindness is endless and His compassion never ceases. In His enormous miracles He has come to our aid to strengthen, to fortify and to make us tougher, more so every time, so that we hold on with all our might and with all our senses to the true tzaddik, to his holy teachings and to his holy name. I have taken shelter in God, and I trust that all of us will merit to be counted among the Rebbe's holy assembly in This World and the Next, forever. *Ashreinu!* Fortunate are we! How good is our lot! Even after all we are going though, still — *Ashreinu!* The *mitnagdim* will perish and a thousand like them, and not one word of his holy teachings or conversations will be annulled! As long as the breath of life is in us, as long as our souls are in us, we will thank and praise God that we have been worthy of being in the Rebbe's holy portion! Our lots have fallen in pleasant places!

The words of your father, waiting for salvation.
Noson of Breslov

Greetings to all our comrades with a great love! Especially

to my friend whom I love as myself, the distinguished young man, progeny of a tzaddik, Reb Nachman, the son of Chayah, may he live. May God make me worthy of seeing him face to face. May he merit to walk in the ways of his holy ancestors, may their merit truly protect us, so that he may have eternal good.

Noson, as above

I need not tell you to give this letter to our true friends to read and then put it away, well out of the reach of outsiders. For no outsider must taste what is sacred.

185

With thanks to God, Sunday, Behar, 5595.

To my dear, beloved son, Reb Yitzchak, may his light shine. Greetings, life and all good in This World and the Next.

I received your letter. You already know that I cannot go outside and therefore had no-one with whom to send you a response. May God have pity and turn the whole thing into great good for all of us. Those who rise up arrogantly against us will don shame and disgrace; and those who favored the justness of my cause will sing, rejoice and constantly say, "Let God be exalted!" Thank God that He helps me be happy most of the time over that enormous, miraculous and eternal kindness of His: that I merited to hear the things that I did and to write them down in books — "to inform people of His mighty deeds"!

Letter #185

The truth is that all of you too ought to be rejoicing every day over this. For it is no small matter. It is your eternal life! God forbid that a single word should grow old for you! These words are always flowing and every single one of them is a well of fresh water, cool water to a weary soul. They are new every moment of every day! They give life to every soul that wants to live, and they revive it with delicacies of every kind! They reveal the greatness of the Creator and the light of His Godliness in a way that is simply inexpressible! For each person perceives them in a different way, according to his heart. And beyond all this, they rise up to the Infinite Heights and reach down to the lowest levels. "You have done much, Lord, my God. Your miracles and thoughts are for us!" The Doer of Miracles Who has helped me so much thus far will not abandon me now either. He will help me and save me soon, and He will subjugate our enemies and bring them down beneath us. You, God, Who performs wonders, for Your sake and the sake of the true tzaddik — cut them down literally to the ground! Salvation is in God's hands.

Your tremendous yearning for the Shavuot of our awesome and exalted master, teacher and Rebbe whose truth and holiness shield us each day, particularly when we are gathered together, along with your crying out, are making an impression, with God's help. If we merit it, I will tell you about it face to face, God willing, this coming holy festival of Shavuot. But you, [my son,] and all of you, need to long and desire very much for the holiness of the true Shavuot, that we will all be able to gather together and to pray to God very much that it be with peace and tranquility and that "You will guard my life from fear of the enemy," and the lives of all of us. You must long and desire that we will merit to joyfully speak words of truth which give life to the soul forever — words which emanate from the holy and awesome flowing stream. May He Who hears the prayers of every mouth hear our prayer and save us, for His Name's sake.

The words of your father, waiting for speedy salvation.

Noson of Breslov

186

With thanks to God, Sunday, the 3rd of Sivan, 5595.

My dear, beloved son.

You have already heard about the great and wondrous act of salvation that God has done for us. You will hear more from the carrier of this letter, our friend Reb Sender, may his light shine. At present I have nothing new to say, and besides, it is right before prayers. May God help me so that when you arrive safely tomorrow, God willing, I will merit to joyfully tell you about God's salvation. May we merit to see God's salvation more and more, and may the truth be revealed in the world!

The words of your father, giving thanks for the past and petitioning for the future. As God has begun to show His lovingkindness, may He likewise finish well for us, quickly, in every way, and in every place that our truly pious and God-fearing comrades, may they live, are located — especially in Uman. Our enemies will see and be ashamed! We will rejoice in God and sing praises to the Holy One of Israel!

Noson of Breslov

187

With thanks to God, Sunday, Torah reading Shelach Lekha. 5595.
My dear, beloved son.

I received your letter with the two gold pieces. May God have compassion and quickly send a complete recovery to your daughter, may she live. May she soon regain her full strength. The deliverer of this letter will tell you what has happened here. It is certainly all for the best. As regards the persecution, harassment and beatings that they have perpetrated against every single one of you in Tulchin, you can understand for yourselves how to conduct yourselves and assert yourselves in their presence. Do not be ashamed or look down on yourselves! Do not be afraid or daunted before them! God is with us to save us! Do not fear them! The deliverer of this letter will tell you everything. I have absolutely no time to go on. Stand up and look at the salvation of God! For just as He has begun to save us, we hope that, with the great power of the elder of holiness, He will also finish quickly and grant us complete salvation! Our enemies will see and be ashamed!

The words of your father waiting for salvation.

Noson of Breslov

188

With thanks to God, Wednesday, Shelach, 5595.

My dear, beloved son.

I received your letter along with the note from Reb Henoch and the two gold pieces. At present there is nothing new to report. You have already heard that Reb Nisan, the son of Reb Kalman, spent twenty-four hours in jail and was released on Monday. The youths are still pushing ahead with some stone-throwing, but they are already quite scared because on Sunday they [the police] searched for them and wanted to detain them. Yesterday Moshe, the turncoat, was at the house of the Rav [Reb Aharon] here and he cried and pleaded for his life for some time. His mind is as unstable as it has been for some time, but now he is even more confused and is suffering very, very much. May God have pity on him and take away his madness. May he wholeheartedly return to the truth and may he endeavor to rectify the enormous damage he has done, of which he is a little cognizant even now amidst his madness. May God have compassion on him and on us, to rescue us from our enemies and those who pursue us without cause. May He "give truth to Jacob." May God send a full recovery to your daughter, may she live, among all the other sick people of Israel.

Be careful, my son, now too, to remember the World to Come every day — both in general and in all the details of your life. This is an obligation for every person, no matter who, through everything that happens to him. Everything that happens to a person every day is all hints to draw him closer to God, from wherever that person may be. For God contracts Himself from Absolute Infinity into the minutest details [of Creation] (*Likutey Moharan* I, 54). Remember this well and guard this memory vigilantly each day. Just remembering it is very good. And all the great upset and tempest of this tremendous *machloket* that has risen up against us is all the result of the envy [*Ra Ayin*] stirred up against the true tzaddik who is working to remind the world every day about the World to Come. There is no-one who speaks about and works for this the way he does. So that since we have at any rate been rescued, through God's wondrous kindness, from opposing and attacking him, it is incumbent upon us to accustom ourselves to walk in his holy pathways and to remember the World to Come every day. There is a lot to say about this, but I do not have the time. Besides, it is impossible in a letter. This will suffice for now for one who desires truth.

The words of your father.

Noson of Breslov

189

With thanks to God, Monday, Korach, 5595.

My dear, beloved son.

I received your letter today. But even before that, Reb Isaac, may his light shine, informed me about your youngest daughter's ailment. I am extremely pained over the distress and suffering you are having. Nonetheless, I cannot restrain myself from admonishing you a little, that after so many years you are still crying out bitterly every time something happens to you. I have told you a thousand times: the world is full of suffering and pain! Our master, teacher and Rebbe said, as you know, that "this [world] *here* appears to be Gehennom" (Likutey Moharan II, 119). King David as well cried out, "I am ready to suffer and my pain is continually before me." And there are many other similar statements.

It is without a doubt absolutely true that a person must cry out to God in a time of trouble, and also that he should tell a Torah scholar about his pain, so that the scholar can pray for him. In particular *you* should tell your father, for who will pity you more than I? But on each occasion, the way you cry out is inappropriate. It is as if, God forbid, the whole world has fallen upon you; as if, God forbid, *your* sufferings are greater than those of everyone else in the world. It is just not so, my dear son. You have to remember very well every time what the Rebbe said on the verse, "In suffering you gave me relief" (Likutey Moharan I, 195); and in particular to bring yourself to joy all the time, that you have been saved from what you have been saved by not being an opponent, God forbid, of truth such as this. For he is our support and our hope, in This World and the Next. You must look at what our antagonists will do when they face suffering much worse than yours! What are *they* going to inspire themselves with? The fact that they break windows, spill blood and persecute Jewish souls so terribly for no good reason?

You must realize, my dear son, that the things I say are not intended to be just words, God forbid. They are meant to be practiced and for a person to save his soul with them, particularly in times of trouble. It is crucially important that a person force himself to find the relief, the positive, amidst all the world's distress and suffering; because "man was born to suffer," as we have already discussed a great deal. I constantly go back and look, and I never find any vitality or hope, any refuge or escape from everything that comes upon a person in This World except the power of the true tzaddik. If it were not for the salt, the world could not endure the bitterness (as explained in *Likutey Moharan* I, 23). How great are the kindnesses and wonders that God has done for us, that we have merited to be saved from opposing true good such as this, who sweetens all the bitterness of the world. He is our support and our hope forever.

I do not need to tell you that if you ask me, I would not agree to call the doctor even now. But it is hard to stand up against one's family in this matter and prevent them from calling the doctor. But do not be upset over this. God in His compassion can cure a person even if they *do* call the doctor. For His miraculous ways are far beyond our grasp! Try to find a way, though, to talk to the doctor with understanding and to persuade him to keep his prescriptions to an absolute minimum. And if, God forbid, he wants to make an incision there, do your best to get him to abandon the idea. For I am absolutely opposed to this. Rather ask him if perhaps he couldn't soften the area with some sort of medicinal treatment. Salvation and compassion are God's. May He quickly send from Heaven a complete recovery for your daughter. I am extremely busy, because I plan, God willing, to travel to Uman tomorrow. May God give me a safe journey.

I do not have time to continue. Fortify yourself, my son, and be strong! Bring yourself to joy any way you can, and trust God. He will not abandon us, for the sake of His Great Name.

The words of your father, waiting for salvation.

Noson of Breslov

190

[Publisher's note: Reb Noson did not make it then to Uman. His son, Reb David Zvi, was due to marry his stepsister, Dishel's daughter Chanah — with Reb Noson acting as parents of the bride and groom. During the sheva berakhot, the week of celebration following the wedding, Reb Noson was arrested and subsequently exiled from Breslov. The next few letters tell the story.]

With God's help, Wednesday, Balak, 5595.

My dear, beloved son.

I received your letter just now, and I really feel for the great pain you are having over your daughter, may she live. May God have compassion and from Heaven heal her quickly, in spite of the fact that you are using a doctor, all of whom together add up to nothing. Even so, "God is good for everything," for all ailments and for all things (Likutey Moharan I, 14:11). His power to save is great and we have no-one to lean on but Him: that He will act for the sake of His great compassion and for the sake of His true tzaddikim and save us quickly in all that we need to be saved. Amen. May it be His will.

"There are many thoughts in a man's heart, but God's plan will be accomplished." Before the prayers today I began thinking about advancing the marriage until right after Shabbat and

I am seriously considering doing so. However, I have not yet spoken about this with anyone, because I still want to think about it some more. You can imagine how preoccupied I am with this right now and so I cannot write you much at all. You just do your part and be quick about encouraging our comrades in Tulchin to send me money for the garment for my son [Reb David Zvi, the groom], may he live. For it is very likely that the marriage will take place right after Shabbat. It just now occurred to me to have the wedding tomorrow, God willing. I will most likely send a coach for you if it is to be tomorrow. If it is after Shabbat, I will inform you as soon as possible, or by a messenger. May God do what is good and guide me on the path of truth. May He finish matters well for me. You are receiving letters for Odessa. You understand for yourself how to proceed. Salvation is in God's hands.

The words of your father who is extremely busy and waiting for salvation.

Noson of Breslov

Greetings to all our comrades with a great love; to every one of them according to his own high level. I have a great deal to say to you, but I cannot say it in a letter. In addition, I am extremely preoccupied right now, as my son, may he live, will tell you. Please, come to my aid at a time like this — more than your means allow you — as you can understand yourselves the great need for this. May God open your eyes and fortify your hearts to think very, very carefully about yourselves in This World, and to come up with strategies every day about how to find a way to draw close to God and to His holy Torah, or at least, about how to escape from the pit of destruction. May He show you whom to join up with in this passing shadow so that there will be hope for your ultimate end and you will not toil for nothing, God forbid. The truth is its own witness.

> Their true, eternal friend, speaking for their benefit and their true, eternal success.
>
> *Noson, the same*

191

With thanks to God, Friday, Torah reading Balak, 5595.

May happiness and joy overtake my honored and beloved son, the distinguished Reb Yitzchak, may his light shine.

The time for song has arrived! Today is my son's *chuppah*, may he live! I am therefore sending a carriage for you. If your wife, may she live, can come too — so much the better. You, at any rate, should come with your son, may he live; and if another one of our friends wants to come too — even better. May God grant us much happiness, joy and all good. Let us celebrate and rejoice in His salvation! Regarding the garment for my son, may he live, I have not yet spoken with my son, Reb Shachneh, since I received his letter at night.

I am all ready to pray right now. So you do as you wish, and God Who is good will finish everything well for us, in accordance with His will and the will of those who fear Him. I am beset on all sides by my many cares and concerns. I have, without a doubt, never had such a day in my life — to have to make a wedding for my son, may he live, in circumstances such as these, amidst upset, poverty and straits such as these, with a *machloket* such as this, and amidst such doubts and uncertainty. All this, in addition to what is in my heart that I cannot express. But the many marvelous "expansions" and favors to be found in all this are also impossible to express! And the scale of good far outweighs the bad! The greatest of them all is what we have merited to hear about every single detail of all the above! [referring to the salvation that amidst all the suffering they have remained true to the Rebbe's teachings]. So in spite of it all — *Ashreinu! Ashreinu!* Happy are we!

The words of your father, waiting to see you soon amidst joy!

Noson of Breslov

192

With God's help, Sunday, Torah reading Pinchas, 5595.

My dear, beloved son.

I received your letter and there is nothing special to report. After you left, the celebrating did not continue much longer — only about two hours. Thank God, everyone was very happy. As for your yearning for joy — this is very good. Also, where you are now, you should be happy and rejoice in God's salvation! For everything that is happening to us through God's lovingkindness and enormous wonders, is a matter of no small significance! Anyone who considers everything that has come upon us in recent times will realize that the little joy that we merited now in Breslov was a great miracle indeed! I see with my own eyes that God's lovingkindnesses are never-ending! Indeed there is still hope that we will be able to attain total joy, that is joy from performing the Commandments — true Jewish happiness, in This World and the Next, forever!

> The words of your father who yearns for joy with all his heart. Joy is the main thing! "Let happiness and joy take over!"
>
> Noson of Breslov

193

With thanks to God, Sunday, Matot and Masai, 5595.

Peace, life and all good to my dear, beloved son, the distinguished Reb Yitzchak, may he live.

I am going to relate to you, my dear son, a little of what has happened to me since Wednesday of last week, Torah reading Pinchas. But I am warning you and I ask you: do not become frightened or worried in the least. "God is with us. Do not fear them!" Last Tuesday, which was the 17th of Tammuz [a fast day], Reb Shlomo from Brahilev came to my house. He is the father of my son-in-law, Reb Barukh, may his light shine, and he brought with him his son Reb David whom he married off in Nemirov last week. His brother-in-law, Reb Barukh, also came to my house. I saw that this was the hand of God and that it would be appropriate for me to host one more *sheva berakhot* celebration. As you might have expected, I spoke with my in-law and his son some of the words of truth that are in my heart.

Letter #193

That Wednesday, about two hours before the Afternoon Prayers, as I was talking about the Rebbe's holy teachings with some of the young people (my in-law's son among them), into my house came Reb Shmuel Weinberg and he appeared rather upset about something. He called me aside and told me that someone had told him in the utmost confidence that an official had been appointed to oversee "my case" and he added a few more details. God helped me and I was not too frightened. I did, however, immediately become quite discomposed, because I had intended to go away on Thursday in any event, and after this news, I wanted to hurry things along even more. In addition, I was forced to borrow nine silver rubles on collateral. I spent seven of them right away to "mitigate" the situation a little [bribing an authority] and the rest I spent on traveling expenses. In the meantime the Reb Shmuel whom I just mentioned read my travel document and discovered that it had expired. I was highly uncertain about how to proceed. Meanwhile, the messenger came and brought me your letter. I answered you briefly that I was going to set out early the next morning, since my plan at that time was to travel in the direction of Nemirov and wait either there or somewhere on the way until my travel documents arrived.

"There are many thoughts in a man's heart, but God's plan will be accomplished." For God arranged events such that I delayed here until today, when my brother Reb Yudel brought me a permit. The document, while it had the stamp of the [Nemirov] community, had not yet been stamped by the administrator, since he was sleeping when Reb Yudel left his house. I therefore had to send Reb Nachman of Tulchin on foot to Nemirov for this purpose; and on Thursday too he went to Nemirov on the same errand.

[Publisher's note: In 1821, Reb Noson opened an illegal printing press in his home in order to print the Rebbe's writings. Censorship was in force then and to print elsewhere was too costly and time-consuming. In 1824, someone informed on him to the authorities and the press was closed. His opponents, knowing that the press had been idle for over ten years, nevertheless used this as a weapon to indict Reb Noson as an anti-government activist, along with his "many other" anti-state crimes. Details of the press, its closure and impact on Reb Noson's troubles during this period are found in Eternally Yours, *Volume One, and in* Through Fire and Water, *Parts IV and VII.]*

Late yesterday afternoon the [state-appointed] investigator came to my house inquiring about the printing press. They told him that it has been many years now since I had a press. He left my house in silence, without saying a word. He never even came to the upper room of my house where I was, but stayed down below. The way it looks, there is nothing to worry about, with God's help. So I am now waiting for the travel document, and after that I will be able to go, with God's help. I wanted to write a little more, but several matters have since come up.

So, my son, you can understand for yourself that everything that is happening where you are, and here, and in Uman, is all really one and the same thing, and all that is happening throughout the entire world is all interlinked and interconnected. God's wonders and thoughts are profoundly deep. So that if indeed we are suffering greatly and they are chasing us from every direction, this in itself is what comforts us in our destitution. For since every one of us sees that wave after wave of troubles are constantly washing over him, "one abyss calls to the next"; still, how great are God's kindnesses that He has saved us from being persecutors of sincere, righteous men who every time flee to God, His Torah and the true tzaddikim! We must rejoice over *this* very much every day! *Ashreinu!* Happy are we that we are among the pursued and not among the pursuers!

That scoundrel Mordekhai Sherer, may his name be obliterated, has undoubtedly drowned already in the deep pit of this-worldly desires. But this is not enough for him and he has gone on to ignite himself even further "with a fire that will burn him *slowly*" by raising his hand to strike a man better and more righteous than he. Woe to him! Woe to his soul! Woe! Woe to all those who support him! The truth is that if Reb Itzik were more resolute he could uproot him by filing a suit against him. After all, the world is not a free-for-all! But while it is extremely hard to take their abuse, insults and intimidation, what can we do? It is all really for the good. Our transgressions are responsible for all this and we must accept it as expiation and forgiveness for our sins. For we are certainly not *worthy* of coming close to a light such as the Rebbe! This is why we have to suffer all this. But God has already helped us very much, and He will continue to help, protect and save us, so that it will all come with great kindness. God in His compassion will certainly show us a favorable sign, and our enemies will see and be ashamed!

In addition to all these troubles, my livelihood is extremely tight and moreover, I had to borrow money for this whole affair that I described above. I must also take care of everything needed for my son's wedding, may he live [Reb David Zvi].

Last Friday I was extremely anxious about all this, but just then God eased things for me. A letter came for me from Reb Zev in Vinnitsa and with it he sent ten silver rubles. While this is really only a small sum, I saw God's miracles in it. For God's kindness is never-ending and in suffering He gave me relief. My hope is in Him that He will help me, and all of us, and that He will save us in every way that we need to be saved — body, soul and financially, physically and spiritually.

Fortify yourself mightily, my son! See and understand well how a person is pursued every moment, especially anyone who wants to draw near to holiness! We have nothing but the few points of good that we grab every day through some crying out, some prayer, some study, some good wish, longing or yearning, or some mitzvah that we are worthy of performing, some charity or act of kindness. A person has nothing but the present day, as the Rebbe said on the verse, "*Today*, if you will listen to His voice!" (Likutey Moharan I, 272). Do not say, "When I will have leisure I will study. Perhaps you will never have leisure." Especially since we already know that the desire itself is very good — that the main thing is desire! I do not have time to continue, but I intend to write you another letter before I leave here. May the Master of Compassion have compassion on us and may we be worthy to give each other good news from now on.

The words of you father who prays for you.

Noson of Breslov

[Editor's note: I will describe a little, less than a drop in the ocean, of what *happened to our teacher, Reb Noson, of sainted memory, after the time of the above letter. Immediately after he wrote this letter, on Monday, he was summoned by the above-mentioned official. The official questioned him about the accusations which the slanderers had brought against him — namely, that he was still printing in his house and so on. He, of course, responded that this was a lie, presenting the official with clear evidence to that effect. But the slanderers had given the official a great deal of money and he was therefore unwilling to accept the evidence. He then called forth twelve of the slanderers and, while holding a holy object in their hands, they swore false oaths and testified against our teacher. Though he gave clear evidence to the contrary — it was to no avail. Subsequently, on Wednesday of that same week, he was taken to prison. They tormented him very much by placing him together with thieves and murderers. On Sunday, the punishment they imposed placed Reb Noson in very real danger, until God, in His kindness, caused him to find favor in the eyes of the prison warden, and the head of the prison decided to alleviate his suffering. He placed Reb Noson in a room by himself and allowed him to receive all the books that he needed every day: a volume of the TaNaKH, a volume of Shulchan Arukh, a tractate of Talmud, Zohar, the writings of the Ari, and other books, on both the Torah's revealed teachings and the mystical. Writing supplies were also brought for him to the prison, because even there he so attached himself to God that he was worthy of conceiving original Torah ideas (*Likutey Halakhot, Yoreh Deah, Hilkhot Yayin Nesekh 4*). He stayed there for about eight days, after which there was a great and awesome miracle and the entire situation reversed itself. The informers and the official changed their minds and he was released on bail. The legal action continued however, and on that Rosh Chodesh Elul they banished him from his home to Nemirov, as described below. The story is too long to describe in all its details, but anyone reading the letters from the years 5595-5599 will learn a small part of it, and will thereby strengthen himself in whatever befalls him. For he will see for himself how God never abandons a person, no matter how much his enemies may assail him. "For You are on high forever, God." You always have the upper hand.]*

194

[Publisher's note: This letter was written after Reb Noson's release from prison.]

With thanks to God, Sunday, Va'etchanan, 5595.

To my dear, beloved son. Peace, life and all good.

I just now received your letter. For the moment I have nothing to say as you will probably be here next Shabbat, God willing, and then we will talk face to face. At the moment, speech must be restrained as in (Psalms 32:3), "I fell silent, mute." We must fulfill, "Let him put his mouth into the dust [in supplication], maybe there is hope." Maybe. Maybe. If you write me a thousand times about the intense bitterness of your heart, I know that I have already endured bitterness thousands upon thousands of times greater. May God have mercy from now on.

As for the rest of our comrades, practically all of them will need to endure what they will. As I have seen, and I see it now, always until this very day — all the bitterness, sorrow and suffering that come upon each person, every moment of every day, are all rooted in the destruction of the Holy Temple. For *there* is the essence of holiness, the main *tikkun*, rectification, of everything. From the time that the House of Our Life, Our House of Holiness, Our House of Splendor was destroyed, each day is worse than the previous, as our Rabbis, of blessed memory, taught (Sotah 48a). What can we say? What can we utter? Then there is each individual's own personal destroyed Temple, i.e. the Temple of Wisdom and Understanding. Who will stand up for us?! We have no-one to lean on but God's great compassion elicited through the power of the true tzaddikim who are constantly drawing forth new compassion. With this we have the hope that we need not, God forbid, despair of crying out and screaming, particularly during these bitter days.

Letter #195

"If only our heads were filled with water and our eyes were a well of tears," so that we could pour out our prayers like water before God, until He consoles us and saves us from now on, with true consolation and salvation, forever.

The words of your father, writing with an inconsolable bitterness in his heart, until God looks down from Heaven and sees.

Noson of Breslov

195

With God's help, Sunday, Torah reading Va'etchanan, 5595.
My dear, beloved son.

I just now received your letter and there is nothing new to report. We have not done anything yet, because we simply have no idea what to do. Many are rising up against us and we have no-one to lean on but our Father in Heaven. Still, we will probably attempt to take some action in this matter — whatever God in His enormous compassion guides us to do. For one must receive the counsel of *what* to do from God through His great compassion and lovingkindness. Salvation comes from God.

We are presently in a time of very great suffering, and these days of *bein hametzarim* [the three weeks from the 17th of Tammuz to the 9th of Av] are in any case a time of distress for Israel. Right now, the only vitality I have comes through the holy teaching of "in suffering You gave me relief" (*Likutey Moharan* I, 195). For amidst the sweep of pain and sorrow I see awesome gifts of relief every day! This is beside the fact that my hope is in God that He will soon rescue me from these straits entirely! He will certainly not abandon me, or any of us, and everything is definitely for our good in This World and the Next, forever. The news you gave me about that money is also an incredible relief and help at such a time. How great are God's kindnesses! They are never-ending! His compassion never ceases! How I hope to God that everything will be all right, with God's help! At the moment though we need salvation and very great mercy.

My friend, Reb Itzele from Heissen stayed here over Shabbat. God helped us and yesterday, Shabbat, we spoke many words of truth that arouse and fortify the heart very much; to be tenacious and adamant in all one's good points; to grab everything we are able while in This World, and to remember that we have nothing in the world except the unification of God's Blessed Name every day. For the Unification of God's Name encompasses all the other devotions that a person accomplishes every day according to his level. Belief in God includes everything and is the foundation of everything. Time rushes by in a flash. No matter what we do, it keeps on passing. The days of our lives are pure vanity. In the end we will have nothing but the holy faith that we merited through God's mercy to receive face to face from the true tzaddik of the generation — the holy faith that our holy ancestors planted in our midst long ago.

Therefore, even now *Ashreinu!* Happy are we! How good is our lot! Reb Feivel was certainly right every time when he proudly intoned "*Ashreinu!*" Now too, we need to inspire ourselves with this, so that we will have strength to recite the *kinot* with all our hearts and so that each one of us can break his heart as he should over his own individual share in the destruction of the Temple and over the sufferings of the Jewish People as a whole and individually. May God pity us and may we merit to be among the mourners over Jerusalem and thereby to see its joy, and may we constantly see the sprouting of the seeds of salvation. May He show us a favorable sign. Let our enemies see and be ashamed! May they fall and not get up! Our souls will rejoice in God and His salvation! Let all our bones say, "God, Who is like You?!" You rescue the poor man from one stronger than he!

> The words of your father, sighing, downcast and speaking with a very broken heart. But nonetheless I truly do encourage myself with all I said above, to adamantly fortify myself and to wait for God's speedy salvation.
>
> *Noson of Breslov*

Warm greetings to all our comrades with a great and mighty love. Fortify your hearts determinedly, all you who hope in God! "It is a time of trouble for Jacob and he will be rescued from *it*." From *it*, indeed, because through the trouble itself great salvation will come! With amazing lovingkindness, the trouble will turn into great relief through the power of the elder of holiness! Thank God, we have someone to rely on! There is hope that our end will be a good one in This World and the Next forever!

196

With thanks to God, Wednesday, Ekev, 5595.

My dear, beloved son.

I received your letter on Sunday with the eighteen gold coins. I was delighted to hear how well you are doing. Now you can see the miracles of God — that it is just now, when I traveled despite such difficulties, that things are taking a turn for the better. Look and understand the ways of God! Impediments do not even exist. And when a person is determined and breaks all the barriers regardless of what might happen to him, all the impediments become help and salvation!

Be strong, my son! Be strong! You should be rejoicing over the Shabbat that you merited to be with me, because, thank God, you had a very large share in all the good that took place then. May God fortify your heart, and the hearts of all our comrades, to walk the straight and true path! May we merit the wisdom to choose at all times the path that is really and truly the straight one, in accordance with God's will and the will of those who fear Him. May we merit to fulfill, "Let us search out our ways, examine them and repent"; and likewise may we fulfill, "Let us raise up our hearts in our hands to God in Heaven" — both of these verses in accordance with all that we talked about last Shabbat. May God allow us to know what He wants and truly to do it always, all the days of our lives. Amen.

The words of your father.

Noson of Breslov

197

[Publisher's note: This letter tells of Reb Noson being exiled from Breslov to Nemirov. His opponents pushed for exile to Siberia. The exile to nearby Nemirov was thus a blessing in disguise as it kept Reb Noson near the center of Breslover Chassidut. Furthermore, it was a telling blow to his enemies that, even after all their bribery and false testimony, their charges were not accepted as being truthful.]

With thanks to God, Monday, Torah reading Reay, 5595.

My dear, beloved son.

I received a letter from you yesterday, as well as one last week through Reb Yitzchak Yehoshua. I was quite pleased by them, and by yesterday's letter in particular. I am sure you heard the same thing that we heard here, that, God forbid, the official has received the answer that I must, God forbid, leave here and go to Nemirov. Numerous false rumours are also circulating and I am quite frightened. But by God's lovingkindness I strengthen and encourage myself very much through the use of our "methods." Thank God, even if this does happen, at least it does not put me in danger. My hope is in God that, even if I do, God forbid, have to live in Nemirov for a while, I will certainly return safely home. At the moment, though, the anticipation and waiting are difficult, since people are saying that tomorrow or Wednesday the verdict will be released, God forbid. May God have compassion and save us in His kindness, and may everything turn into good. May the Almighty give us compassion. May He Who said "Enough!" to His World, say "Enough!" to our troubles! Have pity on us, God. We have had our fill of disgrace!

I ask you, my dear son, apple of my eye, do not be afraid or anxious. Just pray to God about this. Take it from me and act wisely: Use this opportunity to force yourself all the more to express yourself before your Creator and Protector. We have no strategies and no tricks. All we have is prayer, supplications, crying out and screaming to God; and God has great power to save. At the same time, you will also have the chance to express before God everything else in your heart.

Everything that happens to us, especially this and every year, is all great hints which force each one of us, wherever he may be, to draw closer to God. The main thing is that from now on, none of us should be remiss about placing his supplication and prayer before God every day, no matter who he is. He must not let his thoughts upset him. Nor must he become discouraged by his urges, his confused state of mind and all his distractions. Rather, he must fortify himself in all the ways we have spoken about so much, and especially with the teaching of *Azamra!* For this holy and extremely awesome pathway must be new for each person every day! By putting this teaching into practice, every person can inspire himself constantly wherever he may be and can express himself before God very much — or at least a little. And this is the foundation and essence of everything! Now stand up and look to God's salvation! I hope to God that in His great kindness He will soon save us for the sake of His Name. He will rescue me, and all of us, from the hands of our haters and pursuers. He will put down our enemies beneath us and everything will turn into good soon!

Noson of Breslov

Extend my greetings to all our comrades with a great love!

198

With thanks to God, Saturday night, Shoftim, 5595.
My dear, beloved son.

I received your letter on Friday along with the letter from Reb Chaim. You should know now that on Friday I was again summoned to the official. He showed me that he had transcribed my declaration from my letter into his language and he read out his version to me. I also called Reb Chaim who read it to me as well, and it accurately reflects what I wrote. May God have compassion and may it all turn out for the best. It does not appear right now as though any answer at all has come from Kaminetz [about the charges and trial].

Thank God, I spent Shabbat here. May God give me salvation and may I continue to live here as long as I wish through God's great lovingkindness. Now, though, we must pray to elicit salvation and compassion so that the verdict will be in my favor and I will be found completely innocent in the trial, just as I am, in truth, completely guiltless in this matter. The whole thing is just slander and lies. May my enemies stumble and fall! May they be ashamed and completely confounded! Salvation is all in God's hands. This same official told me himself that all this has to be sent to Kaminetz, to the state prosecutor, and that afterwards there will be another investigation. In the meantime, we have a respite during which we can *use* all this to draw close to God and to pray before Him. For we have nobody to flee to but God.

The days of the great trial and judgment of Rosh HaShanah are rapidly approaching, and we have already blessed the arrival of Rosh Chodesh of Elul [which falls this week]. *This* is the trial we must shudder in fear of, for it pertains to our eternal lives and it is impossible to bribe with money or appease with words. All the fear that I am presently experiencing over this trial of mine is in order for me to remember and not to forget the fear of the judgment of Rosh HaShanah and, even more so, the day of the great and awesome Final Judgment.

We must elevate all our worries and fears, and not be afraid or daunted by anything but God. We have to know and believe that all the anxiety and fears that come upon a person, especially the kind that we have right now, are meant to remind us to tremble and shake in fear of God. For when a person remembers the fear of God, even though each person knows in his heart that he is far from being innocent, he can immediately rejoice and be truly alive! For "the fear of God, increases one's days" and "fear of God gives life." The perfection of the right kind of fear is that a person's great fear leads him to joy, as is written, "rejoice with trembling." And this is effected by the power of the true tzaddik. For when we begin to be scared and tremble over how much we have done wrong, we immediately encourage ourselves and bring ourselves to joy, that we rely on a great and awesome power such as this! What is more, we ourselves have also merited to grab every day many points of good with which to encourage ourselves! In this way a person can achieve clarity of thought in order to grow all he can in every way possible. He can daily renew and strengthen his desire and yearning for holiness; and, through the power of speech, he can bring these desires from potential to actual. We truly can say *Ashreinu!* that we know about all this and much, much more! We will never be ashamed, after knowing about truth such as this! We must always remember what the Rebbe said, "What do we have to be ashamed of?!" I cannot write any more.

    The words of your father, waiting for salvation.

Noson of Breslov

199

With God's help, Sunday, Shoftim, 5595, Breslov.

My dear, beloved son.

    I sent you a long letter this morning. Afterwards, the order came from the police that I must leave here for Nemirov. It was only with difficulty that I managed to get permission to remain here a few more days, as Reb Nachman of Tulchin, the carrier of this letter, will tell you. At the moment, I have to encourage myself with the teaching, "In suffering You gave me relief" — with the gifts of relief contained *within* the suffering itself. A person can live a true life in Nemirov too! God is my hope that I will soon return here. Beyond this, you can understand for yourself how busy and preoccupied I am right now. I cannot go on at all.

    The words of your father, waiting for salvation.

Noson of Breslov

200

[Compiler's note: This letter was written after Reb Noson was banished from his home to Nemirov.]

With thanks to God, Monday, Teitzei, 5595, Nemirov.

Warm greetings to my beloved son, the apple of my eye, Reb Yitzchak, may his light shine.

I have no news to tell you. You know everything that is happening in Breslov better than I do, and the bearer of this letter, Reb Nachman of Tulchin, will tell you what is happening here in Nemirov. "Know this today and place it upon your heart, the Lord is God" in Breslov *and* in Nemirov. His Rulership is everywhere. Everything they have done to me is all for the good, thank God. And while I can remotely comprehend only a tiny fraction of this, I believe that the rest is all for the good in This World and the Next, forever.

My brother Reb Yudel came at night from Breslov and he told me about the enormous, bitter and treacherous informing taking place there, as they turn *themselves* over to the deepest pit of hell. By God's lovingkindness, I was not frightened by it. To the contrary — thank God, I celebrate, rejoice and exult over our portion and our lot. Now, now, we ought to be saying *"Ashreinu! Ashreinu!"* a thousand, ten thousand times a day! Our mouths should never stop saying *"Ashreinu!"* "Happy are we!" that we know about this true tzaddik who enables us to feel a little of the sweetness of that praise, what it means to be able to say *"Ashreinu!"* All of Israel, and we among them, say it every day. But how few are they who notice it and who feel the sweet loveliness of the words they are pronouncing with their mouths! Praise God Who had compassion on us in His great and marvelous lovingkindness so that we are not opponents and we have drawn a little close to the point of truth, which allows us to summon our strength and to rejoice in the eternal goal! And most important is the holy belief in God and in the true tzaddikim. *Ashreinu!* Happy are we! How good is our portion! that we have merited to escape opponents of truth such as this, and to be in his portion and his lot forever! This is our share, this is our comfort in every hardship. This is our salvation and our hope, in This World and the Next, eternally.

Now I must certainly put forth many prayers and supplications, and converse very much with my Creator concerning our enormous hardships and the grave danger we are facing. But more than this, we must strengthen ourselves to trust God, to wait for salvation and to rejoice in our mighty hope. For, thank God, we have someone to lean on; and God will certainly not abandon us for the sake of His Great Name. "Even when I am old and gray, God, do not abandon me, until I declare Your strength to the generation and Your might to all who are to come. Your righteousness, God, reaches to the Heavens."

> The words of your father, waiting for salvation at all times.
>
> *Noson of Breslov*

201

With thanks to God, Sunday, Nitzavim, 5595, Nemirov.

My beloved son and apple of my eye.

The carrier of this letter, Reb Nachman Tulchiner, will tell you how busy I am right now. But my love for you and your desire for my letters compel me to write you at least these few lines. Fortify yourself, my son, and be strong! Trust God; He will not abandon us. We have to review every day and remember what the Rebbe wrote on the verse, "In suffering You gave me relief." From this I draw all my vitality right now. The enormous favors that I find amidst our tremendous suffering are what give me the life and inner strength not to despair of praying, crying out, supplicating and waiting for His salvation at all times. God will surely help us and save us for the sake of His Great Name, through the power of the elder of holiness upon whom we lean in This World and the Next.

The words of your father, extremely busy and waiting for salvation.

Noson of Breslov

Letters from 5596 (1835-36)

The year in review

Before Rosh HaShanah, Reb Noson requested a travel document to allow him to travel to pray with the *kibutz*, the gathering of the Breslover Chassidim on Rosh HaShanah, in Uman. The permit was never issued, but Reb Shmuel Weinberg managed to have one signed by a non-Jewish official in Breslov, unknown to Reb Noson's opponents. He slipped out of Nemirov but upon his arrival in Uman the authorities were informed that Reb Noson was without travel documents and issued a warrant for his arrest. After showing his permit, the judge permitted Reb Noson to stay in Uman until right after Rosh HaShanah, when he was to return to Breslov under police guard and to prove to the Breslov authorities that he had a permit. Upon doing so, he was allowed to return to Nemirov, to continue his exile until his case was decided.

Having seen that the opposition to Reb Noson brought no tangible results, the Savraner Rav decided to travel to Kaminetz himself and use his considerable influence to have Reb Noson tried, convicted and banished to Siberia. His plans went awry and the Savraner himself was forced to flee Kaminetz and spent his remaining years in exile, in the city of Titchalinik, where he passed away in January of 1838.

Meanwhile, Reb Noson settled into rented quarters in Nemirov. His followers were reluctant to gather in large numbers as this had been one of the charges against him, so they visited him infrequently and in small groups. Still, his enemies would inform the police even under those circumstances. The reader will see these fears in several of the letters of 5596. Details of Reb Noson's trip to Uman, his arrest and humiliating return trip to Breslov, of the Savraner's plot and its failure and of Reb Noson's suffering are found in *Through Fire and Water*, Part VII, Chapters 39-41.

202

[Editor's note: Upon Reb Noson's return from Uman, he spent the night in Ladizin. His opponents surrounded the house where he was staying and began throwing rocks. Everyone in the house was in danger, and especially our teacher, of blessed memory. Just then a new trouble arrived but this provided a remedy for the stone-throwing and prevented them from killing him. For the local official came and imprisoned Reb Noson. In this way he escaped being murdered. He was held there for about twenty-four hours and by a miracle was released.]

With thanks to God, Thursday, the Eighth Day of the Ten Days of Repentance, 5596.

My dear, beloved son.

I arrived here safely in Breslov yesterday. You have no doubt heard already what happened to me in Ladizin. By God's kindness I escaped. "All Your breakers and waves have passed over me." At the moment I still do not know where I will spend Yom Kippur.

Just now as I am writing you, the order has arrived from the police that I must travel to Nemirov immediately. All this is certainly God's lovingkindness and miracles. I am prepared to set out at once. As far as I am concerned, they are doing me a great favor, because the enormous dangers that I have experienced thus far are simply beyond description. I am trusting in God's kindness that I will return safely home and, with God's help, soon. At the moment there is no time to talk about this because the holy and awesome day, Yom Kippur, is rapidly approaching and I am very busy. God willing, after Yom Kippur I will write you a somewhat longer letter. Fortify yourself and be strong, my dear son! See and understand that everything is pure vanity! Many of the things that you were frightened of are, no doubt, already behind you. As it turns out, it was really for nothing that you neglected what you did because of needless worry. So it is with every person every day. I spoke about this at great length a few years ago on Shavuot, how the Evil One finds some postponement and distraction for every day, particularly in these times with all that we are going through. Therefore, remember well that a person has nothing in the world but the present day — "Today, if you will listen to His voice!"

The words of your father, praying for you, that you will be sealed for a good year, a good, long life and peace.

Noson of Breslov

203

With God's help, Sunday, the day after Yom Kippur, 5596, Nemirov.

To my dear, beloved and learned son, Reb Yitzchak, may his light shine.

I traveled here from Breslov the Thursday before Yom Kippur. I left a letter there for you with my son, Reb Shachneh, may he live. At the moment there is nothing new to report. Thank God, I was here for Yom Kippur, with Reb Itzele of Heissen and Reb Nachman of Tulchin and, thank God, everything was peaceful. We prayed as we wished and no-one said a word. May God have mercy from now on and may there be peace and truth in the world. I am sending now for my wife to come here with my small children, may they live. While I obviously do not have proper lodgings, I must send for them. I have no sukkah to eat in here either, and I cannot eat in a sukkah at my brother's house, because he [himself] is in rented quarters. I cannot explain everything.

At the present time, it is undoubtedly necessary to draw encouragement just from the kindnesses *within* the suffering itself. For they are downright miracles! What is more, in several respects they themselves constitute new developments, kindnesses and great miracles even more than the favors contained in them — so that I hope to leave the troubles behind completely and soon to return safely to my home.

Right now nothing is preventing me from prayer and study — just worries and internal distractions. And to repel these a person must constantly be fighting. For even now, all the distractions and fears which trouble us are all really for naught. This is particularly the case during prayer; because thinking about these things when we should be thinking about something else, God forbid, certainly serves no useful purpose at all! In this area every person must battle constantly to settle his mind and banish from his thoughts all his worried musings and preoccupations. The most crucial time for this is when a person is praying, because it is precisely *then* that all the distracting thoughts come forth and begin to make themselves heard (see Likutey Moharan I, 30:7).

I have written you this in order that you should glean hints, according to where you are. For though you do have worries, concerns and activities connected to your livelihood which distract you, I know that there are a number of areas in which confusion, worries and fears trouble your thoughts for nothing, as you yourself are aware. I have already spoken about this a great deal, but it is necessary to recall all I have said many times every day. Even when you are working, you must remember God and His Torah; yes, even in the post office, and on your way there and back and at similar times. "If a person should say to you, 'Where is your God?', tell him, 'In the great city of Rome'," as is explained in the lesson "Who is the man who desires life" (*Likutey Moharan* I, 33) and in other places. *Ashreinu!* How fortunate are we to have merited to hear holy and awesome words such as these! A man who desires life will hold onto them. Study them over and over! There is nothing better.

I do not have time to go on any longer. Thank God, Who has helped us to be happy again and again. We trust His Holy Name that we will rejoice and be happy over His salvation in This World and the Next! We can really and truly be happy!

Noson, the son of Reb Naftali Hertz, of blessed memory, of Breslov

204

With thanks to God, Sunday night, Noach, 5596, Nemirov.

My dear, beloved son.

I received your letter the night of Hoshana Rabba and I was delighted. How very much I longed to see your handwriting! Everywhere you turn, in every direction and with every move, you can see God's miracles and His direct supervision. It never occurred to me that no-one would tell you, and that you would not know where I was for Yom Kippur until the day after. I even had a letter all ready the Thursday, before Erev Yom Kippur to let you know my situation. Everything is from God though — pain, God save us, its alleviation, knowledge, good news and its opposite, God forbid. He made everything good in its proper context and time. All the labor that a man toils at under the sun is futility and vanity. And while it is sometimes necessary to make certain efforts in accordance with God's will, toiling and struggle are most certainly pure futility. I have already talked about this in relation to the verses (Ecclesiastes 3:1-8) which read, "Everything has its time and every purpose has its season... What does a man gain from all his toil?" There is much to say about this, but it is impossible in a letter. Besides, it is growing dark and I have no time.

All that has happened every day from Rosh HaShanah until now is just beyond description. Praise God, after all the suffering and hardship, it has really all been with amazing lovingkindness. Thank God, the holiday passed here peacefully. God also helped me to dance very much in the study hall on the night of Simchat Torah and afterwards — all peacefully, and even with a little respect. Nonetheless, many of the impudent from the "nine-hundred and seventy-four generations" who simply cannot suffer tranquility are to be found here too; and they broke one glass pane in my window on the night of Simchat Torah as we were having our meal. Most of the city is furious with them, but the culprit is still unknown.

During these times the only way to encourage ourselves is with the conversations with which God favored us in the past: how the entire world is replete with suffering and how joy is what alleviates it. We have already spoken about this a great deal, but even I have to constantly remind *myself* about it. My hope is in God that He will surely not abandon me, or any of us. "It is a time of suffering for Jacob, and he will be delivered from it." My son, Reb Shachneh, along with Reb Nachman, may they live, are presently in my house and I really have no time. Yesterday I trekked from lodging to lodging and, thank God, I have quarters with a little space. Everything is with kindness, as in "in suffering You gave me relief." Had we come into the world only to hear this teaching, it would have been enough! For through this, you can see the kindnesses of God and His enormous, immeasurable miracles! "He performs deeds of incalculable greatness, miracles and wonders without number!" And this is in addition to all the things God does which remain hidden. For He alone does great wonders! "I considered my ways and turned my steps to Your testimonies" to say what our Rabbis instructed us, "everything that Heaven does is for the best." We have no-one to lean on but our Father in Heaven.

You should know, my son, that I received from my son, Reb Shachneh, on your behalf the money that is due to me from you, i.e. twenty-one gold coins. Be sure to send it to him immediately. I must begin now to fortify myself with new trust in God concerning my livelihood and my many needs here in Nemirov. For, as you realize, my friends and supporters are now far away. Salvation is in God's hands: God, Who has tended me from the beginning and has performed wondrous kindness with me to draw me near to such good, such truth and such light, and this is my share for all my suffering. This is my hope and the hope of my children and descendants forever and ever. God will be with me always, through the Rebbe's great merit and power. Even when I am old and gray, God will not abandon me, "until I declare Your strength to the generation and Your might to all who are to come."

The words of your father, waiting for salvation.

Noson of Breslov

205

With thanks to God, Monday, Lekh Lekha, 5596, Nemirov.

My dear, beloved son.

I received your letter today [text missing]...very... I am presently in the middle of prayers, before *Uva L'tzion* and I cannot write much. The deliverer of this letter, your brother-in-law, my friend Reb Yosef, may his light shine, will tell you everything in person. Most likely you have already received the letter I sent you yesterday with the special carrier. Reb Shmuel Weinberg is presently here with his brother's whole wedding party. I need to speak to you as well, but I have no time. Just talk the matter over carefully with your brother-in-law and our real friends. Perhaps you will find someone to speak with him. Perhaps some salvation will sprout so that the fire will die down. May

Letter #206

He Who makes peace in His High Places make peace for us and for all Israel. Amen.

> The words of your father, praying for you.
> Noson of Breslov

206

With thanks to God, Sunday, Vayeira, 5596, Nemirov.

My dear, beloved son.

I received your letter on Friday from the bearer of this letter. Concerning the letter to the Rav [it is not known who he was], what I really intended was that there would be someone in your community who could speak to him as my advocate, along the lines of what I wrote in my letter. But since, from what you say, there is no-one there to do this, "I have considered my ways, and turned...to Your testimonies" to rely on God alone and take no action whatsoever. I definitely do not want you to deliver the letter yourself. I never even considered this. Still, I am returning you the copy which belongs to my son, Reb Shachneh, may he live, so that you will have it. Maybe it will prove useful. Maybe there will still be someone who will direct his heart to Heaven and take upon himself to try to diminish the *machloket*. God will do what is good.

I do not have time to write any more. The deliverer of this letter will tell you everything in person. Thank God, He is with us, and in His kindness gives us much relief in the midst of our suffering. The carrier of this letter, Reb Nachman Tulchiner, will tell you about some of the sufferings and the favors. We have to fortify ourselves and start anew. I trust God that the good is really dominant and that all this is a great favor. We must fortify ourselves and start anew every day to follow the Rebbe's holy paths, and to draw life and encouragement from God's amazing kindnesses — that we merited to avoid being opponents of the point of truth! With this alone we can be alive and joyful even now, until God grants us complete relief, and we can leave behind our suffering entirely; and everything speedily will turn into tremendous good, happiness and joy!

The words of your father, praying for you.

Noson of Breslov

207

With thanks to God, Motzay Shabbat, Rosh Chodesh Kislev, 5596.

I received your letter last Thursday and I was really delighted. I was slightly upset, though, by your failing to mention in your letter whether you received the letter that I sent you from here last Monday night, [Torah reading] Toldot, with Reb Chaim Noson Tzeses, who was traveling to Odessa by way of Tulchin. I gave him my letter to you, and I enclosed with it a letter for you to send to Kremenchug to Reb Efraim, may he live. These letters should have reached you on Tuesday. You did not confirm this, though, and I am extremely upset over it. Therefore be sure to let me know regarding this immediately. I was also surprised that you wrote that I should destroy your letter. I do not know what secret was written in it. To the contrary, it is full of words of truth! I read it over twice and you inspired me with your words which came sincerely, right from your heart. May God soon fulfill your heart's desires for good that you may be a truly religious and righteous man. This is what I so much long for. The truth is, though, that even the longings and yearnings are also very precious.

It is explained in the Rebbe's holy books that the desire and yearning for holiness is of great value, especially when a person articulates his desires in detail every day (see *Likutey Moharan* I, 66:2). Fortify yourself determinedly, my son, to follow this practice of speaking out your yearnings for holiness every day! Force yourself to make this a regular practice! Believe that, regardless of anything else, your words themselves are extremely precious to God! For God desires *your* prayers too! All the universes with all the great devotion that they are constantly performing for God in awe and fear, is nothing as far as God is concerned compared with one meditation or prayer uttered by a lowly human being in this world, as explained in the lesson "The one who has compassion for them will lead them" (*Likutey Moharan* II, 7). And if someone is at a very low level because his actions are not proper — when *he* expresses himself before God or performs some religious act, God cherishes it all the more! It is God's greatest honor, when those who are very distant from Him are drawn to His service, as explained in the Rebbe's holy books (see *Likutey Moharan* I, 10:1; ibid. I, 14:1).

Furthermore, you have to believe that all that is said in the Rebbe's holy books about the great pride and joy that God takes in even the most inferior Jew, is also applicable to you! Above all else, force yourself with everything you have to rejoice with all your might every day that "He did not make me a heathen" and that "He separated us from those who err." We really and truly can say "*Ashreinu!*" Happy are we!

It is impossible to write any more in this context, because I do not know with whom this letter will be sent.

> The words of your father, praying for you and waiting for salvation.
>
> *Noson of Breslov*

Greetings to all my comrades with a great love! Regarding my health, you should know that I was not well last week. It was all related to the abdominal ailment, God save us, that I have had for some time now. I never had a flare-up though that went on for as long as the one last week. May God have compassion on me and protect me from now on from this illness and from all the sicknesses and ailments in the world. A person can see, every hour, every moment, that it is impossible to survive in this world except by keeping to the holy path, the true path of the Torah that we received from our master, teacher and Rebbe, of blessed memory. For every single word of his teachings we should be saying, "If we had come to the world only to hear this... it would be enough!" What can we say?! What can we say?! "His kindness to us has been great, and God's truth is forever!"

Noson, as above

[Compiler's note: The reader should know that it was from the abovementioned ailment, God save us, that Reb Noson passed away in the year 5605. He had this condition from the age of forty and it grew worse in his old age until it took his life. Woe for our affliction! Woe for the ailment that has stricken us! Woe for what is lost and can never be recovered! This alone comforts us — praise to the Living God for the remnant that survives him as an eternal memorial, i.e. his holy letters and his holy books. Praise to the Living God!]

208

With thanks to God, Tuesday, the 2nd of Kislev, 5596, Nemirov.

My dear son.

I had already sent you a letter on Saturday night, when your letter arrived with the post on Sunday. I was delighted — particularly with the fact that you spoke with Reb Nachman, our Rebbe's grandson, may he live. Be sure to make an effort to speak with him frequently and make yourself available to him. You will understand on your own how to conduct yourself. I already wrote you that, thank God, I am feeling better, with God's help. I was not actually sick, God forbid, last week either. It was just that condition that I have had for some time now. This latest flare-up, though, went on for a long time. With God's mercy it left me before last Shabbat. May God have compassion on me and protect me from now on from this illness and from every kind of sickness and pain in the world. May He heal me body and soul. Things are so pressured that I cannot write any more. Thank God, I had guests last Shabbat and I spoke words of truth. Thank God Who has helped me thus far. His lovingkindness never ceases.

Fortify yourself determinedly, my son, and encourage yourself every day with the great lovingkindness and miracles that God showers upon every single one of us every single day! Believe that it was not for nothing, God forbid, that our Sages fixed that we should say every day [in the daily prayers], "for Your miracles that are with us every day, for Your wonders and favors that [are with us] at all times." A person who looks at this with sincerity and faith will be able to discern it a little. This is particularly the case for us, who have many assailing us, and the Holy One, Blessed be He, saves us from their hands. God is our hope that we will soon leave our troubles completely behind us, and go from suffering to great relief! Let our enemies look on and be ashamed. Let it come swiftly, quickly, right away!

The words of your father.

Noson of Breslov

Warm greetings to all my companions with a mighty love; especially to my friend, whom I love heart and soul, the illustrious and honored Reb Nachman, may his light shine, grandson of the crown of our heads, of sainted memory.

209

With thanks to God, Tuesday night, Vayeitzei, 5596, Nemirov.

My beloved son.

I received the letter that you wrote on Wednesday, [Torah reading] Toldot. You should know now that I was informed by Reb Shmuel Weinberg that the letter that I sent you with Reb Chaim Noson Tzeses of Nemirov fell into the hands of out-

Letter #209

siders. What happened was that this Reb Chaim Noson forgot to give you the letter [in Tulchin]. He remembered as he was traveling away from Tulchin and so he sent it to you with someone else. The letter was already opened in Bartnik and I do not know where they are. While I am indeed pained by this, my comfort is that, thank God, I have nothing to be ashamed of in what I wrote there. I did not speak, God forbid, against a single Jew. I only reminded you to keep your mind constantly on the World to Come every day, in a general way and through all the details of your life (see *Likutey Moharan* I, 54:1). Thank God, I do not need to be ashamed about this in the least! Still, were I to have known that this was going to happen, I would not have given the letter to a carrier. But, after the event, it is certainly all for the good. Who understands God's ways and His wonders? So be sure now to write to this Reb Chaim Noson, tell him what happened, and ask him to write and tell you to whom he gave the letter. Perhaps you will be able to recover it. God will do what is good.

Thank God, I am well, with God's help. Chanukah is rapidly approaching and, without a doubt, the dedication of the Temple [which took place on Chanukah] is effected every year in accordance with the *Selach Na!* plea that we make on Yom Kippur, as our master, teacher and Rebbe revealed to us (see *Likutey Moharan* II, 7). In the end, the Holy Temple will definitely be rebuilt, may it be soon in our times, and its entire construction will have taken place through this process. Little by little, each year it is being built, until it is finally completed, may it be soon. Therefore, every year, each Jew must have a share in the dedication of the

Temple, and his share is in accordance with his *Selach Na!* plea on Yom Kippur.

Even now it is necessary to pray that our Yom Kippur's *Selach Na!* be accepted. For a person must return to God every day, which is the aspect of Yom Kippur's holiness which we draw into the rest of the year. The more we succeed in doing this, the more efficacious is our dedication of the Temple. The dedication of the Temple, in turn, creates an illumination of "the son" and "the student," i.e. to make known God's greatness and kingship both to "those who dwell on high," people on high spiritual levels, and to "those who dwell down below," people on low spiritual levels. The essence of this illumination is to reveal to all the very inferior and most abject people in this lowly world that "the whole world is full of His glory," to proclaim "Rise up and sing, you who dwell in the dust!" *Gevalt*, dear brother! Do not let amazing, original words such as these grow old for you! They really and truly are completely new for me every day, every moment! I am constantly astonished at wonders and new original ideas such as these! They are very, very sorely needed by every person, to revive him, rouse him, awaken him and stand him up, wherever he may be! *Ashreinu!* Happy are we to have merited to hear all this!

I cannot elaborate any further in this context. But I could not resist giving you these few brief, but potent reminders. May they make a good impression on your heart, motivating you to fulfill them with simplicity, straightforwardness and sincerity. Thus you will always enjoy good in This World and the Next eternally.

Noson of Breslov

Extend greetings to all my comrades, particularly to the learned Reb Nachman, may his light shine, grandson of our master, teacher and Rebbe, of holy, sainted memory. Fortify him and strengthen him! Rouse him and awaken him! In this way you too will be awakened and you can "receive from each other." If you wish, you may show him this letter. Do as your good sense dictates.

210

With God's help, Wednesday, Vayeitzei, 5596, Nemirov.

Greetings to my beloved son-in-law, who is as dear to me as my own son, the distinguished young man, Reb Barukh, may his light shine, and to my modest daughter, Chanah Tsiril, may she live, and my granddaughter, Esther Shaindel, may she live.

I received your letter before last Shabbat. I was greatly pained to hear about my daughter's toothache, which came on top of my other worries and tribulations. May God have mercy. Thank God, I heard this week that the pain had stopped. May God have compassion and rescue her from now on from all sickness, ailments and pain. May He give you livelihood, life and, above all, peace. Amen.

I was really pleased by what you wrote in your letter, because I could see your longing for the ultimate goal. May you always genuinely feel this way all your life, to fear God, and to trust that He will certainly never abandon you, or any of us. For God's lovingkindness never ceases. From now on beware, my dear son, of getting into arguments and disputations with the other young men. They too, like most young people, are argumentative. This quality causes many disagreements and conflicts and is a very great impediment to entering the path of truth. Contentiousness is the result of impure blood which has not yet served God (Likutey Moharan I, 75).

Get into the habit of always drawing yourself to genuine simplicity [*temimut*]. Study Torah, pray, talk to your Creator, and cast these childish ways aside! In particular, do not pose complicated questions and enter into any sort of philosophical investigations at all. You are forbidden to entertain questions even about me, God forbid! Because God knows that my only motivation is pure truth, to steer you on the true path of the Torah, the path our ancestors have always followed, as I received it from the mouth of our master, teacher and holy Rebbe, of holy, sainted memory. Consider very carefully the absolute truth about what my intention and the intention of all of our comrades is with regard to what we are doing. Are we motivated, God forbid, by a desire for the shallow honor which is popular nowadays, or for wealth? God knows and anyone with a brain in his head can understand that, thank God, we, and I, are untainted by this or anything like it. I do not have time to write any more.

> The words of your father-in-law, speaking truly and sincerely for your eternal good.
> *Noson of Breslov*

My dear daughter. For God's sake, do not worry. Believe in God that He will not abandon you. Look at those who are worse off than you. Many young men are only temporarily supported by their fathers-in- law, and some do not even have *that* little. Listen to me and do not worry about tomorrow. If possible, you might yourself try to work out some livelihood. It might be good for you to ask my son, Reb Shachneh, to talk to me when he is here about some suggestions I might have. Perhaps you could work out some income for yourself. But, for God's sake, right now do not worry at all. God is great, and the Giver of Life also gives sustenance. I do not have time to write any more. Be well and happy. My dear children! Thank God, *we* are not tearing up holy books! What is more, we are studying them! Thank God, we have something to study! Praise God, I have already given you a good inheritance for eternity. No rich man in the world can give an inheritance such as this! Thank God, we have absolutely nothing to be ashamed of!

The words of your father, speaking sincerely.

Noson of Breslov

211

With thanks to God, Tuesday, Vayishlach, 5596.

Greetings to my dear, beloved son, the learned Reb Yitzchak, may he live. Peace and all good to him and his household.

I received your letter from yesterday just now, around noon, and I was delighted. While I am indeed pained by what you are going through, I nonetheless know that no person escapes it. For while no two people are alike and it is impossible to make comparisons, everyone *is* equal in that each person must endure suffering very, very much every day. If, as the Rebbe said, in the future each person will be told everything he went through every day, then apparently each person must go through a great deal every day (see *Rabbi Nachman's Stories* p.229). Look carefully at what our Rabbis, of blessed memory, said on the verse, "And He formed..." [*vaYITZeR*] (Berakhot 61a), "Woe to me from my Maker [*YoTzRI*] and woe to me from my [Evil] Urge [*YiTZRI*]." It emerges that the essence of the Evil Urge is contained in the fact that a person is compelled to suffer this harassment and war every day, this "Woe to me from my Maker and woe to me from my [Evil] Urge!" And thus it happens with everybody, every day. But a person can encourage himself with this very fact, in that at least he still *feels* these two "Woes!" There are people who do not even feel any more, and whose hearts do not even grieve over all that happens to them! The Rebbe said explicitly that a person ought to feel encouraged that at least he is feeling his pain, as is written in *Likutey Moharan* (II, see Lesson 48:1). Thank God, you encouraged me with what you wrote about how you inspire yourself through the teachings and advice that you have heard from me. This is the way! This is exactly what you should be doing! Study them over and over!

At the moment there is nothing new to report. You will hear everything from Reb Nachman of Tulchin who set out from here yesterday. I was surprised that you mentioned nothing in your letter about my son's hat that I gave to Reb Zev who lives here. That was the whole purpose of my last letter, though as a result of it I gained the few words of truth that I wrote there. But you did not even give me a response about it. You know that the possessions of a person who wants to come close to God, and my possessions in particular, are all extremely valuable and are very closely bound up with the service of God. I need not go on about this, because you understand it for yourself. Besides, the past is gone. Just see to it now that the hat gets here quickly. I already spoke with the abovementioned Reb Nachman about this and I urged him on this matter. Also be sure to send me immediately the second section of *Choshen Mishpat*. I need it very badly; so, for God's sake, do not ignore my request!

As I already wrote you, I found out that the letter that I sent you with Reb Chaim Noson was already opened in Bartnik. It was Reb Yaakov Shtramvasser who told this to Reb Shmuel Weinberg. It seems to me that you know this Reb Yaakov. Therefore you must be sure to discuss this matter with him as soon as possible. Maybe you can persuade him to tell you where the letter is. If it is possible to recover the letters, you should certainly do everything you can to get them, and keep me posted about your efforts. We believe that God is supervising everything, and everything is surely for the best. While it took a great deal of time and effort until I was able to send those letters, God is certainly behind everything. His thoughts are wondrous and His wisdom is very great. A person can see God's miracles in everything every day aside what we believe [that miracles occur daily]. It is impossible for a person to understand anything [that is happening around him] for God's thoughts are very deep. *Ashreinu!* How fortunate we are to have seen and heard all this!

The Rebbe would frequently say that we really know

nothing and that his ignorance was even more unique than his knowledge (see *Tzaddik* #112, #283, #341). It is impossible to explain all this in writing because each individual will understand it differently according to his own perceptions. Through God's enormous compassion, the Rebbe also placed in *us* this awesome teaching which every single one of us needs every day, through all the setbacks in the world. For he concluded there by saying, "Even when it comes to *you* people and to wherever each one of you has fallen, [there is a phenomenon whereby a thing undergoes a complete and total transformation and becomes something else entirely]" (see *Rabbi Nachman's Wisdom* pp.106-7, #3). In other words, God's greatness is unfathomable and people know nothing at all. Thus there is hope for our final outcome, even for the worst of all people. The main thing is that a person never give up crying out and pleading (*Tzaddik* #565). Remember all this every day! I had not intended to write you about all this now, but your enormous desire and your good heart's burning for the truth compelled me. May God illuminate your eyes and the eyes of all those who desire the truth, so that my words of truth enter their hearts. For these words are extremely awesome, beyond all estimation!

The words of your father, looking forward to rejoicing over you in This World and the Next, eternally.
Noson of Breslov

Greetings to all our comrades with a great and mighty love, in particular to my dear, learned friend, Reb Shimshon, may his light shine. All these words were meant for you too! Take heart and be strong! This World is utter vanity, and nothing remains of a person except his Torah, prayer and good deeds! Even if everyone knows this, it does not change the fact that it is absolute, clear, pure and undeniable truth which a person must remember every single day! Today I studied the verse (Isaiah 40:6), "A voice says 'call.' What shall [I] call? 'All flesh is [like] grass, and all [a man's] kindness [like] a flower of the field'." Rashi comments on this verse, "All those who elevate themselves will have their greatness overturned and will be as the grass. Or, alternatively, 'all flesh is like grass' [can mean] that the end of man is to die." When I studied this today, it was as if I were seeing it for the first time! May you really take these words to heart simply and sincerely. "Do not be afraid because a man grows rich..." Today I realized that someone who is sincerely looking for the truth will constantly see that all the books are crying out and issuing fearsome proclamations to return to the truth.

I am holding myself back with all my strength from writing any more through the mail, especially during these times. May God give truth to Jacob.

212

With thanks to God, Monday, Vayechi, 5596, Nemirov.

Greetings to my beloved son, dear to me as my own heart and soul, Reb Yitzchak, may his light shine.

I received your letter through Reb Nachman of Tulchin at the beginning of Chanukah. You understand for yourself that it was simply impossible to answer you until now. First of all, I must devote a great deal of time to our comrades during these days. Secondly, I had no-one with whom to send you the kind of response I wanted. You already know that the work that I have with each one of the few people who come to me is far more monumental a task than engaging in business, litigation or other such pursuits with thousands of people. Matters which pertain to true religious devotion are above all else, and it was therefore impossible to take the time to sit down and write you the kind of letter you deserve. In addition to this, I really did not know what to write you. You already know and have heard everything, and the Rebbe has already restored our souls with words of perfect rightness — splendid pearls of wisdom. I know for a fact that many people more righteous than yourself have also endured everything you are experiencing. Many of them were well-known figures and leaders of their generations. In practically every case the primary cause was sadness and depression, which trips up a person in all sorts of ways. It saps the strength and intensifies the physical urges. It brings on downheartedness and discouragement. It is responsible for all kinds of internal distractions, which, though they cannot be described in writing, an intelligent person can easily recognize.

No matter what — God forbid, God forbid that this matter you wrote me about should get you down! It certainly *is* necessary to cry out to God over our having come into "deep waters" such as these. But God forbid that a person should allow himself to become excessively frightened by it. Anxiety and depression are more harmful than anything! God forbid! God forbid! This is especially true since we, thank God, have someone to lean on who can rectify everything! How exuberantly you can rejoice that you merited to be there on Rosh HaShanah and to be at the Rebbe's holy gravesite! It is unnecessary to go on about this right now. Fortify yourself and be strong, my son! Bring yourself to joy using all the things that you know! Do not think about this matter either beforehand or afterwards. For God is very great and His greatness is unfathomable — there is a phenomenon whereby everything is turned into good.

Thank God, He helped me this past Chanukah, Shabbat Chanukah in particular, and through His kindness I spoke words of Torah and had holy, awesome conversations that really gave life to the people who heard them. You may hear a few of them from the deliverer of this letter, Reb Nachman of Tulchin. In particular there was what I said about the verse, "You desired absolute truth; teach me the wisdom which is hidden" (see *Likutey Halakhot, Ribit* 5:26). You need what I said very much right now. For the primary cause of your downheartedness and sadness is too much truth. You *know* the truth about how far away you are and about how much wrong you have done. But since this truth wants to distance or discourage you, God forbid, you have to throw it away! It is impossible to explain all this now; the page is too short and there is not enough time. You can hear it from the carrier of this letter. How terribly I missed you when you were not among us this past Shabbat Chanukah! My consolation is that you were here for the Shabbat before Chanukah. In my opinion, you had a large share in our Shabbat Chanukah, because the Shabbat that you were here before Chanukah did much to prepare the ground for Shabbat Chanukah. I cannot explain the whole thing though.

I do not have time to write any more because it is almost the time for the Morning *Shema*. "May God bestow His lovingkindness by day" on me, and on you, that you may merit to fortify yourself in serving God wherever you are and in everything that you go through. What each person must endure is indescribable. The main thing is to fortify yourself and keep going! Thank God, *we* have plenty to fortify ourselves with all the time!

The words of your father who is praying for you.

Noson of Breslov

After I wrote this letter, your letter arrived, sealed with your stamp. I recalled that I had received another letter from you before Chanukah, and I took it out and read it again. All your letters speak the same language! They cry out sorely over the bitterness of This World, which is so full of the pain that overtakes each person. It is never the same for any two people, but everyone suffers great bitterness. All the different kinds of bitterness that every individual goes through, whether in body, soul or money, all emanate from the all-inclusive evil, the desire which includes all others, which is referred to in the verse (Ecclesiastes 7:26), "I find [this] woman to be bitterer than death; her heart is snares and traps, and her hands are shackles." But you and I have *this* to rejoice over: we know about the salt that sweetens the bitterness of the world about which it is said, "if it were not for the salt, the world would be unable to endure the bitterness" (see *Likutey Moharan* I, 23).

Even if you are suffering very greatly, my dear son, you should encourage yourself with this fact alone, that at least you are feeling the bitterness, and this is why you are crying out so much. For the very bitterness you are experiencing is the result of the eternal covenant of salt which sweetens the bitterness; and precisely *because* the bitterness is being sweetened, you are feeling it all the more. It is just like all types of medical cures which are very often harsh and painful: when the bandage is placed on the wound, it starts to hurt even more. For it is known in the science of healing that the illness and its cure are like two opponents and that there is a fierce battle raging between them. The illness sees that the patient is trying to cure it by taking some medicine or by applying some kind of bandage from the outside. Therefore, as soon as the medicine begins to take effect in its effort to drive off the illness, the illness immediately rouses itself in a mighty countereffort against the medicine. This is why it is very difficult to determine exactly the right way to cure something, and it is also one of the reasons not to make use of doctors.

Precisely the same principle applies to spiritual sicknesses, only much, much more so, because "the greater the person, the greater his evil urge." So that whenever a person makes an effort, great or small, to fight against the sickness of his soul, the opponent then mounts a commensurate counterattack from within and without. This is the reason that so many countless people have stumbled and fallen [away]. Our master, teacher and Rebbe, of blessed memory, has already spoken about this at great length; and he has strengthened every single person very much with the most wondrous encouragement, and inspired us with precious gems of wisdom. Thank God that we have a doctor such as this, an absolute master at healing our souls completely and right up to their final end! Besides his precious cures, his great power itself surpasses all else! God illumined my eyes just now as I was writing, and I was able to write these words, wondrous, new, straight and true. There is still much more in my heart to say about this, but it is impossible to express it in this context. Besides, time does not allow it. This will suffice for now to give life to your soul forever. A wise person will hear and draw instruction. Fortify yourself, my son, and be strong! Believe in yourself and that your hope is not lost! Your efforts will not go unrewarded! Just fortify yourself with the utmost determination in prayer and supplication always! Then you will have delight, forever and for all eternity!

Noson, the same

213

With thanks to God, Saturday night Shmot, beginning of the week of Va'eira, 5596, Nemirov.

Greetings to my honored, beloved son, Reb Yitzchak, may his light shine.

I received your letter this past Friday night. It is now immediately after Havdalah and I am sitting down to write you this letter. Maybe I will be able to send it to you with someone traveling to the fair. I do not yet know if I will be able to find one of them to be the carrier. As far as answering your cry —

God has already supplied us the cure in advance of the illness with the many holy words I have related to you, both in writing and in person, from our holy, awesome Rebbe, of sainted memory. They are all life-giving gems of wisdom that can inspire even me, even the whole world, and even you, in whatever situation we are right now! There is no subject in the world that is not covered in his holy teachings!

Thank God, you have heard from me very much and understood very much. You have also seen very much in the Rebbe's holy books and in the books in which God has allowed me to generate new ideas based on the Rebbe's holy words. So you should certainly know for yourself how to encourage yourself, even now. For it is a basic principle which I have talked about many times that, even if I were to say many inspiring words of truth and elaborate on them all at great length, every person still has to draw inferences and conclusions from them about how to encourage himself in his present place and time, according to who he is. For even if our mouths were "as full as the sea" with words of truth, it would still be impossible for a person to explain to his friend or student every single detail of what he needs to cure the pains of his soul, and to strengthen and fortify him through every last detail of everything that he goes through in even one day; let alone a week, a month, or a year — and certainly not for his whole life! A person must understand for himself from the holy words that *are* spoken how to receive strength and advice to bring himself to joy amidst the sweep of pain and grief, God forbid, and how to turn all kinds of sorrow and sighing into joy! *We* especially can do this since we have a good strong foundation with which to bring ourselves to joy and to encourage ourselves wherever we are and whatever we go through. For God gave us the merit of knowing about and drawing close to a light such as the Rebbe, or, at any rate, of not opposing him! Know and believe, my beloved son, that these are not just words. You have to inspire yourself with this every hour of every day!

My son, the real truth is that you worry too much. This is the work of the Evil One trying to fill you with downheartedness and depression, God forbid. The downheartedness and depression themselves are extremely harmful to someone in your situation! I am really angry with you, my son, for not listening to me, especially since all my words come from the Rebbe and are said in his name. Know and believe that the Rebbe is telling you not to think about this at all anymore, neither before nor after. The suffering is bad enough while it is happening, God save us! God is my hope that through this you will escape. No matter what, though, do not think about it at all! Be extremely careful to do as I say and do not trouble your mind over this in the slightest. Just study Torah, pray and go about your business. Relax your mind with things that cheer you and bring yourself to joy with silliness. You have no idea what is going on in the world! The greatest members of the Jewish People also experienced such things.

How terribly distressed I was when you wrote that you have been neglecting Torah study and that you have been missing the study sessions that you set for yourself at the beginning of the winter. What you are doing is not good. Not good at all! And it is certainly not becoming to us. Is it for nothing that I have spent so much time talking, practically until my throat was dry, about how a person must never give up on himself or become discouraged, and must never give an inch, through whatever should happen to him?! And after all this you write me such stupidity, rooted in improper humility, saying that you know yourself that coming close to holiness is beyond your grasp, and that this is the reason these things come to trouble you so much!

It certainly is true that no person *deserves* to attain holiness and to serve God, Who is Great, Awesome, Lofty and Exalted; particularly not people who are as full of wrongdoing and sin as we are in these generations. But the true tzaddikim have already told us, and our master, teacher and Rebbe in particular, that the essence of God's greatness is that the person who is most distant from Him and the most attached to physicality can and should serve Him. This is God's greatest pleasure and delight! For wherever we find God's greatness, we also find His humility. I have already told you many times that this mistake is very commonly found among young people. Each one thinks that this principle does not apply to him, given how dirty and sullied he is, and how much wrong he has committed. But the truth is just the opposite! It applies *especially* to him! But why should I go on talking to you anyway, when you do not heed my words, all of which are the words of the living God? For I received them from the fount of living waters, "the stream which flows forth, the source of wisdom," as expressed in the verse, "Deep waters are the counsel in a man's heart. Deep,

deep. Who will find it?" It is precisely through straightforwardness and simplicity that each person, wherever he may be at any given time, can plumb these "deep waters" and discover this council. A person's principal test and the essence of his refining process is that, through all the declines and falls, and through all the things that he goes through, he should not become distanced from God, from Torah or from prayer.

I have been looking lately into the most recent volume that I wrote, which speaks about the ideas I innovated, with God's help, last Shavuot and during that period (see *Likutey Halakhot, Hekhsher Keilim* 4). They are wondrous words indeed which constantly give life to the soul. I therefore yearn very much for you to receive them. God willing, when you are here, remind me and I will give them to you. For the teachings which I have originated most recently are, without a doubt, indispensable for you.

Thousands of pages would not suffice to tell you about God's greatness and the lovingkindness and miracles that He performs at all times; particularly the kindness that He has done with me in the recent past, when, in the midst of troubles and persecution such as these, in His wondrous kindness, He has showed me enormous relief. Reb Nachman of Tulchin has doubtless told you about Shabbat Chanukah. On Shabbat Torah Reading Vayigash there were also a few guests, and on Shabbat Torah Reading Vayechi, God helped us and we were very joyful, with God's help. There was a Brit Milah at my brother Reb Yosef's, may his light shine, and God brought it about that they had to send a carriage for my son, Reb Shachneh, who was honored with the mitzvah of *periah*. So he was here for Shabbat, along with the people from Breslov, Reb Shmuel Meir and Reb Gedaliah from Ladizin. Thank God, I danced a great deal at my house, and afterwards at a celebration over the child at my brother's house as well. I could tell you a lot about this, but it is not possible in this context. I need the ten gold coins very much, because I do not have a *zuz* [penny] in my whole house. Be sure to send me them quickly, as soon as you possibly can.

[section missing]

May the One Who created day have pity and compassion on me. May He reveal profound advice to me every day as in the verse "He reveals profundities from out of the darkness," as is cited in the lesson "Sound the Shofar-Faith" (*Likutey Moharan* II, 5). Thus may I know how to act each day, particularly with regard to everything that is taking place right now with us, and with me in particular. It is impossible to say very much about this, though. How great are the deeds of God, Who gives a weary man such as myself the strength to bear what I am presently suffering! You know much of it, but there is more than that which I know myself. Were I to describe it, no-one would believe that a person could suffer so much.

Come! See the might of your master! [Rebbe Nachman]. How very deep are his thoughts in that he shone forth in advance holy words — hints conveyed by the movement of hand, and a radiance such as this — which are capable of sustaining and inspiring me even now, to the point that I can also sustain and inspire you and others. May we merit to feel "the wind that blows in the six joints of the arms and the six joints of the legs." My heart lifts up my legs with truth and perfect faith, and I dance for joy! (see *Likutey Moharan* I, 10:6). Thank God, I, you and all those who desire the absolute truth have something to be happy about indeed!

I cannot continue. I have not yet sung *"HaMavdil"* and *"Eliyahu,"* since I hurried to write you these words immediately after Havdalah. May God finish for me. Sending you a letter — both writing it, and even more, having it delivered — is also an extremely difficult and exhausting labor. It is all a result of the controversy, which makes us afraid to send words of truth, lest they jokingly make a mockery of them, God forbid. But it is all for the best. For in this case too, the impediment is there to build up desire; and because of it God helps me, and even more inspiring words of truth emerge! For the only way to draw forth words of truth is by breaking down barriers, both from the side of the transmitter and from the side of the receiver.

All your downheartedness and depression too is all just another barrier setting itself in your way. It has to be broken. For above all, you must work to break depression, which is more harmful, God forbid, than anything else! *Gevalt!* Do not be afraid, my beloved son! Do not be afraid! God really is with you! Remember what our master, teacher and Rebbe, of blessed memory, said, "God is great and we know nothing of it at all. Even when it comes to *you* people and to wherever each one of you has fallen. But there is a phenomenon whereby everything turns into good, for His greatness is unfathomable." You must really believe and know that these words of the Rebbe's are also directed at you, the way you are right now! Even someone thousands and tens of thousands of levels worse, God forbid, is also included in these words. And were this worst person to hear these words, he too would inspire himself with eternal life forever, and would not throw his life away! But what can we do? This is exactly why they have arrayed themselves against us so vehemently, and especially now. However, this is also reason for you and me and all of us to rejoice very much, since we are able to hear and believe in holy, true, awesome, profound and straightforward words such as these! What can I say?! What can I say?! With these words and words like them, anyone with a brain in his head ought to turn all kinds of distress and sighing into joy!

>The words of your father, who yearns to bring you to joy, and waiting for salvation.
>
>*Noson of Breslov*

214

With thanks to God, Tuesday, Erev Rosh Chodesh Shevat, 5596, Nemirov.

My dear son.

I received all your letters. I cannot tell you, my dear son, the enormous pain I have over this matter. I wrote you a very long letter Saturday night after Shabbat. I had a great deal of difficulty writing it and I sent it with the post. I have no idea why you have not yet received it. You can imagine how terribly I am suffering over this and I have no idea what to do. For me this is one of the most painful things of all, until I am forced to "turn it into joy." It is certainly for the best. Who knows God's ways and His wonders?! In that same letter I also wrote a great deal about how much effort I must expend before I can get a letter to you — all because of the controversy which makes us fear that band of scoffers. Through this I also wrote words that give comfort. But it is all certainly for the best.

I cannot write very much right now because the carrier of this letter is in a hurry, and I have not yet finished my studying after the [Morning] Prayers. You will probably hear something to encourage and inspire you from the carrier of this letter. You should also see to it that you cheer yourself with the little bit of bad news that you hear from him as well. For we already know that everything is for the good, and barriers exist for the sake of desire. Surely God will not abandon us and, if there are also a lot of barriers here too, God will undoubtedly finish all He has begun. For everything that we as group, and every one of us individually, is presently going through is no insignificant matter, especially since we know what is happening with the rest of the world too — and to our opponents in particular. They are filled with sorrow and pain even more! I cannot go on about this.

I have already discussed the truth with you at very great length, how you must remember carefully what is written in the holy books that the world is full of sorrow, as is written (Ecclesiastes 2:23), "And all his days are sorrow and pain." You already understand this a little. But you have yet to look very carefully at this, and to realize that God has not the slightest desire for the world to exist for the sake of all of its vanity and futile pursuits. All the vanity only exists for the sake of free will. What

Letter #215

God really intended and what He really desires is every good movement and every good point that every single Jew grabs every day, which the true tzaddikim will refine and elevate and build into wondrous, awesome constructions! There is no life or existence, except through the true tzaddikim! Even if you already know this, it is still neccessary to repeat it every day, and to remember that there is no such thing as time, as is explained on the verse "I gave birth to you today" (see *Likutey Moharan* II, 61). I cannot write any more.

The words of your father, praying for you and waiting for your speedy salvation.

Noson of Breslov

215

With God's help, Tuesday, Terumah, 5596.

Greetings to my dear, beloved son, the learned Reb Yitzchak, may his light shine.

The carrier of this letter is in a great hurry right now and I do not know what to write you. Reb Nachman of Tulchin will tell you a little of what has happened here. Be strong, my son! Be strong! Bring yourself to joy any way you can! Cast aside your many musings, worries and concerns! Remember that everything is vanity and there is no such thing as time! If you still go through what you do, we have a "grandfather," in whose great power we are confident! It is necessary to review this with yourself constantly. I know that you are planning to be here for a Shabbat soon, so I will not continue. May God grant you success in This World and the Next. May you merit to spend your days in Torah and the service of God.

The words of your father, waiting for salvation and praying for you.

Noson of Breslov

216

[Publisher's note: Reb Avraham Ber, Rebbe Nachman's grandson, was married to the daughter of Moshe Chenkes in 1830. But after hostilities against Reb Noson began in the previous year, 5595, Moshe Chenkes demanded a divorce. This letter refers to the engagement of Reb Avraham Ber to the daughter of a follower of Rebbe Nachman, Reb Ber of Tcherin.]

With thanks to God, Wednesday, Tetzaveh, 5596, Nemirov.

Warm greetings to my dear, beloved son-in-law, the distinguished and learned Reb Barukh, may his light shine.

I received your letter yesterday from a man from here. I, and all of us, were really delighted. God sent the carrier of this letter to me today, but I do not know who he is. Therefore I cannot, as you realize, write you a long letter containing many words of truth. Out of my intense love for you, though, I am writing you these few lines.

Thank God, all of us here are alive and well. You should know that our distinguished friend, Reb Avraham Ber, may he live, set out yesterday for Uman with his chaste mother, Adil, may she live, and with a number of our comrades. There they are to meet with the wealthy Reb Ber of Tcherin who is coming there with is daughter, may she live. The engagement is to be

Letter #216

completed there and the *chuppah* will take place soon. This Reb Ber was in Breslov himself regarding this matter, and he begged them with enormous pleas and supplications to agree to make the match with him. He is laying out more than two thousand *kerbelich* (rubles) for the dowry. Thank God Who has helped us thus far.

That divorced shrew and her father, along with her shrew of a mother, are all grinding their teeth. Their envy and rage is cutting them up like swords inside them. May God, in His mercy, continue to knock them down, time and time again, until they acknowledge the truth. Then they will tear out their hair and lacerate their faces in grief over all the evil they have done to themselves by forfeiting a precious treasure such as this. Even that scoundrel Moshe's own people ridicule him for losing forever a good man such as this. I cannot continue. May God have compassion on us. May He speedily save us through the power and merit of the holy days of Purim which are rapidly approaching, that we may be worthy of escaping all our enemies and all those who persecute us for no reason. May all our enemies be ashamed and utterly confounded. Please let me know regularly how you are doing.

> The words of your father-in-law and father, extending greetings to your learned honor, with a mighty love.
> *Noson of Breslov*

Greetings to your father, my friend whom I love as myself, the learned and distinguished Reb Shlomo, may his light shine, and to all his family as well. Fortify yourself and be strong, my friend! Trust God. He will not abandon you. He has taken care of you your whole life and He will not abandon you, even when you are old and gray. Rise and call Him! He will quickly strengthen you. God hears the prayers of every mouth, and the only power we have rests in our mouths.

The words of the one who advises you for your eternal good.

Noson, the same

217

With God's help, Monday, Pikudey, 5596.

My beloved son and dear friend.

I received your letter on the Fast of Esther, as many of our comrades who were here as guests were gathered around me. I was quite preoccupied with the preparations for Purim, in addition to my nagging anxiety about our enemies with which you are familiar. May God have compassion and protect my life from the fear of my enemies. In spite of all this, I read your letter carefully. I felt pain at that time that cut me to the quick. But the true, simple, wondrous and profound methods of the master of true advice fortified me and strengthened me to let the joy of Purim prevail over everything. Thank God, we were quite joyful on Purim, and on the Shabbat following, and I spoke words of truth that flowed forth from the wellsprings of salvation. You will hear a fraction of them from the carrier of this letter.

Letter #217

As for your lament, what can I answer you, my dear son? I have already written you *so* much! You have already heard a great deal, and our books are in your hands! Study them over and over! There you will find strength and encouragement, salvation and solace for everything that you, and all of us, are going through. You will be one of the hopeful. I was speaking with a person here and I asked him (Job 15:7), "Were you the first person born?" This is what Job's friends said to him in response to his bitter complaint. Rashi explains their question, "Were you the first person born" to mean, "Were you born before Adam, the first man," that you know what has happened to every person in the world? Each person can also apply this to what he is going through, both in the area of his physical needs and livelihood, and with regard to his own personality traits and behavior. *Were you born before Adam, the first man, that you know what is behind what every person is going through?* The whole reason a person comes into the world is to go through all that he must! He has to be strong as a rock and bear everything. Whatever he goes through, he must hope and wait for God, and under no circumstances must he despair of God's mercy. I have already talked about this a great deal and time does not permit me to elaborate right now.

My son! Get the upper hand and throw off all the fears and dejection, both regarding the past and the future! Just fortify yourself to constantly grab whatever Torah, prayer or mitzvah you can! Trust in the great power of the elder of holiness who has the power to rectify everything! Bring yourself to joy constantly that you merited not to oppose him and his followers who hail in his holy name! We have already talked about this a great deal, but you need to remember it every day, especially at a time of pressure and stress, God forbid. I too, in my destitution, with everything that I must endure, derive all my vitality, hope and strength through this, as you are already somewhat aware.

The words of your father, waiting to hear good news from you.

Noson of Breslov

218

With God's help, Wednesday, Parashat Vayikra, 5596.
Greetings to my dear beloved son, the learned Reb Yitzchak, may he live, and to all his family. Peace and abundant salvation.

Only through great effort and inconvenience did your letter reach me yesterday. At the moment I have nothing new to report. As for your lament over your sufferings — I am surprised at you, my dear son. You already know, and you have heard so often, that a person must inevitably suffer a great deal. It has already been explained in the Rebbe's holy books that each person has to have some suffering each day, and that the greater a person's understanding, the greater his suffering, God save us (Likutey Moharan II, 77). Look it up.

If sufferings such as the ones you described in your letter keep a person from serving God, then it seems that all hope is just about lost, God forbid. For it is not possible to escape sufferings such as these. While it is undeniable that they are an impediment and a hindrance, we have already spoken many times about how it is possible to grab good every day. For "there is no day without some good." It is just that "every day has a fence surrounding it, and not every person can come into that good" (see *Likutey Moharan* I, 84). I spoke about this at length on Shavuot a few years ago. If the barriers and distractions have arrayed themselves, so that it is hard to perform practically any devotion, well, the shepherd of Israel has already informed us that will, desire and yearning, in and of themselves, are also very good and that the desire itself [to study] is considered as if the person actually studied from a book (*Likutey Moharan* I, 142).

A person has to have faith that everything that happens to him is really a great favor! For is it possible to explain in a book or conversation that if a person's partner were to buy a share in a house and he cannot... because of his children and so on — would you believe that this too was for the best? But the Torah has informed us that a person is obligated to believe that *everything* that happens to him is for his good. It is either to atone for his sins, to remind him to return to God or to motivate him to pray over it. For it could be that whatever has happened will force a person to turn to *hitbodedut* in order to express his pain to God about this particular thing, but, once having begun, he will move from one subject to another until he has poured out his entire heart before God. All these reasons are in addition to the concealed wonders of God, i.e. the way that He precisely calculates everything that He brings upon a person, so as to give him free choice. From precisely this thing the person will understand hints encouraging him to draw closer to God, wherever he may be.

I have already talked about this a great deal and it is explained frequently in the Rebbe's holy books. But a person must pay close attention to this every day and then apply them to his own situation. For it is impossible to explain everything in every detail. Above all else, we rely completely on the power of the elder of holiness himself, on which rest all our hopes. Thank God, we have someone to lean on! "Thank God, when we lie down; thank God, when we rise up" that we have merited to be in his portion! The holy days of Pesach are rapidly approaching. May God help us and all Israel so that the right hand will cause the darkness to pass from our eyes (see *Likutey Moharan* II, 83). Then we will be able to see the miracle of all the kindnesses that God has showered upon us, that neither written nor spoken words can describe!

The words of your father, waiting for salvation.

Noson of Breslov

May God lead us on the straight and true path and may we be privileged to avoid any trace of *chametz* [leaven], physical or spiritual. May we merit to be happy in the joy of the approaching holy festival and may the holiday be completely new for us! May we see ourselves as if we ourselves went out of Egypt this year, as is written, "In every generation a person must see himself as if he himself went out of Egypt." May God help us to truly fulfill this, in particular persecuted people such as us who see the miracles of the Exodus from Egypt and the Splitting of the Red Sea every moment of every day! May God help us see revealed miracles and may the truth be revealed in the world for everyone to see! Our enemies will see and be ashamed! Our souls will celebrate in God and rejoice over His salvation! Amen.

219

With God's help, Tuesday, the Second Day of Chol HaMoed Pesach, 5596.

My dear son.

    I received your letter yesterday, and out of my love for you I will give you a brief response, despite the fact that it is Chol HaMoed. My beloved son, you really uplifted me with your words, for I can sense that your heart has awakened to understand a minute fraction of the greatness of the Creator, even amidst the enormous suffering and hardship that we are going through. The truth is that these very things are His mighty and awesome deeds! But it is impossible to elaborate on this right now. The post office is still stationed in my house. This too is certainly for the best. It is necessary to believe without a doubt that "He will not quarrel with us forever, and He will not always be at odds." The day will certainly come when they will look upon our joy and be ashamed!

    Even now, thank God, we have nothing at all to be ashamed. Please, I beg you, my dear son, throw off your sadness! Distance yourself from worry and grief with all the strategies you know! You complain and cry out too much in your letters. You already know that for such items you must set aside an hour every day to cry out bitterly over whatever you are going through. The rest of the day you must fortify yourself and be simply and straightforwardly happy that "He did not make me a gentile, etc." On the contrary, the fact of the matter is that all the bitterness that a person experiences can enable him to understand God's enormous kindness and wonders whereby He gives us life and sustains us amidst such great bitterness. For "were it not for the salt we would not be able to endure the bitterness" (see Likutey Moharan I, 23:2).

This is the meaning of the mitzvah of eating bitter herbs [on Seder night]. It is in order to remember how "they [the Egyptians] embittered their lives." For even at a time of redemption, salvation and relief it is necessary to remember and not forget the bitterness. This enables one to rejoice in one's salvation; because given the enormity of the bitterness that we see in the world, everything is good and sweet [by comparison]. However, if a person does not remember the bitterness, and wants to fulfill his desire for all the vanities of the world, he will always be lacking and will never in his life see good.

All this is related to what I talked about on the night of Shabbat HaGadol [the Shabbat prior to Pesach]. You will certainly hear about it from our comrades and will enjoy it. I am deriving all my vitality from this idea right now. It is similar to the teachings of the Rebbe on the verses, "Love your neighbor as yourself, I am God" (Likutey Moharan I, 165) and "For the sake of peace I have great bitterness and You desired..." (Likutey Moharan I, 27:7). But "the words of the Torah are poor where they are and rich somewhere else"; and when you discuss them at length you feel to a greater extent the advice that flows from them. For God's sake, do not let them become old and hackneyed for you! Study them over and over, and let them be totally new for you every single day! Remember well that we are passing through This World, and it is full of barriers and impediments from the many enormous *kelipot* that have a hold on it, because it is the World of *Asiyah* — Action. But it is all a passing shadow, a dissipating cloud, nothing more than a breeze. All our vitality and all our support comes from the true tzaddikim who did not look at This World at all (see *Rabbi Nachman's Stories* #13; The Seven Beggars, The First Day). "The sound of joy and salvation is in the tents of the tzaddkim!"

The words of your father, cautioning you and urging you to always be happy, particularly during this holy festival. May the One Who performs miracles and wonders in every generation do miracles for us now as well and rescue us from all our enemies and persecutors. Let us celebrate and rejoice over His salvation!

Noson of Breslov

Warm greetings to all our comrades with a great, eternal love, forever and ever! "Great waters could not extinguish this love...!"

220

Peace, life and blessing to my dear, honored and learned son, Reb Yitzchak, may his light shine forever — and to all our followers. Peace and abundant salvation.

I received your letter yesterday. I do not have enough time to answer you and I also do not know what to write. Nonetheless, your enormous desire compels me to interrupt my studies after the Morning Prayers, and to shorten them for your sake. Maybe God will help and send words to my pen that will inspire and encourage you. Then this will be considered teaching Torah to others, which is preferable to all other Torah study; particularly when it is great Torah such as this which emanates from the "flowing stream" and leads a person to action — which is the highest level of all!

I have already written you a great deal, both what is inscribed in the Rebbe's published holy books, and the original teachings that God has helped me to develop based on them, which have been bound into handwritten folios. You have them all. There are also the many letters that I have written to you and, in particular, the many things that I have been telling you in person for so many years now. What [else] new can I tell you?! You know that you can receive an answer for every one of your cries from what you already know and have heard! Nonetheless, I am forced to do your will and give you a response for precisely this purpose — to remind you and urge you to carefully remember at every moment of every day all these holy, true and perfectly direct and simple teachings. Yet, despite their simplicity, they are very, very deep. They contain level after level of deep, true wisdom extending up to Infinity and reaching down to the very lowest levels. Nothing can be added to them and nothing taken away.

You need only look into them and pay attention to what they are saying, and on each occasion you will find life-giving gems of wisdom of all kinds. They contain true advice which will strengthen you and those such as you and those worse than you and those better than you — each person according to what he is — rich, poor and in between, young and old, healthy and weak, God forbid. Through all the different seasons that a person goes through, without a single exception, a person can find in these teachings sound, true wisdom that enables him to hold his ground at all times and to prevail against all those who are standing up against him, trying to harry him into losing two worlds, God forbid! For a person is confronted daily by many obstacles which try to annihilate him completely. Yes, many, many rise up against him from every side, as it is written (Ecclesiastes 9:14), "There is a small town containing a few men. A great king came and surrounded it, and constructed a great fortress."

I have already spoken about this, but you still need to pay attention to the words of this verse and, how the king, who is the Evil Urge, "an old and foolish king," surrounds a person on every side and builds up great fortresses against him. It would be impossible to stand up against him, were the Holy One, Blessed be He, not to help a person every day. This is what the Rabbis, of blessed memory, said, "A person's [Evil] Urge is renewed in him every day and, if the Holy One, Blessed be He, did not help him, he would not be able to prevail" (Sukkah 52b). Yet a person also has a certain form of free will.

For we have long known that in no place will you find awesome, true advice such as you will in the Rebbe's holy books and in the words which flow from the holy words of the Rebbe that I received from him orally and from his books. Remember this well and take heart! Strengthen yourselves and be men! Do not be what they call *shlamazelniks*— "losers"! Look and see that the suffering of the world in general is much greater than your individual suffering. Everything that is happening to you, and to all of you, has already happened to everyone who sought to draw close to God, both in this generation and in previous ones. Moses, our teacher, warned us (Deuteronomy 32:7), "Remember the days gone by; understand what happened in previous generations." This is a commandment and an obligation for every Jew. For anyone who is not a fool can understand from what he has heard and seen in books the nature of this whole drama that is taking place under the sun with every single person in every generation, and how countless, countless people have been diverted as a result of these distractions and preoccupations, God save us.

Fortunate are those who were steadfast in their devotions! The key for all the people who held their ground was that they truly fortified themselves, because they understood what is happening in the world, and they did not allow themselves to fall, under any circumstances! But never has there been anyone who can help a person fortify himself with such wondrous strategies as the way our master, teacher and Rebbe can! For he strengthens, sustains and restores all souls, even those who have sunk very low, with profound and direct advice of all kinds. And all his counsels are taken from a place "where the mind cannot comprehend." To start speaking about them means going back and explaining all his holy books. Therefore "consider your ways and turn your feet to His statutes" — to the original Torah teachings that the Rebbe revealed to us! Study them over and over! Grow old and gray with them, and never leave them! For there is nothing better. I cannot go on any longer.

The words of your father and your true eternal friend, who seeks your good and success in This World and the Next, forever and ever.

Noson of Breslov

Greetings to all our companions with a great love! These words were said to all of you, and to anyone else who desires pure truth! Fortify yourselves and be strong, all you who hope in God!

221

[Publisher's note: This letter refers to the opponents of Breslover Chassidim searching for faults in Rebbe Nachman's teachings. Here Reb Noson replies to the attacks and his answer is included in a discourse in Likutey Halakhot, Milah *5:24-28).*

With God's help, Wednesday, the 25th day of the Numbering of the Children of Israel, 5596, Nemirov.

Warm greetings to my honored friend whom I love as myself, the learned and illustrious Reb Shmuel Weinberg, may his light shine.

I received your letter on Monday of this week. I had already heard the noise of their slanderous attack before Pesach, in which they distort the words of the Living God written in *The Aleph-Bet Book* [Daat, B:1-2]. So it was no news to me. I already heard several years ago that the *mitnagdim* had found an opportunity here to go astray, and to press on in their campaign of opposition. For a person is led in the direction he wishes to go. The Torah has two powers, "For the worthy it is an elixir of life; for the unworthy, a deadly poison." Each person can find in the Torah what he wants. We have likewise seen that the heretics explain the essence of our holy Torah, Moses' Torah of Truth, in accordance with their own evil ideas. How much more so do they do this with the rest of the holy literature.

In recent generations, this phenomenon was particularly prevalent with the books of the Baal Shem Tov and his holy students, with which the opponents, the *lomdim* [lit. "learners"], found fault. Despite the fact that a few of these opponents were tzaddikim and giants in Torah knowledge, they looked for and found what they thought to be the case — as if, God forbid, the writings of the students of the Baal Shem Tov, known as *chassidim*, are against the Torah, God forbid. But if those opposing us had taken exception to this one statement alone, I would certainly be able to respond to them. But, as is perfectly well-known, they opposed us intensely even before this, shamelessly taunting, abusing and mocking us without limit and for no reason — simply because the hearts of all the Rebbe's followers, both those who hailed in his holy name during his life and those who became attached to him after his passing, burn with a great, holy fire for God and His Torah, and to pray with intensity. The Rebbe's followers take heed of the fact that This World is absolute vanity, having no substance. They accustom themselves to follow the Rebbe's holy advice, which is included in the 613 "counsels" of the Torah and which direct a person to walk the path of truth, the path that our holy ancestors have always followed! What can we say?! What can we say?! How fortunate we are to have been saved from their error! God gave us life as our lot, to draw close to a light of holiness and truth such as this!

You should know, my friend, that during all this uproar about what is written in *The Aleph-Bet Book* some intelligent men were here. They had no connection whatsoever with our group; they simply decided to look at the truth, and they laughed at this allegation. They said that, even if there were no way to refute it, who would ever think of attacking a well-known tzaddik such as the Rebbe over some difficult or curious statement that they found in his books?! We have already heard, they said, many more perplexing questions than these about all the famous tzaddikim! On the contrary, they said, there *is* no tzaddik who does not evoke enormous wonder and puzzlement. They also cited what the Rabbis, of blessed memory, said, "For the worthy it is an elixir of life; for the unworthy, a deadly poison." One of them also made a nice analogy about this, but I cannot put down everything they said in writing.

The real truth is that they can see for themselves the holy intention of our master, teacher and Rebbe, of blessed memory. He is not talking, God forbid, about knowing the nature of the world through studying the works of scientists and philosophers such as Aristotle and Plato, may the name of the wicked rot. The Rebbe is referring to the underlying secret of Nature, which is rooted in the letters of the Torah and in their various combinations, as can be clearly understood from the section prior to the one under discussion. Look it up. If a person looks carefully at what is written in this preceding section, he will be able to experience a faint glimmer of understanding of the greatness of our holy, awesome Rebbe, of sainted memory. Look at every single word there. They are all counted and measured with great precision.

In particular, look at what is written there at the end, "One who merits to understand the Torah will understand the significance of all the differences between all created things. He will also understand [the significance of] what they have in common, i.e. their origin and their end, because in their origin and their end they are identical and without distinction." Let the Heavens look on aghast! Rouse Yourself, God, and awaken to the Rebbe's judgment and his cause! Who has heard or seen awesome wonders such as these?! If the attacker would focus on the truth, and put aside his own evil desire to be victorious in spite of the truth, he would see in these words the greatness of the Creator, the greatness of the holy Torah, and the greatness of the Rebbe, of blessed memory. I cannot go on about this here.

In the context of what I just quoted, though, we understand

what immediately follows, "Know that a person has mastery over the world in direct proportion to his knowledge of Torah and Nature." This refers to a knowledge of Nature as it is rooted in the letters of the Torah. For it is the Torah that governs Nature. Immediately following this it is written, "Daniel was extremely wise and 'no secret escaped him'. He knew the lion's nature, and Nature itself follows and is under the dictates of Torah knowledge." There is no doubt that the phrase "no secret escaped him" does not refer, God forbid, to scientific knowledge, as mistakenly thought by those who say that Aristotle was as wise or wiser than Daniel! God save us from evil ideas such as these! Rather we are "believers and the children of believers" and when the verse says about Daniel that "no secret escaped him" we understand that it is referring to supreme mysteries, hidden, concealed secrets (see Daniel 4:6; and *Chullin* 59). If a person indeed knows Nature according to hidden mysteries such as these, Nature will certainly be "enslaved to him." This was exactly the miracle that God did for Daniel.

But our opponents want to turn things upside down. All their teeth gnashing is to libel, defame and undermine all of Judaism! The whole reason they want to deny and discredit Daniel's unique knowledge is that they can then deny, God forbid, the actual miracle itself. May their mouths be filled with gravel for speaking such utter nonsense, trying to pin such utter absurdity on such a true, holy and awesome tzaddik.

It is well-known that the Rebbe struggled tirelessly all his days to inculcate the Jewish People with straightforward, simple faith, without any sort of convoluted ideas! He also, as is known, revealed many marvelous, awesome teachings on this subject. Take a book and look into it! All the enormous and bitter suffering that the Rebbe went through, and all the fierce opposition that he and his followers face, is only because he wants to eliminate all the foreign ideas and atheism from Israel, and to bring perfect faith into the world, as is known to anyone who merited to stand before him. Who could possibly think that he would contradict himself, God forbid, after what he wrote many times in his holy books to strengthen our belief in the miracles that the tzaddikim perform even now (*Likutey Moharan I, 186*); all the more so what he wrote to strengthen our faith in the miracles of tzaddikim of former times, may their merit protect us, as is found in the lesson "The depths covered them" (*Likutey Moharan I, 9*) and in many other places (*Likutey Moharan I, 7,40,42,116*). The truth is there for those who want to see it. Precisely this is the essence of the miracle performed for Daniel — that God in His mercy had compassion on him as a result of his many prayers. Thus Daniel merited a great understanding of the nature of the lion at its supernal root up above, until the lions were subordinated to him and did him no harm at all.

It is known that all the miracles that God performed for the tzaddikim were a result of prayer (*Megillah 27a*). Nonetheless, each miracle occurred as the result of favorable circumstances arranged by God so that, in most cases, the miracle was brought about by the direct command of God. For instance, when He sent the locust it is written, "Stretch out your hand to bring the locust" (*Exodus 10:12*). And similarly with the plague of boils it is written, "Take a handful of soot from the oven." We find the same in connection with other miracles [in Egypt]. Also in the case of Elisha it is written (2 Kings, 4:41), "Take flour and throw it into the pot...and there will be nothing harmful in the pot." Now God is perfectly capable of performing a miracle without anyone having to do anything. But this is His way. Who can understand His magnificent deeds?!

Similarly with Daniel, this amazing miracle was the result of his prayers. However, the circumstance through which God performed the miracle was that, at the time Daniel was thrown into the lions' den, God granted him sufficient presence of mind to enable him to mentally cleave and be bound to God and His holy Torah, until he knew and comprehended the secret of how Nature is governed by knowledge, i.e. by knowledge of the letters of the Torah and their various combinations. This is what saved him. Anyone can understand that it is an amazing miracle indeed that Daniel's mind was steadfast at such a time of crisis. Daniel, thrown into a den of roaring lions, nonetheless kept his presence of mind sufficiently to be able to comprehend the lions' nature at its upper root according to the exalted secrets hidden in the Torah and included in God Himself, and thus he was saved.

It is unquestionable that no-one living today could stand up to this. The very fact that "no secret escaped" Daniel was an amazing miracle in itself, and this he merited through prayer. For it is stated explicitly that he prayed about this and that he also ordered his companions Chananyah, Mishael and Azaryah to pray. "Then the secret was revealed to Daniel in a night-time vision." Similarly, when they wanted to throw him into the lions' den, he prayed to God until He enabled Daniel's mind to grasp the secrets and mysteries from which the nature of the lion draws all its strength. Through this the lions were made subordinate to him and he was saved from them. This is the essence of perfect faith: to believe that Nature is governed by God and that Nature itelf *is* Divine Providence [*hashgachah*]. Someone whose belief in this is complete is able to alter Nature. For he knows the truth, that there is actually no Nature at all. God governs His World according to this particular order — i.e. that dry land should be dry land, and sea should be sea. This is what the world calls Nature. But when God wishes, He changes this order and turns sea into dry land. This is what our Rabbis, of blessed memory, said, "The One Who told oil to light, can tell vinegar to light" (*Taanit* 25a).

So we see that all miracles occur only as result of the belief that the entire order of Nature is governed by God, Who directs and sustains His world through the letters of the Torah and their various combinations. Anyone who knows all this can perform awesome miracles and change Nature, because he knows that everything happens by God's will. All this occurs through prayer. For only through prayer is it possible to attain this knowledge with any degree of frequency. The Searcher of Hearts knows the truth, that we cry out to Him in truth more than our opponents. "May He Who answered Daniel in the lions' den [also] answer us" — especially now, when we are between *their* teeth, which is worse than in the mouths of lions. As our Rabbis said (cf. *Zohar* I, 185a), "Better that a person throw himself into [fire or into] the lions' den than be placed [directly] into the hands of one's enemies." We have no-one to lean on but our Father in Heaven. "May He Who answered Daniel" and all the tzaddikim, pious, righteous and pure of heart, also answer us, and rescue us from their murderous tongues! May those who seek my life be humiliated and ashamed! May all our enemies be humiliated and utterly confounded! Soon they will repent and be ashamed! Amen. May it be His will.

I was extremely surprised at you, my dear friend, that this question [raised against the Rebbe] actually started to bother you! Even if there were to be some hard-to-answer or puzzling question, it is already well-known that the tzaddik is bound to be surrounded by such mystery. For "he likens himself to his Creator," as is explained in his holy books (*Likutey Moharan* II, 52). I have written all this to remind you and your comrades to begin anew crying out to God that He should allow you to truly come close to him, since you see that they are still coming at you.

May the Master of Mercy have compassion on me and on you. May we merit to walk in His pathways of truth, so that we will never be ashamed. Let us be glad and rejoice in His salvation!

I cannot say any more in this context.

> The words of your true friend, eternally.
>
> *Noson of Breslov*

Greetings to all our comrades with a great love; in particular to my friend and brother whom I love as myself, the illustrious and distinguished in piety, Reb Naftali. Greetings and abundant salvation to him, to all his family and to all his followers!

Please, my dear brother, write me a letter immediately, in your own handwriting, in order to restore my soul at a time such as this. "It is a time of suffering for Jacob, and he will be saved from it."

Noson, as above

222

With thanks to God, Thursday, the 26th day of the Numbering of the Children of Israel, 5596, Nemirov.

Warm greetings to my beloved, honored son-in-law, whom I cherish as a son, my distinguished, learned friend, Reb Barukh, may his light shine.

I received your letter yesterday and I was happy to hear that you are well. The post office is still in my house and I have no idea when they will leave. Beyond this I have no news to tell you. The deliverer of this letter is in a great hurry, so I cannot write much. May God have compassion on your father and on you. May He improve your financial situation and make up all his deficiencies. Most important, may God strengthen your heart to intensify your efforts in studying God's Torah and in prayer, and to trust that God will not abandon you. For there is no other advice for anyone in the world except to have faith and to trust God [*bitachon*]. The primary way to build up this trust is by strengthening one's resolve to study and pray all day. For the world is a passing shadow and, no matter what, our days are going to pass. "Neither silver, nor gold, nor precious stones accompany a person [to the grave] — only Torah and good

Letter #223

deeds," says the Tanna (*Avot* 6:9), to remind a person never to forget his eternal goal! While everybody knows this, it is necessary to review and recall it every day. May God grant you long days and years full of good and pleasantness.

Noson of Breslov

223

With thanks to God, Saturday night, Bemidbar, 5596.

My dear, beloved son.

I received all your letters. At the moment I have absolutely nothing to inform you; but since the deliverer of this letter came to my house, my love for you compelled me to send some kind of note with him. Thank God, we are alive and well. I just this moment finished Havdalah and the days of Shavuot are rapidly approaching. This will be a new Shavuot for me, unlike any I have had for many years now, because I will be in Nemirov and we will be too frightened to gather together to say the *Akdamot*. If our persecutors had only prevented the saying of the *Akdamot* by our holy group, they would still deserve what is coming to them!

> [Publisher's note: Akdamot *is a song/prayer recited on Shavuot morning, extolling the beauty and greatness of the Torah and the great rewards waiting for those who observe it. There is a known melody that most people use when singing it. In Breslov synagogues it is recited with deep passion and fervor and this is what Reb Noson refers to.]*

Nonetheless, I hope to God that the holiness of Shavuot, the time of the giving of the Torah, will be drawn upon us through

God's great lovingkindness. You, my dear son, should do as you wish with regard to coming here. I cannot advise you about this matter right now. May God in His compassion make us happy with the joy of the giving of the Torah. May we merit, from now on at least, to prepare ourselves as we should for the festival of Shavuot. In the great merit of the Rebbe, may we be worthy of drawing upon us the holiness of the receiving of the Torah. Let us rejoice and be happy over God's salvation!

The words of your father, waiting and bringing himself to joy at all times over the fact that I merited to draw near to and know about our master, teacher and Rebbe, of sainted memory — about a holy and awesome Rebbe such as this, and about Torah teachings such as these! *Ashreinu!* Happy are we!

Noson of Breslov

Greetings to all of our comrades with a great love!

224

With thanks to God, Wednesday night, Torah reading Shelach Lekha, 5596, Nemirov.

May the Master of Salvation and Consolation comfort my dear son, my heart's delight, the learned and distinguished Reb Yitzchak, may he live, with all his children, may they live for many long, good years to come. Amen. May it be His will.

Just this evening, your learned brother-in-law, Reb Yosef, may his light shine, came to my home. He brought me a short letter from you. Then I realized your pain, which is also my pain, that the life of your little daughter, may she rest in peace, has been taken. May her soul have eternal life. I did not have leisure at the time to think about my anguish and to console myself, because I had to talk with him. Then it was time for the Afternoon Prayers.

I understand now, looking back, the bitter lament of your previous letter that I received through Reb Mordekhai, may his light shine. I have not yet received the letter in Breslov as you will hear from the deliverer of this letter. I do not need to offer you the customary words of consolation. You understand for yourself that the whole world goes through this kind of experience. Many have drunk from this bitter cup, God save us, particularly during these times in your community. May God protect them from now on. May the Merciful One replace what they, and all His People Israel, have lost. May He comfort them and save them with the consolation of Zion and Jerusalem. The primary consolation, though, for all kinds of suffering, God save us, is the knowledge of the Torah and the true tzaddikim, as is written (Psalms 119:50), "This is my comfort in my destitution; Your word has given me life." And similarly there is the explanation of the verse (Isaiah 40:1), "Give comfort, give comfort to My people" (*Likutey Moharan* I, 21:11).

I know very well, my son, that this is really the essence of your lament in your letter, as you express explicitly. For as you should, you cry out bitterly, "when will you merit to return [to God] through all the hints and proclamations that are calling you to draw closer to Him?!" It is definitely true that a person does need to cry out over this, and to cry out over it every single day. Nonetheless, it is necessary to remember well that the Rebbe, of blessed memory, cautioned us repeatedly to fortify ourselves to be joyful all the time and to turn all the grief and sighing into joy (Likutey Moharan II, 23). Particularly at a time of suffering, God forbid, a person must fortify himself all the more not to let the pain overwhelm him, God forbid. Rather he should console and cheer himself any way he can, and turn all the grief and sighing into joy. Thank God, you have plenty to be happy about even now, though it is impossible to give all the details in writing, especially at such a time as this.

Remember and do not forget everything you have heard from me already; and you should know that God's compassion is even greater and stronger and more manifest than that — [it is] without limit. For His lovingkindness is never-ending. I have now a whole beautiful discourse about how a person's main test and the essence of his free will stems from the fact that he does not comprehend his own situation. For if a person were to realize exactly what was happening to him at all times, if he were aware of his actual position at every moment — if a person were to realize how, even now, every single good movement, thought, etc. is so very precious to God, then everyone would certainly be chasing after God will all their might and they would all be tzaddikim! The fact that this knowledge is obscured is the main test of a person and the essence of his free will. Therefore, the truth is that it is absolutely impossible for a person during his lifetime to accurately evaluate where he stands, as I heard in the Rebbe's name. For it is on this uncertainty that free will depends. But someone who really wants to care about his eternal goal ought to draw strength from just this, and to at least know and understand that he really does not know at all. For "God's thoughts are very deep." Who knows how very much God cherishes your efforts toward good? Precisely because a person is so far away, his every good effort or move, no matter how slight, is extremely precious to God! Especially since our master, teacher and Rebbe, of blessed memory, has already revealed a great deal about this, and "his words are alive and enduring, faithful and lovely, forever and ever." There is more that I could say about this but, for several reasons, I cannot elaborate about it in writing (see *Likutey Halakhot, Shvuot* 2:12-15).

> The words of your father, hoping to hear good news from you always.
>
> *Noson of Breslov*

Greetings to all of our companions with a great love.

The light of day has now arrived, the morning light, "the morning of Avraham." Without a doubt, new and highly wondrous kindnesses are now coming into existence for the first time, as it is written (Lamentations 3:23), "[God's kindnesses] are new every morning, great is Your faithfulness." And yet it is extremely difficult to begin to pray, because every day is "narrow at the top and wide at the bottom" (*Likutey Moharan* I, 60:2) — nonetheless, it is necessary to believe that new kindnesses are born every morning, as it is written, "to speak of Your kindness in the morning." Through the faith in the great kindness and good which God bestows at all times on every person, even the very worst, each one of us can gather the strength to begin anew constantly every day. The key is to banish depression and sadness, and to turn all grief and sighing into joy!

I have already talked about this a great deal, but a person must understand it for himself and force himself with all his might to bring into his heart the joy over the Torah and the mitzvot that we merit every day. Know and believe with complete faith that, despite all the hardships and suffering we have endured, and the vast distance that separates us from our Father in Heaven as a result of our improper actions, *Ashreinu!* Fortunate we are! *Ashreinu! Ashreinu,* that we merit to say the word *Ashreinu!* twice a day! If you accustom yourself to rejoice over this, you may be able, at least once in your life, to really feel in your heart the beauty and joy of *Ashreinu!* — the beauty and joy of, "How fortunate are we that we declare the Unity of His Name!" (from the Morning Service). Then you will understand in retrospect the sweetness and pleasantness of our lot, our portion and our inheritance, and you will feel remorse over the past for not having fortified yourself to be so much more joyful! Finally, though, you will encourage yourself with the small amount of joy that you did feel each time.

My enormous love for you compelled me to originate some words of truth for you, now, in the morning, before praying. May the "lovingkindness of Avraham" bring our souls to happiness and joy over God's salvation!

Noson, as above

225

With thanks to God, Monday, Chukat, 5596.

Greetings to my dear, beloved son, Reb Yitzchak, may his light shine.

My brother-in-law from Maiyaskifka was at my house, along with my brother-in-law Reb Yonah Hirsh and Reb Shmuel, the son of R.M. from Ladizin, all regarding a marriage arrangement with someone from here. They came yesterday, and today, my brother-in-law, Reb Matityahu from Ladizin, came. It is all the hand of God. Who knows His wondrous ways — the way He arranges every thought, word and action every day to send us wondrous hints? (see *Likutey Moharan* I, 54:2). Thus I have absolutely no time now to write a long letter. You are receiving the enclosed letter here for R.S. You should certainly read it, and understand hints from it that you can also apply to yourself. Had you read R.S.'s letter to me, you would have seen and heard cries so bitter that it is difficult to listen to them. As you will see, I have already given him a partial response.

Tell R.S. not to be irritated that I sent his letter to you unsealed. The truth is that I considered sealing it so that you could not read it; but he wrote in his letter to me that I should include my response in one of my letters to you, so I concluded that he did not mind if you saw it. He really should not mind either, because we are brothers, and our enormous love makes us like one man. Happy is he who does not separate himself from us! Through the power of the elder of holiness we are "like a flourishing cypress": anyone who wishes to draw from the spring of fresh water words that give life to the soul forever and for all eternity — may come and partake! And if the barriers array themselves against them like bars of iron and doors of bronze, what can I do? I too have barriers greater than his which try to keep me from bringing him close, especially now, as you know. May God give us good in the future. But it is already known, and it is especially true now, that it is impossible for us to draw near, to come together and to speak the words of truth that we need to speak, except by breaking enormous barriers.

Now, my dear son, fortify yourself and be strong! Bring yourself to joy any way you can! Grab and eat! Grab and eat — food, drink and clothing of Torah, prayer and mitzvot! Remember well what the Rebbe, of blessed memory, wrote (*Rabbi Nachman's Wisdom* p.123), "Happy is he who 'eats' several chapters of Mishnah, 'drinks' many chapters of Psalms and 'dresses' himself in many mitzvot." For besides this everything is worthless. "What advantage does a person gain from all his labor?" While everyone knows this, it is necessary to review it every day, to preserve the memory carefully, and to remember the World to Come every day, in general and in every detail of our lives. Do not let these words become old platitudes for you! Let them always be new!

It was not for naught that our Rebbe, of blessed memory, reminded us with many statements such as these not to sleep our lives away, God forbid! King David, peace be upon him, said, "they are in turmoil over nothing," "human beings are vanity, and people are a lie," and "every man is vanity." King Solomon, peace be upon him, proclaimed, "Vanity of vanities says Kohelet, vanity of vanities." When Rabbi Meir finished the book of Job, he would said "In the end a person will die... Happy is he who struggles for the Torah!" All the *mussar* books say similar things too. But our master, teacher and Rebbe, of blessed memory, revealed strategies and advice by which even the most inferior person can rescue himself! They have no match! Happy is the person who holds onto them! I do not have time now to write any more.

 The words of your father, waiting for salvation.
          Noson of Breslov

 Greetings to all our comrades with a great love.

226

With God's help, Thursday, Balak, 5596.
My dear, beloved son.

 I have prepared a letter and I am now sending it to Lemberg with the post. The postman is in a great hurry now, as it is close to noon, and I heard that you are planning to be here soon anyway, so I will not write much. What I go through every day is just beyond description. How great are the deeds and wonders of God which every day are discernible from afar! Three times a day we make the blessing "Who makes the seeds of salvation sprout." We therefore have to believe that everything that is happening in the world, both on a universal scale and down to the smallest particulars, all represents a sprouting of the seeds of salvation. And to the degree that a person strengthens his faith in this, he merits to receive actual revealed salvation! I have a lot to say about this, but it is impossible to relate it all even verbally, let alone in writing. Nonetheless, each person must believe in this, and God will soon reveal His salvation to us. Let us be happy and rejoice over Him!

The words of your father.

Noson of Breslov

Loving greetings to all our comrades.

227

With thanks to God, Saturday night, Ekev, 5596.

My beloved son.

I received your letter and I was delighted to see the intensity of your desire for good. You understand for yourself that time does not allow me to answer you, as the carrier of this letter is setting out immediately after Havdalah. Nonetheless, I forced myself to write you these few lines, because of your great desire to see my letters.

As regards your thinking today about Rosh HaShanah — while it is good for Rosh HaShanah to be in one's thoughts throughout the entire year, you were not correct in letting yourself suffer pain over the barriers involved. I have already said that you must not think from one day to the next; particularly since, in my opinion, with God's help, you will not suffer now, God forbid, the way you did last year, but rather less. Of course it is impossible to escape with no suffering at all. The truth is that you should be extremely happy that the days

Letter #228

of Rosh HaShanah are approaching and you will merit to be at the Rebbe's holy gravesite! I have already said that things that one knows without doubt have to be done are not considered to be suffering or obstacles. You should certainly not be thinking about what will happen afterwards! I will not go on about this. You have already overcome many obstacles. I hope to God that now you will travel easily for this coming Rosh HaShanah, with God's help. May God allow me to receive a visa quickly and may I merit to be there in Uman soon.

[Publisher's note: Reb Noson was referring to Reb Yitzchak's near dismissal from his job and the troubles he suffered at home after going to Uman for the previous Rosh HaShanah. See Through Fire and Water, Chapter 39].

I absolutely cannot continue and, besides, the carrier of this letter said that you will soon be here. You will hear more from the carrier of this letter.

The words of your father, waiting for salvation.

Noson of Breslov

228

With the help of God, Wednesday night, Torah reading Ki Teitzei, 5596, Nemirov.

My dear, beloved son.

Thus far has God's compassion helped me, and, thank God, they informed me today that they will be giving me a visa. This was the answer that arrived from Kaminetz. It is good to thank God Who has helped us thus far. So may He continue and save us from all our troubles, and may He soon return me safely to my home in Breslov. May He raise us up and may our enemies see and be ashamed! Salvation is God's. Thank God, we have someone to lean on! I am hoping now, with God's help, to receive the visa this week. Then I will travel to Uman, God willing, after next Shabbat, on Tuesday or Wednesday of Parashat Tavo. May God have mercy on me and may He bring me there safely very soon!

I cannot go on any more because the carrier of this letter is in a hurry. You are receiving my manuscript folios. Guard them carefully because, as you know, they are much more valuable than gold or pearls. Fortify yourself now with the salvation with which God has helped us so far, and wait constantly for His salvation, whereby He will allow you to come to Uman for this coming Rosh HaShanah without too much suffering. May God help us, and fulfill our request with compassion this Rosh HaShanah that we be written and sealed for long, good lives and for peace. May He grant that we merit, from now on at least, to follow the path of truth that our splendrous pride, our master, teacher and Rebbe, of sainted memory, taught us.

The words of your father, giving thanks for the past,
requesting for the future, and waiting for salvation.
Noson of Breslov

Greetings to all our comrades with a great love, particularly to my distinguished friend whom I love as myself, Reb Yaakov, may his light shine! May my salvation fortify you and strengthen you — yes, you too — to come to Uman this coming

Rosh HaShanah and to be counted among us. What can I say to you, my cherished friend? One who believes will not have a second thought! Especially since I know that, thank God, your heart is steadfast and adamant in the absolute truth. So do not, God forbid, be remiss about carrying out my words. For This World is a passing shadow, and there is no greater profit in the world than this! I have said enough for an intelligent person to understand.

> The words of your true eternal friend, encouraging you for your eternal good.
>
> *Noson, as above*

229

With thanks to God, Sunday, Tavo, 5596, Nemirov.

My dear, beloved son.

I received your short letter through the gentile who is delivering this letter. The long letter from Friday, I have yet to see. Because of a delay on Thursday I have not yet received my visa. I had wanted to send a carriage for it on Friday, but it was not ready since it was Erev Shabbat and the man who can handle it, with God's help, did not complete the task. At the moment I intend to travel to Breslov tomorrow, God willing. Such was the command of all our comrades in Breslov, who are eagerly awaiting my safe arrival there. With God's great lovingkindness and through His miraculous salvation, I will receive my visa there, and from there I will travel to Uman, God willing. If you can get to Breslov easily tomorrow, so much the better. Most likely I will be staying there overnight. God will do what is good. As He has begun to bestow His lovingkindness, so may He finish for me and let me come safely to Uman — swiftly and right away! May He fulfill our requests there propitiously. May I merit to return safely to my home in Breslov soon and to live there in peace and quiet. Our enemies will see and be ashamed, and the verse will be fulfilled, "They will soon repent and be ashamed!"

The words of your father who is extremely busy and waiting for salvation.

Noson of Breslov

Greetings to all our comrades with a great love. I was surprised that you did not write me any response from Reb Yaakov regarding his traveling to Uman.

Letters from 5597 (1836-37)

The year in review

Reb Noson was forced to remain in exile in Nemirov during this year as his case had not yet come to trial. However, there was a reduction in the hostilities against him. Also, his travel permits were allowed to remain in force and he was able to resume his biannual travel to the Tcherin, Medvedevka area in the Eastern Ukraine. See *Through Fire and Water*, Part VII, Chapters 40-41.

230

With God's help, Thursday, the day after Yom Kippur, The Name of God, 5597, Breslov.

My dear son.

Thus far has God's enormous compassion helped me, and I made the journey safely from Nemirov to Uman; then from Uman to Teplik for Shabbat Teshuvah, and now from Teplik here to Breslov. I spent the very fearsome and awesome day of Yom Kippur here. Who can express God's mighty deeds?! If all the seas were ink, it would still be impossible! God is my hope — and the power to save is His — that I will soon return to my home here through His many miracles and kindnesses which, as we see with our own eyes, are endless and never-ceasing. Even more numerous than these are the hidden miracles which only God knows! These are His concealed kindnesses, unearned kindnesses, from "the treasury of free gifts," that are elicited by the Great *Prastik*, Simple Man, of whom we merited to know a tiny, miniscule fraction (see Likutey Moharan II, 78). Who can comprehend His enormous greatness and exaltedness?!

Just now, God had it that I called my son, Reb Shachneh, may he live, away from all his business. He came and showed me the letter you wrote to him. That letter was the impetus for my writing you these few but potent words now, amidst the many concerns which surround me on all sides. Thank God, I spent the holy Yom Kippur here in peace and quiet without incident, and, thank God, from the day I left Nemirov until now, all has been well. May God have compassion on me and bring me back here safely, and from here to the Holy Land. I have absolutely no time to go on. May God's Great Name be magnified through us. If we had come to the world only to hear the reason that the day after Yom Kippur is called "The Name of God," it would have been reason enough! (see *Likutey Moharan* II, 65). If you are fortunate, you will hear a great deal from me on this subject. Everything that I wrote just now emanates from this teaching. My son! If only you could enter into the recesses of my mind and heart, into that measure of understanding that is in my heart, then you would understand a little of the greatness of the Creator and His awesome miracles and kindnesses which are absolutely without limit! The mouth cannot utter them or the heart fathom them!

Noson of Breslov

231

With God's help, Sunday, Noach, 5597, Breslov.

My beloved son.

The carrier that you sent came here to the house of the *tzaddeket* Adil, may she live, as I was eating breakfast. I immediately received your letter which was sent through my son, Reb Shachneh, may his light shine. I was delighted by the letter from my daughter and son-in-law, may they live. I have not yet received your letter from Thursday. This Saturday night, immediately after Havdalah, I traveled here to see to my affairs for a number of reasons. I expect to stay here until this coming Tuesday, so if you can get here easily tomorrow, it would be very good. At the moment my mind is not at all lucid, so I cannot go on with words of truth and affection.

You are receiving the letter to my son-in-law, may his light shine. Try to send it with a trustworthy man. You can also add to it as you wish. Let me know if you sent this letter of mine to them in Brahilov. It is a great mitzvah, because I know that they are very much looking forward to seeing a letter from me. So far God's compassion has helped me and, with God's help, everything has gone well. Thank God, we also were a little happy on Shemini Atzeret, Simchat Torah, and on Shabbat Bereishit, and I spoke words of truth. All is well, thank God. May God only finish His salvation and may I soon return safely to my home here in Breslov. I am extremely busy and the carrier of this letter is in a hurry, so I cannot continue as I should. There will be other opportunities to write more.

The words of your father, waiting for salvation.

Noson of Breslov

232

Wednesday, Rosh Chodesh Cheshvan, 5597, Breslov.

My dear, beloved son.

I received your letter just now. All day yesterday I was waiting expectantly to see you, but it didn't work out. What can we do, though? Barriers connected with earning a livelihood are constantly upon us. Thank God, though, your desire for truth is strong and, with God's help, there will be another time. We will certainly see each other soon and you will come in joy, with God's help.

It occurred to me this morning to write you anew what was in my heart, but I am too busy right now. The gist of it is, though, that you must view yourself every day as if you had just been born that day. It should be as if you have nothing in the world but that day alone. Do not trouble yourself thinking about past and future. Even if you do engage in business and what you need for your livelihood — and these *do* relate to the future — the main thing is still today. For who knows what tomorrow will bring?!

There is much to say about this, and you have already heard a great deal about it. But you should view these words as new every day! How very much we need to rejoice in our lot, in the enormous kindness that God did for us by removing us from so many errors and so much foolish advice! But I cannot explain this in detail in a letter, and particularly not in these times.

Fortify yourself, my son, and be strong! God is with you even now! All your heart's good desires are noted down on high in your favor. Even more so when you are successful in bringing these desires from potential to actual, and to articulate your good desires every day [in prayer]! For this is the key to everything! God desires *your* prayers and *hitbodedut* too! Not a single word is ever lost! Fortify yourself determinedly, my son, in Torah and prayer and in expressing yourself before God — all you can grab every moment of every day, be it little or much! It does not matter if a person does little or much, just that his heart

Letter #232

should be directed to Heaven. I have delayed here until today, Wednesday, and today or tomorrow, God willing, I will set out for home. I have yet to make any progress in my business here. When you are with me, God willing, I will tell you everything about how I cast my burden on God alone that He will show me the straight path and the good council that I need to return safely to my home here. Beyond this I have no time to continue.

The words of your father, waiting for salvation.

Noson of Breslov

The woman Sarah left following your promise to be in your house. In my opinion, though, right now you are quite distressed about this because another maidservant is not available. Nevertheless, God will surely help you, and you will find one to your liking. Then you will thank God that she refused in this matter, because it is for your good.

God willing, when you are here, I will also speak to you about this. For all the laws of proper human conduct [*derekh eretz*] are related and combined with divine service. For each day is made up of Torah and *derekh eretz* and they are interrelated, as every person can understand for himself. In all matters, the only thing a person can do is wait for God's salvation, and in the meantime to petition Him to send him what he needs. Whether it is something small or large, whatever a person needs, be it food or drink, clothing, shelter, eating utensils, furniture, servants, tuition money, whatever it is, there is no advice and no strategy except to throw one's burden on God that He will send him what he needs. If a person needs to take some action or discover some advice or strategy about what to do, he should rely on God to supply him with it and to supply him with good advice at the proper time. Everything requires good council. For everything involves a great many doubts and all kinds of uncertainty about how to proceed, to the point that a person has no idea what to do, other than to rely on God and ask Him to have compassion on him and send him the good council that he needs.

> The words of your father, whose love for you, along with your desire for good, has compelled me to write these words now. My eyes are to God that you will inspire yourself with this. Really and truly we can be happy! For, thank God, we have a "grandfather!" [Rebbe Nachman]. We have someone to lean on, thank God! All is vanity, all is vanity! "People are vanity, and human beings are a lie." But the Torah teachings that we received in this generation — true, original teachings such as these — they are the words of the Living God, the words of our God which will stand forever! For "the truth stands!"
>
> *Noson, as above*

233

With thanks to God, Sunday, Vayeitzei, 5597.

Greetings to my dear, beloved son, the distinguished Reb Yitzchak, may he live.

I received your letter on Tuesday, [Torah reading] Chayey Sarah, and I reread it again today. How I enjoyed the sweet pleasantness of your words, which came straight from the heart! I have nothing to respond right now, but your enormous desire for my letters compels me to fulfill your request. You already wrote in your letter concerning the matter that I presently have in mind, a little of which you heard from Reb David. It relates to rejuvenation and renewal [*hitchadshut*], how entirely new phenomena are coming into being every hour of every day. I have more than this in my heart, and through the wondrous kindness of God, Who in His goodness renews the Creation every day, I have already written about this.

It is all contained in what the Rebbe, of blessed memory, warned us in a booming voice, when he admonished us that (Rabbi Nachman's Wisdom #51), "It is forbidden to become old!" With this he aroused us to pay attention to the words of the Rabbis, of blessed memory, who gave us a similar admonition on the chapter containing *Shema Yisrael,* on the verse (Deuteronomy 6:6), "and these words which I am commanding you *today.*" They warn us there to "view them [the words of the Torah] as new every day," as is explained on the verse in Rashi's commentary. Likewise on the verse (Deuteronomy 27:9), "Today you became a people to the Lord, Your God," Rashi comments, "Consider it as if you entered into the Covenant with Him *today*!" With this, the Rabbis have indicated to us that wherever the Torah writes "God" in the context of an exhortation to uphold the Torah and the commandments, it means that we should feel as if we were commanded anew today.

This is a very great admonition and it is necessary to recall it constantly, every hour of every day. For every hour wondrous new things are coming into being; not to mention every day, week or month, and certainly every year and *shmitah* (seven year period)! You may have heard what I said recently on the verse (Lamentations 3:23), "They are new every morning, great is Your faithfulness"; namely, a person's mental faculties are renewed every day. I said, through God's kindness, that even if a person does not merit to see and comprehend the enormous wonder of this daily renewal, he needs to believe with abundant faith that certainly wondrous new things are created daily as is written [Daily Liturgy], "He creates daily new things." This is the meaning of "They are new every morning, great is Your faithfulness." A person must have great faith to believe that every morning, every day, God brings about many new things, as in "they are new every morning." Understand this.

A person needs to apply this teaching zealously. He must pay close attention to what we say every day, "in His good He renews the Creation every day," and especially to what is written, "He alone...creates new things, the Master of Wars." God will certainly complete everything as is fitting, and will bestow His eternal good on us abundantly. But it is necessary to wait for salvation every day.

Letter #233

You probably also heard a little of what I said about the verse (Genesis 22:4), "And he saw the place from far off," about how a person must see the salvation [that he needs] literally as a person sees something in front of his eyes, only that it is at a distance. This is the meaning of the verse in its context, as Avraham was taking his son Yitzchak to the *akeidah* to sacrifice him. The S.M. [Satan] wanted to confuse him completely and tried to break his resolve through many temptations and enticements. Finally he [Satan] said, "I heard from behind the curtain, 'the sheep as an offering' and not 'Yitzchak as an offering.'" But Avraham answered, "The punishment of a liar is that he will not be believed even when he is telling the truth," as our Rabbis, of blessed memory, said in the Talmud and the Midrash (*Sanhedrin* 89b; *Tanchuma, Vayeira* 22). See and understand! Look closely and pay careful attention to all that is said there about this test, because the Torah applies to every person in every time (See *Likutey Halakhot, Shiluach HaKen* 5).

Each person in his own way must understand what this teaching contains for him, and learn a lesson about how sedulously the Evil One arrays himself against every person with his devices, even against the smallest of the small, in his attempt to push him away, God forbid. We must fortify ourselves against him with the powerful hope and support that we have, inasmuch as we rely on the power of the elder of holiness! For, because of our terrible weakness, we have no strength except through this. We have to be adamant [in our faith], as if we literally see the object of our expectations with our own eyes, even though it is extremely far off — as in "he saw the place from far off." The place that Avraham saw was the site of the Holy Temple which the descendants of Yitzchak were eventually to inherit. But the place was "far off," because at that moment he was leading Yitzchak to sacrifice him at the *akeidah* and to perform God's will without a second thought. Even though these two events appeared to contradict each other — on the one hand, he sees the site of the Holy Temple which Yitzchak's descendants will inherit amidst such grandeur, and on the other hand, he is leading Yitzchak to slaughter — he did not question God's ways, God forbid.

This is the key: a person must eradicate and banish all the questions, confusions and convoluted calculations from his heart and just do his job and grab all the good that he can, whether much or little. For "it does not matter if a person does much or little, just that his heart be directed to Heaven." He must persist in his good yearnings and desires and rely on the power of the true tzaddikim, that they will certainly finish for us what they have started. If, meanwhile, things are happening with — or to — us we still need to know the truth, that we really do not know anything at all [how things will turn out in the end]. "I said that I would grow wise, but it is far from me." This is exactly the idea expressed in "he saw the place from far off."

It is also written (Exodus 2:4), "And his sister [Miriam] stood at a distance." This verse too contains the same idea. For first Miriam prophesied that Moses would save Israel, and subsequently she saw him being thrown into the river. It is written (*Ramban, loc. cit.*) that the verse is hinting at just this, that she stood at a distance to look and to hope over the final outcome. But the hope for good is only "from afar." This is also the meaning of the verse, "From afar she will bring her bread" (Proverbs 31:14). It has to come "from afar" because the bread of Torah can only be obtained "from afar," as discussed above. We must also know that our material bread, i.e. our livelihood, comes from very far away too, each person in his own way. If we know this we will certainly be strong, as we must, in our trust that God will surely sustain us as is fitting. And if it seems "far off," it is no surprise, because, without a doubt, our bread must come "from afar." For "a person's livelihood is as difficult as the splitting of the Red Sea" (Pesachim 117a). Nonetheless it will certainly come.

Thus, in both material and spiritual matters, it is necessary to put into practice "and he saw the place from afar," and to literally see the object of a person's hope before him, no matter how far off it may seem. Then, precisely because he does this, it may well be that what he is hoping for will come immediately when he least expects it. This is what happened in the case of our father, Avraham, when the judgment was immediately sweetened and the angel said to him "do not lay your hand upon the boy" (Genesis 22:12). Immediately afterward, though, he had to fortify himself in trust and hope for a different, new salvation, i.e. he had to find a wife for Yitzchak. This is what is written "and after these things, Avraham was informed." Rashi comments there, "'these things' are thoughts that he had as a result of the *akeidah*" regarding Yitzchak having to marry. God then helped him and he was "informed" that Rivkah had been born. While this was indeed wonderfully good news, it was still a very remote possibility, because Yitzchak was thirty-seven and Rivkah, his wife-to-be, was only one day old. He then came home and found that his first wife, the *tzaddeket* Sarah, our mother, had died, and he had no place to bury her. It is explained in the Midrash that all these things were part of our father Avraham's tests.

Even now the hope of our father Avraham and of our ancestors, of blessed memory, has still not been fulfilled. For we are now at the lowest level, in the grip of bitter exile, physical, spiritual and financial. What can we say?! What can we say?! If God had not helped us by sending us His true tzaddikim in every generation, we would almost have lost all hope, God forbid. But now, due to the might of the true tzaddikim through whom God has made known His salvation, thank God, our hope is very, very strong indeed that without a doubt, God will finish what He has begun. So that we, small and destitute as we are, must expand our minds and understand hints from all this in order to "see the place from afar." It is impossible to explain all this in writing, but this should suffice for someone seeking the truth.

You should know, my beloved son, that you filled me with life by bringing these words out of my heart and onto paper through your enormous desire for good. While these words have long been implanted in my heart, even more than I have written, and while I have already spoken about them a great deal, they nonetheless were awakened in me anew. While it is true that we talk about fulfilling the dictum to "view [the words of the Torah] as new every day," still this dictum itself must not grow old for us. And so on forever.

Letter #233

The words of your father, forced to close, since the time has arrived for the Afternoon Prayers which Yitzchak, our father, instituted. May the Master of Salvation allow us to fulfill (Genesis 24:63), "And Yitzchak went out to pray in the fields," and may He allow us to express ourselves before our Creator very much every day and to daily strengthen ourselves anew in this practice. No matter what happens in the meantime, from one day to the next, a person should know and believe that no good word is ever lost. "And when its back grew hot, it flipped over" — to disprove and eradicate the view that it is dry land, God forbid [see *Likutey Moharan* I, 2; this refers to feeling that our prayers do not bear fruit; "When it grew hot" — from extensive prayer, "it flipped over" reversed the trend and did bear fruit]. In this area most of all, we must fortify ourselves and fulfill the teaching on the verse, "And he saw the place from afar," as above.

Understand this well, my dear son! Attend to all this with straightforwardness in order to truly put it into practice with all the strength you can possibly muster! For this warning to persist in talking to God relates directly to *you* as well! Even if untoward things are happening to us meanwhile — "you are not required to finish the work, but you are not permitted to neglect it either." *Ashreinu!* How fortunate we are to have [spiritual] tools such as these that we can talk about! How very, very much we must give thanks for the past! "If our mouths were full of song as the sea," it would still not be enough! Through this thanksgiving we will have the strength to cry out and to request every day over the future. Then most of the day will be spent in joy! Thank God, we have plenty to be happy about, after all the kindness that God has done with us and that He is going to do with us in the future! For now too we see from afar our hope and our eternal salvation! Exactly what I said above! Understand these things well for happiness and joy — [so that you can] turn everything into joy!

> The words of your father, waiting from afar for complete salvation soon.
>
> *Noson of Breslov*

Greetings to all our comrades with a mighty love! All these words were meant for them as well, each one according to his own place and time. If they want, they have permission to read these words of mine. For, thank God, we need not be ashamed of these words before the entire congregation of the Jewish People! But the *machloket* necessitates that they be concealed. For just as it is a mitzvah to say something that will be heeded, it is also a mitzvah not to say something that will not be heeded (Yevamot 65b). As for a person who wants to hear the truth, "give to a wise person and he will grow wiser." For words of truth will stand forever!

> *Noson, as above*

234

With God's help, Monday, Vayechi, 5597, Nemirov.

My dear son.

I received all your letters and I was quite pleased. At the moment I do not know what to write you, because I have

Letter #234

already written you a great deal. But your friend, Reb Nachman, the deliverer of this letter, has urged me to write you, so I am compelled to take pen in hand and at least send you greetings. Now, my son, fortify yourself determinedly, and constantly bring yourself to joy! Thank God, the days of Chanukah passed peacefully. I had a few of our comrades as guests, and they struggled with enormous difficulties to get here. Who can understand the ways of God?! I was certain that you and our comrades from Tulchin would be here with me for Shabbat Chanukah. As for the rest, I considered it highly unlikely that they would come. But it turned out exactly the reverse!

We see every day that we know nothing at all! You were under duress, though, and "the Torah exempts duress." The deliverer of this letter will certainly tell you what was discussed here that Shabbat, and you have undoubtedly already heard a little from Reb David. You should know that, thank God, you had a large share in the teaching that I originated through God's salvation that Shabbat. For it was your good desire that motivated me to write you that letter; and it was that letter which sparked many of the true, wondrous original teachings that I innovated and taught this Shabbat Chanukah through God's miracles (see *Likutey Halakhot, Shiluach HaKen* 5). How great are God's deeds! Who can comprehend the miracles and kindnesses that He performs every moment of every day?!

Therefore, my dear son, fortify yourself determinedly and at every moment start anew, especially every morning! Practice zealously what I have said, that it is necessary to believe that God is constantly innovating new things, as it is written, "They are new every morning, great is Your faithfulness," and as we say every day (Morning Liturgy), "Who creates daily new things." You will also hear from the carrier of this letter about the marvelous encouragement I discussed with him, which is contained in the verse (Genesis 46:4), "I will go down with you to Egypt and I will also bring you up" (Likutey Halakhot, Shiluach HaKen 5:23-24). Understand the wonders of God! Most important is that you take from all this something that *you* can apply to yourself, as in "a Chanukah candle for each person is the preferred way [of performing the mitzvah]" (Shabbat 21b). I have no time to write any more.

The words of your father.

Noson of Breslov

Greetings to all our comrades with a great love.

235

With God's help, Wednesday, Mishpatim, 5597.

My dear son.

I just now received your letter. I intend to set out, God willing, on Tuesday, [the week of Parashat] Terumah. As you can understand for yourself, I am not yet clear about what route I will take. May God Who steadies the steps of man, let me travel safely. In my every movement and my every step, I rely on Him alone. I will most likely let you hear from me from Uman and, if I come to Tcherin, I will notify you from there, with God's help. Reb Nachman of Tulchin will be traveling with me until

Uman, God willing, and from there he will return to his home on foot. You will hear everything from him. God will do what is good and He will finish everything for the best as He desires.

    The words of your father, waiting for salvation.

Noson of Breslov

236

With God's help, Wednesday, Vayakheil, Tcherin, 5597.

Greetings to my dear son, Reb Yitzchak, may he live.

I received your letter today before [Morning] Prayers and I was extremely pleased. The postman here is in a tremendous hurry, so I cannot write very much at all. Thank God, I arrived here safely Monday night. On Tuesday, there was a Brit Milah by the son of Reb Hirsh, son of Reb Efraim, may his light shine, and I performed the mitzvah of *chitukh* [cutting]. As you know, it has been some time since I had the opportunity of this merit. Thank God, I spent last Shabbat in Medvedevka, and, thank God, all is well.

Everything that is happening with me though, both overall and in each particular, is all in the category of "he saw the place from far off" (see Letter #233 above). We see wondrous, awesome acts of salvation, and yet all that we hope for is still very far off indeed. We must thank God every day for the past and look closely at all the amazing kindnesses that He did for us when He let us know about the splendrous, sweet and lovely pleasantness of the wonders of His holy Torah and such deep, true advice. Then we must petition over the future and wait constantly for salvation. When I arrived here, I also received the good news, that the wife of Reb Avraham Ber, may he live, gave birth to a daughter. May God allow them to raise her to *chuppah*, to good deeds and to a long, good life. This is all in the category of "...from far off." Remember well what we have said about this! Put your mind to really understanding its meaning in order to strengthen yourself with it every day, that we should not sleep our lives away! For the Guardian of Israel neither slumbers nor sleeps, and He will certainly finish what He has begun. He has finished and He will finish! For You, God, are always on high. I cannot continue.

The words of your father.

Noson of Breslov

Greeting to all our comrades with a great love. All of the above was meant for you too! Fortify your hearts and be strong!

237

With thanks to God, Thursday, Vayikra, 5597, Kremenchug.
Warm greetings to my dear, beloved son, the learned Reb Yitzchak, may his light shine.

I had been waiting for your letter until just this hour. Though I had not yet received it, I was preparing myself to write you, knowing your enormous desire for my letters. Then, just now, I received your letter and was delighted. How great are God's deeds! He governs His World with kindness and with an amazing providence which is absolutely unfathomable! "Lord,

Letter #237

my God, You are very great!" "Very" alludes to the [mystery of the] *tzimtzum* [the contraction wherein the world was created, (see *Likutey Moharan* I, 54:2)], into which it is forbidden to delve too deeply. But, "God appeared to me from afar." On Wednesday of Parashat Vayakheil, I sent you my letter from Tcherin informing you that I had received your letter there. That letter [of yours] also arrived at just the right time, as I was preparing a letter to send to Nemirov.

I was in Tcherin for Shabbat Parashat Vayakheil, and on Wednesday, Rosh Chodesh Adar II, I came here, but Reb Efraim, may his light shine, was not at home. So I have remained here until now, and I will spend this Shabbat here too, with God's lovingkindness. After Shabbat I will travel to Tcherin. I would like to be in Terhovitza for Shabbat Parashat Tzav but, because of Purim and because the roads are not in the best condition, it could be that I will also spend Shabbat Parashat Tzav in Tcherin. If so, with God's kindness, I will be in Uman for Erev Rosh Chodesh Nisan. I truly give myself over to God with every single step and every single move that I make. It is God Who steadies a man's steps and He will do what is good with me as He desires.

As far as this lament of yours, which is now many years old, is concerned — I know your pain, my son. I know it well. I have already written you and spoken with you a great deal. What can I add now? After all your lamenting and crying, the words of the Rebbe's holy teachings are still true. It is impossible to think two thoughts at once, and a person *can* direct his thoughts as he wishes (*Likutey Moharan* II, 50). You even wrote yourself that when you force yourself to do your basic, compulsory studying, some of these distracting thoughts disappear. You can infer for yourself then that, if you force yourself to study more, more of the distractions will disappear! If nonetheless they continue to lie in wait and chase after you every time, well, it cannot be any other way. For it is explained in the Rebbe's holy teachings that "A person's thoughts follow in line with his service" (The Aleph-Bet Book Prayer A:84). See the explanation of this there (disturbing thoughts are aroused during one's devotions).

You must also review frequently everything we have said in the Rebbe's holy name: how one must cry out to God very much and how no cry is every lost no matter where a person is. Even if you cannot cry out and express yourself to God as you should, you should nonetheless do what you can. Then, through the methods I have taught you, you will be able to accustom yourself to express yourself before God as a son expresses his pain to his father.

Above all else, you have to force yourself to stay happy through the pathways you have heard from me and seen in the Rebbe's holy books; namely, "that He did not make me a gentile," "I will sing to God with the little I have left," and through the teaching "Joy and happiness will they grab, grief and sighing will flee," which teaches that one must grab [just the thing that is causing one] grief and sighing and drag it into joy (see Rabbi Nachman's Stories pp.447-51; Azamra!; Likutey Moharan II, 23). We have spoken about this a great deal, thank God. A person must really work [and even force himself] to make himself happy, and he must also bring himself to joy through silliness, as all Israel is accustomed

Letter #237

to do on Purim! Thank God Who has kept us alive until now. The awesome days of Purim are approaching. May God make us happy with His salvation. I believe that God will certainly perform awesome miracles for us this Purim too. For the miracles of Purim are remembered and performed [again] every single year in every single generation.

Bring yourself to great joy, my dear son! For we have merited extremely awesome and miraculous acts of salvation in that we escaped from the trap of being opponents to a Rebbe such as this, to holy teachings such as these, and to momentous events such as the ones we are connected with! Pay careful attention to what is happening in the world and how awesome wonders occur in every generation! The greatest wonders occur in connection with a person's drawing close to the true tzaddik of that generation, as was the case in the time of the Baal Shem Tov, of sainted memory, and after him in the time of the Magid [of Mezritch], of sainted memory. But a *machloket* such as the one against us — there has almost never been one like it! They have risen up against us to swallow us up, God forbid — and over nothing! "If God had not been with us..." You have done much, Lord, my God. Your miracles and thoughts are for us.

With this fact itself you should be able to rejoice exultantly in everything that you go through. For it is a matter of no small significance that we merited to know about the Rebbe and his holy Torah teachings. He is our life and the length of our days! Thank God, we have more than enough to rely on. His power now to save us from all of our enemies, physical and spiritual, is just as it was then — and much, much more! At the very least, start anew every day and fortify yourself determinedly, not to get involved [in these thoughts of yours]. Practice what we discussed in this regard, and believe at every moment of every day that God's kindnesses never end and His compassion never ceases. "They are new every morning, great is Your faithfulness."

I cannot say any more in this context, and it is time for the Afternoon Prayers. If only we could merit to fulfill the verse (Genesis 24:63), "And Yitzchak went out to pray in the field," to really express ourselves to God every day until we are worthy of coming to joy! Let us be glad and rejoice in His salvation!

> The words of your father, waiting to see you alive, well and joyful. As far as your livelihood is concerned, fortify yourself with unwavering trust, because God will surely not abandon you. It is all for your good. Cast your burden on God and He will sustain you.
>
> Noson of Breslov

Greetings to all our comrades with a great love.

238

With God's help, Sunday, the 11th of Nisan, 5597, Nemirov.

My dear, beloved son.

I received all your letters: one in Tcherin, two in Uman, and one I received before Shabbat from the deliverer of this letter. They all speak the same language, crying out over your pain, spiritual, physical and monetary. I have already answered you a great deal, and the Rebbe's books are full of responses to all this. What more can I write you? At the moment my mind is not lucid from my weakness after Shabbat, with which you are familiar. Nonetheless, my enormous love for you and the urging of the deliverer of this letter, our friend Reb Nachman, compel me to write you a few words.

You should know that, thank God, I completed the journey safely. With God's help, I also brought some money, though most of it had been spent at home before I even arrived. Now too, I have nothing to rely on for my livelihood except trust. This is what I heard from the Rebbe's holy mouth in these words (*Tzaddik* #501), "Only trust!" They left his mouth as arrows shot from the hand of a warrior! You, too, and all our comrades — do not worry and do not be sad! God is with us and He will surely sustain you honorably. God will not abandon His People, and those who take shelter in Him will never be faulted. God is our hope that our enemies will see and be ashamed! May God strengthen your hearts to be happy in the joy of the approaching festival.

May you merit to understand and believe that a new Pesach is now approaching, a Pesach that never before existed! For without a doubt, new rectifications will now be performed which never before took place. And if our deeds are not what they might be, God still does His part. For God's kindnesses never end. "They are new every morning, great is Your faithfulness." This is particularly true on Pesach which is the "head" [the first] of all the festivals, when every Jew, great and small, experiences the greatest renewal of his mental powers. This is true most of all for those who take shelter in the shade of the point of truth, whose entire work is to awaken and renew our intellect and mental powers. I have a great deal to say about this right now, but it is impossible in this context. The main thing is to believe in all this, i.e. that unprecedented wonders will undoubtedly take place this Pesach! God's kindnesses are renewed every day. How much more is this true for Pesach, when we went out of Egypt amidst enormous miracles, and when the entire Creation was renewed! Likewise, every single year awesome, new wonders take place! For "in every generation a person must see himself as if he went out of Egypt" (Pesachim 116a).

> The words of your father, writing exhausted. It was only your desire that forced me to write these few but potent words of mine. Rejoice in God and in the power of the true tzaddikim. Sing joyously, all you righteous!
>
> *Noson of Breslov*

You are receiving from the bearer of this letter all that I gave him to give you. May God help us to do acts of kindness for each other always. Warm greetings to every one of our comrades with a great love. These words of mine were meant for all of them! Be strong and fortify your hearts, all you who hope in God!

239

With God's help, Thursday, Emor, the 21st day of the Numbering of the Children of Israel, 5597, Nemirov.

Warm greetings, life and blessing to my honored, dear and beloved son, Reb Yitzchak, may he live.

The special messenger arrived at my house just now as I was waking up, before I had opened the doors. I was shaken when he said that he had been specially and exclusively sent to me. I read your letter immediately and I need not tell you how pained I am. I am extremely distressed, but I trust God that He will quickly send your son, David Zvi, may he live, a full recovery. It could be that he needs to perspire "good perspiration" [by exerting himself in an act of holiness], which promotes healing, life and joy. Then the verse will be fulfilled (Psalms 118:24), "This is the day that God made, we will rejoice and be happy" [the first four words of this verse form by acrostic the Hebrew word ZeiYAH, perspiration, as explained in *Likutey Moharan* II, 6].

You know already not to agree to any kind of medical treatment, whether from doctor or layman. Do not listen to the cries of your wife and friends, and not even to the *tzaddeket* Adil, may she live. Just accept this suffering too with love — that you must listen to their screaming — but do not heed them at all. Only if you are absolutely forced by their relentless insistence that you *do* something (you are familiar with this), should you agree to give him a simple enema or plain suppository. Salvation and healing will come from God. I hope to receive the good news from you soon, at least after this coming Shabbat, that he has recovered his strength, with God's kindness.

Now, my son, I have already spoken with you and written you very much about the tremendous amount of suffering that the wretched human being must endure all the days of his life in This World. It is expressed in the literature in these words: "There is no moment without flaw, no hour without evil," no day, no week, no month, no year — as is written in the *SheLaH*. We believe that everything is for the good, though, because the force of good is greater. A person must be very careful to practice what the Rabbis, of blessed memory, said, "A person should be accustomed to say, 'Everything the Merciful One does, He does for the best'" (Berakhot 60a). And we must be especially careful about what is written in the Rebbe's holy books that "a person must know that everything that happens to him is for his good" (Likutey Moharan I, 4, 21, 250). Having this attitude is a taste of the World to Come, and through precisely *this* a person can call up his inner strength and pray about everything. A person has to say before God, "Master of the Universe! Your intention is certainly good and compassionate. But we do not have the strength to receive compassion such as this! We need You to turn over the compassion to us [and give us what *we* consider compassion], as the Rebbe wrote on the verse, "May God Almighty give you compassion" (Likutey Moharan II, 62).

You have already seen from your own life, from our comrades and from the entire world, that incalculable suffering, poverty and worries of all kinds overtake a person practically every day. This is how it has always been, as I showed you above from the books of our forebearers who wrote, "There is no moment without flaw, no hour without evil, etc." Man was born to suffer. You wrote about yourself that you are "young in days and sated with sorrow and suffering"; well, it is also said about the entire human race, as it is written (Job 14:1), "Man born of woman is short-lived and full of sorrow." Our father Yaakov, may he rest in peace, also said, "The days of my life have been few and bitter."

I have already spoken about this a tremendous amount. But it appears that I have to go back and repeat it a great deal more. There is no end to the changes which take place every day, every year, every month and at every moment — globally, locally, within every family and circle of friends, and with every single individual — as God daily performs deeds of unfathomable greatness and awesome miracles beyond all number or measure! It is necessary to believe, though, and we can see it a little, that the good really is dominant. For God's kindnesses never cease and His compassion is never-ending. His lovingkindnesses in general, and with each and every single individual, are reborn anew every morning.

It is already explained in our books that a person requires deep advice every day, i.e. to cry out from "the depths" — the depths of his heart — as in "from the depths I called You." He must do this until he can plumb these depths and draw out the deep advice which is newly born there every morning, as in "He reveals profundities out of the darkness" (Job 12:22). It is this advice which constitutes the essence of the kindnesses that are elicited every day, and through the advice comes faith, the source of complete healing, as explained in the lesson "Sound the Shofar-Faith" (Likutey Moharan II, 5). The only thing I added to this was that a person needs to effect this every day. For it is written there that this whole process is parallel to the Creation which was dark at first and afterwards light, and this [Creation] reoccurs every day.

It is impossible for me to elaborate on this, because I am writing all this before the Morning Prayers. Daylight has begun to shine and the time for prayer has arrived. So this will suffice. May God help me to pray with concentration, and at least to focus on the simple meaning of the words. Most of all, may He help me to pray in accordance with the teaching "Make a window for the ark" (see Likutey Moharan I, 9; Tsohar) and to be sure to at least say the words truthfully and simply. May God hear our prayers, our pleas and our conversations with Him, and may He help us and save us from all our troubles, difficulties and suffering. May He speedily send from Heaven complete recovery from all our illnesses and pains, and in particular may He send it to your son, David Zvi, son of Chanah, may he live, among the other infirm of Israel. Now too, my dear son, fortify yourself determinedly! Rejoice and be happy over His miraculous salvation, whereby He supplied the cure in advance of the illness, by allowing us to hear original Torah teachings such as these which have no rival! It is impossible to express just how high into the exalted, supernal heights these teachings actually reach. But even on the simple level they constantly revive each person with eternal life! I do not have time to talk about this right now.

The words of your father, pained by your suffering and waiting to rejoice over your salvation soon.

Noson of Breslov

240

With thanks to God, Friday, Erev Shabbat, the 36th day of the Numbering of the Children of Israel, 5597.

Greetings to my dear, beloved son, the learned Reb Yitzchak, may his light shine, and to all his family. Greetings and abundant salvation.

I received all your letters and I was greatly relieved to hear about the [improved] health of your son, my precious grandson, David Zvi, may he live. It is good to thank God for the past, and to request for the future, that he enjoy a long, happy life, spent in Torah and in the true service of God. May you merit to raise him in joy and satisfaction to Torah, *chuppah* and good deeds. It is time for the Morning Prayers and I cannot write much at all, but your enormous desire [for my letters] forced me to put pen to paper for you. Be certain to inform me through the bearer of this letter as much as you can about what is going on there.

God is my hope that everything is really a great favor — that "these [our troubles] are the very things that are making us strong" (*Midrash Tanchuma, Nitzavim*). Thank God, Who has kept us from being prey for their teeth. So much has His compassion helped us and has His lovingkindness stayed with us that we have even merited to hear and collect new Torah teachings such as these! There is nothing like them! They are our life and our length of days, for us, for our whole [future] generations, and for all the generations of "the seed of Israel, Your servants." The Rebbe will finish what he started and will quickly make absolute truth known for the sake of His [God's] Name. Now we must praise the Master of All that we have merited to be in the Rebbe's portion, and that He [God] separated us from those who attack truth such as this. They are attacking their own life-source! For no-one loves Israel as the Rebbe does. Salvation is in God's hands. May He have compassion on His People and may the truth shine within all of them.

There is only one truth; and if they leap over mountains, jump over hills and stretch their tongues until they reach up to the Heavens in order to refute it, God forbid, the truth is still its own witness and will stand forever! "Truth will sprout from the ground." It will sprout *from the ground*, as it says in the Midrash (Shmot Rabbah 1:13) on the verse, "They will rise from the land," literally "from the land." Because when Israel is down on the *ground*, that is precisely when they rise up! Thus it is written (Psalms 44:26), "Our souls are bent down in the dust; our bellies cleave to the ground. Rise up and help us! Redeem us for the sake of Your kindness!"

> The words of one calling from the straits. But I see God's miracles and exalted acts of salvation amidst the straits and great stress, until I genuinely merit to rejoice over them wholeheartedly! Waiting for great salvation through God's lovingkindness.
>
> *Noson of Breslov*

241

With thanks to God, Monday, the 9th of Sivan, 5597.

My beloved son, may he live.

Remember and do not forget everything that happened and was heard this past holy, awesome Shavuot! Pay close attention to the "hands" gesturing hints and signaling to every one of you in your hearts through my words, which emanate from the "flowing spring" in spoken words and in writing (see Likutey Moharan II, 7:10). Fortify yourself with the utmost determination! Joy in God is your fortress at all times! Just fortify yourselves and be strong!

The words of your father.

Noson of Breslov

242

With thanks to God, Sunday, Behaalotekha, 5597, Nemirov.

Peace and life to my honored, dear and beloved son, the learned Reb Yitzchak, may his light shine.

I received your letter along with the three gold pieces last week through the messenger. The following day Reb Gershon from Tcherin, who is now where you are, was here at my house. He needed a favor from me and told me a number of times that after his afternoon nap he would return. He did not keep his word, though, and I have not seen him yet. You should tell him that what he did was not right, when he himself knows the great favor that I did him with my letters. He still needs my help now, with God's help, and he ought to have waited here to see me before he left — even if it meant missing the carriage that he had found. Through him, I had expected to send you a letter, which was very important to me at the time for your sake, and I really needed him at the time to do this for you.

But with all this I see the enormous barriers that confront a person any time he wants to enter my house. You are somewhat familiar with them, and you will know more about them in the future — to the point that Reb Gershon neglected to receive a material favor from me through which he did not receive an eternal, spiritual one either. Nonetheless, you should tell him that I forgive him everything. The only thing that bothers me is the eternal good that he lost. But what's done is done. Now he should be certain to act more intelligently if he wants the truth. I love him now as I always did, and whatever material or spiritual good I can do for him I will not withhold, with God's help. Then he himself should choose. Maybe he will choose what is right in God's eyes and God will do what He deems good. There is no need to elaborate about this. It is just my love for him and for his ancestors, who were truly our friends, that I wrote all this for his own true good. I have said enough for an intelligent person to understand. You and your friends, our comrades, will understand how to speak to him in order to bring him closer and not to distance him, God forbid.

As far as you are concerned, we can only pour out our prayers to God that He send from Heaven complete recovery for your son and daughter, may they live, that He give them back their full strength quickly and save them from now on from all kinds of illness, aches and pains. May you merit to raise them to Torah, *chuppah* and good deeds for many long, good years. Amen. May it be His will.

I have already said a very great deal to strengthen and encourage you not to let your efforts flag as a result of the troubles you go through. I have warned you in advance that all kinds of fear and suffering, God forbid, must inevitably visit a person. For "man was born to suffer," and there is no refuge except God, the Torah and prayer, through the power of the true tzaddik.

My beloved sons, brothers and friends! You have probably heard a little about the great uproar concerning me which broke out after you left. I was forced to send from my home immediately two men who were staying there, Reb Nachman from Breslov and Reb A.Y. Even now, God forbid that anyone should come to my house for Shabbat. It is only permitted during the week. They are boasting that they will inform upon me [to the authorities], God forbid. May God have mercy and quickly rectify everything.

God is my hope that everything will soon turn into good, but during these past days I have had some terrible scares. I have been unwell because of my ailment, God save us, and the great grief that I had from your letters about your children, may they live, was in addition to my financial straits. With all these things, though, God has helped me, and also during these times He has given a weary man such as myself the strength of iron to flee to Him. In His great kindness He has rescued me thus far; and I still have hope in His kindness that He will always save me from frights, dangers and attacks of all kinds, and that He will soon allow me to return to my home in Breslov, for His sake and the sake of the true tzaddikim. "Do not give honor to us, God, but give it to Your Name!" Even now, praise God, I am a little joyful over all the kindness He has done for me and for us. Thank God, Who has not allowed me to be prey for their teeth! I am joyful as well over the kindness that He is going to do in the future for me and for all of you! Just fortify yourselves and be strong! Do not forget everything that happens to us collectively and individually, what happens to each and every one of us, every day, every week and every year. Every day they rise up against us and the Holy One, Blessed be He, rescues us from their hands!

Last Thursday I saw in the *Midrash Rabbah* (Bamidbar Rabbah 7:7) a comment on the verse, "Command Yehoshua! Fortify him and strengthen him," as follows, "According to our usual method we learn only to encourage those who encourage themselves and only to push those who push themselves." I have a great deal to say about this, with God's help, and it is partially related to what I said last Shavuot about the great importance of drawing on one's inner strength, and about how it is forbidden to be lazy or remiss (see *Likutey Halakhot, Pidyon Bekhor* 5:33).

A person must just press on determinedly, and through this he merits to earn his livelihood and to receive an "illumination of desire" during eating (see *Likutey Moharan* II, 7:10). But the above-mentioned Midrash says only to encourage those who encourage themselves, and this is included in what I said then. For while it is true that God in His great kindness fortifies us tremendously through the true tzaddik with wondrous encouragement beyond all measure — and that he is constantly giving us holy hints that God is still right there with us and we must not fear, nor be afraid at all for God is with us, and we should not fear! — nonetheless, a person cannot receive this encouragement unless he himself is strong and prevails on himself not to be lazy or remiss, what they call a *shlamazelnik*.

This is precisely the meaning of the Midrash which says "only encourage those who encourage themselves and only push those who push themselves." This is truly one of God's wonders! For people who are strong are certainly only that way through the power of God Who shines this strength into their hearts through the true tzaddik, the source of all inner strength; this being so, it is all from God and the true tzaddik anyway. Nonetheless, a person has free will and must fortify himself and not be a *shlamazelnik*, God forbid. This is included in what is written in the Rebbe's teachings (Likutey Moharan I, 271), "There are a number of things which depend on [and cause] each other, and no-one knows which comes first." As you know, I have spoken a great deal about this. He also speaks there about holy boldness, which is closely related to marshaling inner strength.

Now, my sons, brothers and friends, pay close attention to all these words! Understand well all the holy signals that they are constantly hinting to us in our hearts about how to find the strength to press forward through all the things that happen to us, be they worldly or spiritual, concerning body, soul or money, children or livelihood, collectively or as individuals —

and also with regard to peace and controversy and to the many countless people who groundlessly hate us. "In return for my love they hated me," and I am poor, pained and stricken. From head to toe no place is untouched — neither physical, nor spiritual — as it is written (Psalms 22:15-16), "I am poured out like water, my bones have come apart. My heart is like wax, it melts in my bowels. My strength is dried up like a potsherd and my tongue is stuck to my palate." If King David, may he rest in peace, said this — what should we say?

Even if a person truly feels all this in his soul until he has just barely enough breath and spirit to stay alive—nonetheless, God's kindness is still very great, even to me. He has pity on me and in my heart I hear hints. "I will say in my heart — I will have hope. God's kindness never ends, His compassion never ceases. They are new every morning, great is Your faithfulness."

For God's kindnesses are renewed every day, as we have discussed a great deal, with God's help. By looking for God's kindnesses in this way a person can find the strength to pour out his heart to God even now and to fully express himself before Him. For when a person sees for himself how very far he is from complete salvation, because of his unworthy deeds which have distanced him from God so very, very much from the day he was born until now, and when nonetheless he strengthens himself through these hints that "the whole world is full of His glory" and that God is still with him, and with many other types of life-giving encouragement — this is precisely the way that he may come to express himself to Him. A soul which is hungry, thirsty, exhausted and drained of strength will find good through these amazing, awesome, true and powerful hints until God in His kindness gives speech to the speechless, and literally opens the mouths of the dumb and creates "fruits of the lips!" Then a person can open his mouth and unreservedly speak about all his needs and express himself to God. However much he fortifies himself, God fortifies him many, many times more, since the measure of good is always greater. Thus this cyclical movement in the direction of good continues until one merits to draw close to God.

Nonetheless, every day, and sometimes many times in one day, it is necessary for a person to fortify himself anew and to remember the traces left from all the times when he marshaled his inner strength in the past. In this way God will save him every time. Only strengthen yourself determinedly!

It is impossible to explain all this exactly. But a person who wants the truth will glean for himself many good hints from all this until he merits not to be a *shlamazelnik*, God forbid. Rather he will be a valiant, vigilant, and stalwart warrior and firm in his conviction to have a share in the dominion of holiness! Then he will draw forth livelihood and wealth, and merit "the illumination of desire" when he eats. And this is what sustains a person's knowledge, as I have discussed, with God's help.

The words of your father and true, eternal friend.

Noson of Breslov

Warm greetings to all our comrades with a great love! These words were meant for all of you too! Strengthen and fortify your hearts, all you who hope in God! For the sake of His Great Name

God will not abandon His people. For God knows the enormous love we have for every Jew, even the smallest, worst and most inferior of them. What can we do though? There are people who stir up strife for nothing. "May the lying lips which speak arrogantly against the righteous with pride and contempt be struck dumb! How great is the good You have hidden away for those who fear You!" (Psalms 31:19- 20) "How" [in Hebrew *Mah*] describes this good, i.e. "the illumination of desire" (*Likutey Moharan* II, 7). Fortunate are the ears that heard all this! Happy the eyes that at least see all this in the Rebbe's holy books with an eye for the truth! They will surely understand the real truth! Words of truth stand forever!

After I wrote this letter, Reb Yaakov, the son-in-law of the *Baal HaMagihah*, came to my house and brought me another of your letters. As you may have expected, I was pained by your letter, particularly by the news that your wife wants to engage in fruitless, pointless stupidity. I have already answered you about everything. You also have to suffer the foolishness of ignorant men and women who want to engage in stupidity, i.e. medical treatments and "amulets."

It is all for the best, though, and this too is expiation for sins. For no pain is ever lost and it is all counted as expiation for sin. My beloved son, may he live, your pain is great indeed, and I am extremely grieved by your suffering, God have mercy. But you are too severe and you make too much of your suffering. Everything I say is to minimize and play down the pain and suffering and to find some relief or easement there within the sorrow, as the Rebbe wrote on the verse, "In suffering, You gave me relief" (*Likutey Moharan* I, 195). What you do every time is to magnify all your various troubles and suffering! You already see in your few short years that it is impossible to avoid suffering practically every day. The Rebbe wrote this explicitly (*Likutey Moharan* II, 77), "Know that every Jew must have some suffering every day." You also see from other people the immense blows, pain, worries and suffering that come upon every single person. Therefore you must not exaggerate the pain. To the contrary! Try to find the "relief within the sorrow itself," God save us. Precisely through *this*, you will be able to thank God for the past and cry out over the future, that He should rescue you in His compassion from all kinds of pain and take you from trouble to full relief and send complete recovery to your son and daughter soon. Amen. May it be His will.

As for the outcry here, I have already told you a little, and I cannot describe it in detail. Praise God, though, we have many supporters. Even on the physical level they constitute a majority. And this is beside the many who are with us in the spiritual realm. But arrogance and audacity [*chutzpah*] is "kingship without a crown" (*Sanhedrin* 105a) and even the arrogant themselves are constantly full of remorse. I see on each occasion, though, that God also wants our prayers, and this is why these things continue to happen. It is all to remind us to pray before Him. Then, in the process of praying about this, we will also pray for our own needs. The main thing is to draw close to God. This is the foundation of everything — and everything that happens to every person hints at this. God is our salvation and our hope that everything will soon be rectified and that everything will turn into good, with God's help.

Noson, the same

243

With thanks to God, Sunday, Korach, 5597, Nemirov.

My dear, beloved son, the learned Reb Yitzchak, may his light shine, along with all his children, may they live.

I received your letter on Tuesday [Torah reading] Shelach and I was extremely pleased. I had been waiting and yearning all the time to see your letter. My hopes were disappointed, though, as your letter did not come until that Tuesday. Thank God Who has helped me thus far that you had good news for me about your children's health, may they live, and that you received my letter. Thank God Who has helped me thus far, and praise God, things have now quietened down here a little. Nonetheless, I am still constantly afraid whenever our comrades gather together [here], and I have no idea how to act in this matter. Thank God, last Shabbat I had four righteous guests here and, thank God, I spoke words of truth and was somewhat joyful. Everything I said was related to the Midrash I wrote you about (see the previous letter), "only encourage those who encourage themselves." I am pressured right now — and besides I do not know with whom this letter will be sent, since I am sending it to Breslov, so I cannot go on.

The words of your father, waiting for salvation soon, for the sake of His Holy Name.

Noson of Breslov

Let me know the good news about what is going on.

244

With God's help, Friday, Erev Shabbat Devarim, 5597, Vinnitsa.

Greetings to my dear, beloved son, the learned Reb Yitzchak, may his light shine.

I received your letter yesterday upon my arrival here and I was delighted to see your enormous desire for my letters. Perhaps you will receive some good point — some point of good by which you will start afresh from now on — forever. This is the reason I have forced myself now to send you this letter, even though I have nothing new in particular to tell you and it is also already getting towards afternoon. Thank God, I arrived here safely yesterday before midday and, thank God, all is well. If you want, you can send me a letter to Uman and I will be sure to let you hear from me again from there, with God's help. May God give me a safe journey and may He guide me on the paths of righteousness for His Name's sake. I am too pressed for time to go on at all with words of truth. It is not necessary to go on about the truth anyway. For "truth endures," and one word of truth is worth more than thousands and tens of thousands of words containing an admixture of falsehood, as explained in the lesson which talks about the preciousness of words of truth (*Likutey Moharan I*, 192).

> The words of your father, extending loving greetings to your learned [person], praying for you and waiting to hear all good from you. Greetings to all our comrades with a great love.
>
> *Noson of Breslov*

245

With God's help, Friday, Erev Shabbat Ekev, 5597, Uman.

My dear son.

I received your letter in Vinnitsa and another one here upon my arrival. It is now already close to the arrival of Shabbat, but your enormous desire compels me to write you these few lines to tell you that, thank God, all is well. I read your letter carefully, but time does not allow me to answer you now. I have already provided you in advance, though, with an abundant response in the form of my writings, the words I have spoken and, in particular, the Rebbe's holy books. "Study them over and over. Grow old and gray with them. For there is nothing better." Nothing can be added to them and nothing taken away.

Remember very well that you are now in this passing world and there is no comprehending what is happening under the sun, particularly in these generations. As King Solomon said (Ecclesiastes 8:17), "Even if a person claims to be wise, he will not be able to find [its meaning]." Every moment of every hour of every day is full of trials and tests and refinements for each and every one of us. We have no-one to lean on but our Father in Heaven and on the power of the elder of holiness. What can I say to you, my dear son? I understand your letters well and I know your pain. But as it appears, you have not yet understood even *me*, let alone our master, teacher and Rebbe, of sainted memory. Remember well all that I have said and implied to you on countless occasions about how a person must inevitably endure a very great deal at all times! And there are innumerable variations between one time and another, and among individuals. Be strong! Be strong, my dear son! Even your cries in your letters are not lost! Nonetheless you must zealously fortify yourself to make yourself happy any way you can! The time of Shabbat has arrived, and it is impossible for me to continue.

The words of your father.

Noson of Breslov

Greetings to all our comrades with a great love!

246

With God's help, Tuesday, Reay, 5597, Uman.

My dear, beloved son.

I wrote you a letter on Friday, Erev Shabbat. Subsequently, last Sunday, I received your letter through the post. At the moment I have nothing at all new to say, as my mind is not at all clear. Just know that I intend to travel, God willing, to my home after Erev Rosh Chodesh and I want to be in Breslov for Shabbat Parashat Shoftim. May God guide me safely on the road of truth and rightness. I already answered you in my letter of last Friday, and that can also serve as a response to your letter that I received afterwards [on Sunday]. I believe that awesome, wondrous new things are taking place every single day. How great are Your works, God! As we say every day, "And in His good renews the Creation every day. How great are Your works, God!" To a small extent I can see with my own eyes awesome new things all the time; but it is impossible to explain all this, especially in a letter. I am only reminding you about this because we have already spoken about it a great deal and you need it very badly every day in order to strengthen yourself and to begin anew constantly every day! May God fortify our hearts to prepare ourselves from now on to merit a good new year this coming holy Rosh HaShanah. My mind is extremely tired now and it is impossible for me to go on at all. Only your love compelled me to write to you even now.

The words of your father, waiting for salvation.

Noson of Breslov

Greetings to all our comrades with a great love!

247

With God's help, Sunday, Tavo, 5597, Nemirov.

Greetings to my dear, beloved son, the learned Reb Yitzchak, may his light shine.

I received your letter just now. Thank God, Reb Yisrael from Lipovec was here last Shabbat, and there were four or five other guests as well. Thank God, I spoke words of truth about the lesson "When you go out to war" (Likutey Moharan II, 82) on the subject of "in order and out of order." You too certainly need these words very much, because everything that is happening to you — which conflicts with your will — is all that this teaching calls "out of order."

The path of *teshuvah*, repentance, which is effected in [the month of] Elul, is the rectification for this. The essence of this path is to know and believe that God is in every place and at every level, even at "the Ten Crowns of Impurity," as expressed in the verse, "If I ascend to Heaven, there You are; if I go down to hell, You are here" (Psalms 139:8). This is explained at the end of that same lesson in *Likutey Moharan*. Look it up. The key is to nullify oneself as in *Mah?* (What?) — as in "What are we? What are our lives? What is our power?" (*Morning Liturgy*). Thank God, I spoke some original words of truth about this; may God allow me to write them down (see *Likutey Halakhot, Edut* 5). Because of your love and desire I have written to you that which I spoke about. Perhaps you will glean some practical advice from it too. For all the Rebbe's words are deeper than the sea and they are full of advice for every person, on every level, at any time. Just strengthen and fortify yourself and be determined to really be happy!

Even though it is some time since I have written you about this idea, it is nonetheless clear truth! Thank God, we have plenty to be happy about, no matter what! No matter what! And this is the key — always to be mindful of the marvelous kindness that God did for us when He brought us near the place that He did, so that all the groaning and sighing will turn into happiness and joy! For, in spite of everything, I know about a teaching such as this which explains the underlying reason why things go against a person's will, i.e. "out of order!"

Look at this! Has such a thing ever been heard?! To give such a Torah teaching on these words — "out of order" — a thing which every person experiences?! There is no-one [beside the Rebbe] who can give a Torah lesson about it, especially such a wondrous lesson! For this lesson rises up to the infinite heights and descends infinitely low to raise up those people who are at the "Ten Crowns of Impurity," the lowest possible point. God's compassion has reached them too in this generation, to rouse, to awaken, to support, sustain, rejuvenate and cure them, to give them life and to bring them to joy! No matter how you are, you are still no worse than they are, God forbid, God forbid. And you have an additional quality to endear you, my dear son — that you know about all this, and so very much more! *Ashreinu!* How fortunate we are! How fortunate are our ears, our eyes and our hearts that we saw, heard and understood all this! We still have hope for every true, eternal good in This World and the Next forever!

The words of your father, writing hurriedly before my afternoon nap, which I particularly need on Sundays. My mind is very distracted right now, but nonetheless it was by the hand of God that I wrote you these words now, which I had not even thought of writing at first. Your desire is "an arousal from below," so that through God's compassion these words of truth — which also encourage *me* tremendously now — were written. Praise to the Living God!

The words of one waiting for salvation.

Greetings to all our comrades with great love.

Noson of Breslov

248

With thanks to God, Sunday, Nitzavim-Vayeilekh, 5597, Nemirov.

My beloved son.

I received your letter just now and I have no answer for you. My nephew Reb Isaac set out for home today. Be sure to see him. Maybe he will tell you about some of what was said here this Shabbat, because, thank God, he heard many words of truth which you did not. Now perhaps you will "receive from one another," and it could be that by telling you he will also be awakened. I already know that, even after I speak awesome wonders such as these, it is still very difficult for a person to truly be influenced by them without God's salvation. For precisely this reason it is necessary to speak a great deal, both with other people, particularly with one's true rav, and also with one's self, to seek and to endeavor to bring to light one's hidden, concealed good point. This good point is deeply hidden within a person every day, in accordance with one's deeds and according to what is taking place that particular day [throughout the Creation] from the highest of all levels down to the lowest. For God's thoughts are very deep indeed. We are obligated to fortify ourselves to look for, to seek, to search out and to bind ourselves to the good point which relates to our heart at that particular time. I have spoken about this a great deal, how the Rebbe, of blessed memory, in the lesson "And you will be for Me a kingdom of priests" (Likutey Moharan I, 34) was careful to insert the words "at this time." He wrote there that "each person must bind his heart to the point which relates to his heart *at this time.*"

On Thursday, the time came for [your] payment to P.M., and this particular cause for agitation had to take place on Thursday, [the week of Torah reading] Tavo, 5597, while you were in Tulchin. [Now] this day has already come and gone and nothing remains of it except whatever good point each person grabbed out of it. [What he grabbed was] in accordance with the distractions and barriers which then confronted [him as well as] each one of the inhabitants of the world. The truth, if we look at it, will make our hair stand on end. Yet it is still the truth. We have only to encourage ourselves with the holy teaching of *Azamra!*, "I will sing to my God with what I have left!" Through this we will have the strength to look and to search. And the greatest good point of them all is that we are preparing ourselves in our thoughts to be at the holy site of the Rebbe's holy resting place for Rosh HaShanah. This is my comfort in my destitution. Over this, my heart will celebrate and rejoice! There is still hope to attain the pathways of life at least from now on. May God grant us true, eternal success on our journey, in This World and the Next, forever.

The words of your father.

Noson of Breslov

249

[Editor's note: This was copied from a letter written to the learned and distinguished Reb Efraim from Kremenchug. Much of it is missing.]

...As for writing you words of truth emanating from the "flowing stream, the source of wisdom," time simply does not

Letter #249

allow and the page is too short. I have already said a great deal, and more than this needs to be said every day. If you imagine that you do not have anyone to talk to, I have often chided you about this already, that you must only look at the good in each person. Then you will always have someone with whom to speak words of truth from the point in the heart, so as to "receive from each other." You should also express yourself before God in order to receive from that point within yourself. All these points in turn must receive from the "universal point," the words of our master, teacher and Rebbe, of blessed memory, that you have heard from me and from his holy, awesome books. Study them over and over!

Be sure to bring yourself to great joy every day that you merited to know about a true light such as this. If I had only come into the world to hear this teaching about these "three points" which I mentioned here, which flows from the holy lesson "And you will be for Me a kingdom of priests" (*Likutey Moharan* I, 34) — it would have been enough! We must likewise say this in absolute sincerity about every single word [of his teachings] — not to mention every complete lesson and story! No matter what, we can still say *"Ashreinu!"* "Happy are we!" We really and truly can say *"Ashreinu!"* May God grant salvation and may everything be well, through His great kindness. For God's kindnesses never end and His compassion never ceases; and this is what encourages me every moment of every hour of every day.

For I believe in everything that I just wrote with perfect faith, that [God's] kindnesses are newly created every morning.

This is what Rashi comments on the verse (Lamentations 3:23), "They are new every morning, great is Your faithfulness," which immediately follows the verse, "God's kindnesses never end, His compassion never ceases."

I already spoke at length about this last winter, but it is still necessary to talk about it a great deal and to put it into practice by knowing and believing every day that new awesome kindnesses are coming forth each day. Through these kindnesses, God will finish, in accordance with His will and the will of the true tzaddikim, until we all truly return to Him. Then everything will be transformed into good. For God is great and His greatness is unfathomable. The essence of His greatness is His attribute of kindness, which is called "greatness" (Tikkuney Zohar 67b). Thus it is His kindness, which is His greatness, that is unfathomable. Understand this well! Then you will be able to summon your inner strength very much and always be joyful, especially during prayer! Prayer requires extra fortification. So every time you stand up to pray put everything that has happened until that time completely out of your mind. Just trust in God's great kindness, as is written (Psalms 13:6), "I trust in Your kindness; my heart will rejoice in Your salvation. I will sing to God, for He has treated me kindly." Then you will pray in joy and happiness. I cannot go on any more right now.

The words of your true friend eternally.

Noson of Breslov

Greetings to all our comrades with a great love!

Letters from 5598 (1837-8)

The year in review

Reb Noson began this year still exiled in Nemirov, without any change in the charges against him. However, in Tevet, 5598 (January, 1838) the Savraner Rav passed away. With his most powerful opponent gone, Reb Noson began serious efforts to return to Breslov. Before Purim (March, 1838), several tormentors of Reb Noson began suffering. Attributing this to their treatment of Reb Noson, they began to assist Reb Noson in his efforts to have the charges against him dropped. Only Moshe Chenkes stood in his way and refused to allow Reb Noson to return to Breslov.

Around Shavuot, Reb Noson went back to Breslov again in an attempt to receive permission to return to live there. Moshe Chenkes heard about this and said (literally), "Only over my dead body!" He immediately went to the office of the Governor of Breslov in order to stop Reb Noson's return. During his visit with the Governor, he took violently ill and died the next day. Upon witnessing this, the townspeople gathered together to rescind any and all charges against Reb Noson. Briefs were filed in his favor and forwarded to Kaminetz. But further delays occurred, and his return permit was not issued until shortly after Yom Kippur, 5599 (October, 1838). The letters of this year reflect some of the above. For further details, see *Through Fire and Water*, Chapters 40-41.

250

With thanks to God, Monday night, the 2nd day of Chol HaMoed Sukkot, 5598.

My dear son.

I received your letter just now. Out of honor for Chol HaMoed (the Intermediate Days of the Festival), I did not intend to answer you but from what your brother-in-law, may his light shine, said, I understood your enormous yearning for one of my letters. In addition, all my words are Torah teachings which touch upon actual practice and to the rescue of the soul, so that it is a great mitzvah to write you even on Chol HaMoed.

The bottom line is this: you must know that it is absolutely forbidden for you, God forbid, to think about this matter at all, not beforehand and not afterward. Simply put it out of your mind. I heard from the Rebbe's mouth that this matter is similar to... [missing]. I have said enough for an intelligent person to understand. Thinking about this and getting depressed about it are extremely harmful, and accomplish absolutely nothing. In any case, you certainly need to talk a great deal to your Creator and express yourself before Him every day. Then, in the course of talking, you will surely become aware of your soul's pain. For this does not come about by itself; rather it is the result of what has happened to you previously. In all these things we have someone to lean on, namely, on the power of the holy elder. With his great power we can still express ourselves before God, and God is full of mercy, since only He knows our [evil] urge.

I have already spoken about this a great deal, but it is necessary to review every day what I heard from the Rebbe's holy mouth: "God is very great indeed. There are things taking place in the world about which we know absolutely nothing at all. Even when it comes to you people...." You have certainly heard about this from me already, but you are still in need of great compassion if you are to really feel the wondrous, awesome greatness of these words. The essential message is that we understand nothing at all and that, just as we can damage, we can also repair. Thank God Who has bestowed His abundant kindness on us, so that we do not oppose the one who "repairs" so much. I cannot continue for a number of reasons. May God allow you and me to be happy in the joy of the coming holy festival. Let us be happy and rejoice over His salvation!

The words of your father.

Noson of Breslov

Warm greetings to all our comrades with a great and infinite love, forever.

I repeat my warning twice and three times: do not be the slightest bit sad over this! Put the entire matter out of your mind and do not let it upset you in the least! Just fortify yourself to be happy! Go back and start again to apply the holy teaching of *Azamra!* (Likutey Moharan I, 282) and view it as completely new. Through this you will be able to be happy and strong. Hope to God and He will rescue you in all your affairs. If we had only come to the world to hear the lesson *Azamra!* it would have been enough! And do not forget that, thank God, this Rosh HaShanah you were amidst such a holy, awesome, congregation! The Rebbe already advised us that a person who is with him for Rosh HaShanah ought to be happy the entire year. He said this explicitly: "Eat delicacies and enjoy sweet drinks. Joy in God is your strength!" (Nehemiah 8:10). This verse refers to Rosh HaShanah."

251

With thanks to God, before dawn on Friday, Erev Shabbat, 5598, Nemirov.

Greetings to my dear son, whom I love heart and soul, the distinguished Reb Yitzchak, may he live.

I received your letter yesterday, Thursday, near Minchah-time, through one of our comrades, who arrived as a special messenger regarding our work [this most probably refers to Reb Noson's return to Breslov]. May God conclude them for the best. For the time being we still need many prayers and supplications that, in His amazing compassion, God will quickly bring matters to a favorable conclusion. Salvation is in God's hands. Until now, His compassion has helped us in the most amazing and awesome ways, the likes of which have never been seen or heard! "You have done great deeds, Lord, my God; Your miracles and thoughts are for us!" Now, too, may He not abandon us, and may He not forsake us. For the sake of His Great Name, may He quickly do our desire and complete it favorably. Amen. May it be His will.

I did not think yesterday that I would be answering you

today because, as a rule, I am busy with Shabbat from Thursday on. The essence [of my preparation for Shabbat] is how can I make a "new beginning" at least from this Shabbat. For it is necessary to make a start every day; how very much more so on the holy Shabbat, which is the vitality of all the days of the week! Shabbat is entirely *teshuvah*, repentance, in love and joy amidst the delight of Shabbat, as in "love amidst delights" (see *Likutey Moharan* I, 58:7).

Every person knows in his own soul how very far we are from Shabbat. But every single Jew, according to the good point which still remains in him, has the holiness of Shabbat drawn over him. Yet Shabbat and Yom Tov require preparation, as our Rabbis, of blessed memory said (Beitzah 2b). The essence of this preparation is the desire to simply and literally remember Shabbat every single day and to fulfill the injunction to "begin thinking of Shabbat on Sunday," as is written (Exodus 20:8), "Remember the Shabbat to make it holy," i.e. "Remember it from Sunday on" (Beitzah 16). How much more does this apply with the arrival of three days prior to Shabbat, and especially from Thursday when every Jew is preparing himself for Shabbat, and everyone is running and laboring to buy flour, meat and the like for Shabbat! Who can estimate the glimmer in his own heart and what awesome delights it produces in all the [supernal] worlds! Every Jew does this, with God's help, and we too are among them! We can truly say *"Ashreinu!"* How fortunate we are, all of us, that we merited a good and precious gift such as this which was "stored away in God's treasure house and its name is Shabbat"! We must, without a doubt,

Letter #251

fulfill this simply, with no needless sophistication, and in great joy. But the main thing is for a person to prepare himself heart and soul and to think about how he can merit to draw upon himself the holiness of Shabbat at least now, and to petition God about this very much. It is impossible to explain all this in detail, particularly in this context.

So with all these things, I hardly expected to answer you immediately, especially given the great suffering I have over my effort [to be allowed to return to Breslov]. How I yearn that it should turn out well! In addition to this, I am suffering for each one of our comrades due to my apprehension at the troubles which are prevalent right now. May God in His compassion guard each one of them — "in the shade of Your wings You will hide us." In spite of all this, as I was reading the Torah portion, "the [Hebrew] text twice and the *Targum* once," your enormous desire for my letters came to mind. I said to myself, here I can fulfill the greatest mitzvah of all, "teach them to your children," as well as fulfill "tell your children and your children's children," which the light of our lives, of blessed memory, enjoined us explicitly (see *Rabbi Nachman's Wisdom* #209). Thus I resolved to answer you at once.

Thank God, I reminded myself and you about the holiness of Shabbat, which includes and is the root of all holiness. There is much to say about this. But the main thing is to summon one's inner strength and to ask God to enable one to receive every single Shabbat with great joy, love and with a good disposition; to banish and distance, at least for that day, all forms of sadness, grief and sighing, particularly the anxiety and worry over livelihood, and to forget and put everything out of one's mind — until one merits to extend the joy of Shabbat into all the other days of the week. Then on the weekdays too he will fortify himself to always have strong faith, and he will rejoice in God with his good points, as in "I will sing to God with what I have left." Praise God, we need not be ashamed to mention this awesome teaching of *Azamra!* thousands of times every day! It is our very life!

Now, my dear son, apple of my eye, my heart and soul's delight, I have not even started to respond to your letter yet; but, praise God, through His awesome kindness, I have already answered you a great deal! In fact you can use everything I have written so far to encourage yourself constantly, and you can receive advice from these words of mine every day! For Shabbat itself is wondrous advice for everything, as in "Shabbat protected Adam, the First Man," as our Rabbis, of blessed memory, said (Zohar II, 138). The light of our eyes, of blessed memory, explained in the awesome story of the Exchanged Children (see *Rabbi Nachman's Stories* #11, pp.268*ff*) that when a person is banished from the Holy Garden, i.e. from the Garden of Eden, he must station himself by Shabbat, the King to Whom peace belongs. Even if the concepts [in this story] are far more exalted than I can comprehend, not to mention what you can comprehend, I know clearly that the Rebbe's primary intention was on the simplest level — namely, that a person should station himself by Shabbat, as I wrote above. There is a great deal to say about this too.

You should know, my dear son, that I too feel as if I never

in my life endured as much as I have since last Rosh HaShanah, and especially during Sukkot, and it really is the truth. But I know that every time I suffered whatever I did — "all Your breakers and waves have passed over me" — there were always differences on every occasion, waves and great floods that had never been before. Similarly, each person experiences new things on every occasion, whether good or bad, God forbid. All the same, "the measure of good is greater," and God has also bestowed His kindness upon me and you in great abundance. For He has helped us with His wonders, favors and miracles every moment of every day, evening, morning and afternoon, and especially on the holy festivals.

This is particularly so in "the month of *Eitanim*," which is "*Eitan*, strong, with mitzvot." This is the extremely holy and awesome month of Tishrei. For in Tishrei we merited awesome acts of salvation. We were also able to grab some happiness and joy, to sit in a sukkah every day, to hold in our hands the "weapon of war," the staff of valor, the very holy and awesome etrog, lulav, hadas and aravah, to cry out "Hoshana! Hoshana!" every day, particularly on Hoshana Rabbah, and to rejoice on Shemini Atzeret and Simchat Torah! All this through the power of our extremely holy, awesome and exalted Rosh HaShanah, when we merited to congregate at the the Rebbe's holy burial place. *Ashreinu!*

Happy are we to have merited this! Happy are the ears and eyes that hear and see the holy, awesome letter combinations that the Rebbe revealed about the inner meaning of the month of Tishrei, whose name is formed by the acrostic in the verse

(Psalms 74:13), "In Your strength You shattered the *Sea; You Broke the Serpents' Heads*" [in Hebrew the initial letters of the italicized part of the verse spell "Tishrei"]. And then there are the acrostics formed by the verses, "You know the *Soul of the Stranger, Because you were Strangers*" [spelling "Tishrei"] and, "*Who can Comprehend the Thunder of His Strength*" [spelling "strangers"] (see *Likutey Moharan* II 8:4, 11).

"Who can comprehend" is right! Who can comprehend how people as far away as we are merited to draw near to a light such as this?! To know about letter combinations such as these — especially in conjunction with this entire holy lesson in which these combinations were revealed! I am telling you the truth, my dear, precious son, when I say that every time I reminded myself of the inner meanings associated with the word "Tishrei" as brought out by these awesome and exalted letter combinations, I drew tremendous strength in the face of everything that is happening to me. Any intelligent person's heart ought to at least have a sense that in Tishrei a fierce war is raging with every single person. And we anticipate this war by crying out the whole month of Elul, "If an army should encamp against me, my heart will not fear. If a war should rise up against me, in this I will trust" (Psalms 27:3). "In this I will trust" indeed. For I trust in everything that I wrote up to now: the holiness of Shabbat, the holiness of Tishrei, and so on.

And it is all the power of the holiness of the true tzaddik who revealed all this and who is still working at it! For the tzaddikim are greater after their passing than they are in their lifetimes (*Chullin* 7). It is also written in the holy Zohar (III, 71a) that "were it not for the prayers of the tzaddikim who have died and who pray for the living, the world would not continue to exist for one moment." So we have in our favor the further point that, praise God, we know about the true tzaddik who is engaged in our rectification along with all the tzaddikim who lie in the ground from the time of our ancestors. May the merit of them all protect us always. Amen.

You wrote that while the hardship and distress are striking, it is impossible to feel God's kindness, but that afterwards, when they have eased somewhat, then a person sees the miracles of God's kindness. I have known this for a long time now, and I spoke about it with our master, teacher and Rebbe himself who told me that it was indeed the case. Nonetheless, his intention was that a person should fortify himself to find some easement or favor *during* a time of great duress, until even then he feels God's kindness and miracles. At the least, even if he does not feel this kindness, he should have total faith that without a doubt God is good to everyone at all times; and, as He has already helped him a great deal, He will surely not abandon him now. This is the essence of the war — to turn precisely the grief and sighing into happiness and joy! I have already spoken about this a great deal and there will be other opportunities when God will open my eyes to speak about this — "to learn and to teach, to guard, to do and to fulfill." I have no time to continue.

Now my son, perform the mitzvah of loving your fellows, and copy this letter word for word and send it immediately to Kremenchug, to my friend Reb Efraim, may his light shine. I do not have time to write him myself, mostly because he has been remiss about writing to me. I have often rebuked him about this.

Do all this at once and write me immedialtely through the post that you received this letter and if you have indeed sent it on to Reb Efraim.

Also let me know immediately if my nephew Reb Isaac is alive. I heard a distant and not very happy rumour, and I do not know the truth. This too is a powerful signal and should stir us to fortify ourselves in everything I wrote above, until we quickly and completely merit the *teshuvah*, the repentance, of Shabbat. Thank God, I began [the letter] talking about Shabbat and I am ending it on the same note. All vitality from beginning to end is the holy Shabbat. Thank God, they have already kneaded the holy *challah* for the holy Shabbat and the light of day is approaching. May the Master of Compassion and Kindness sate us in the morning with His kindness and good. "God's kindnesses never end and His compassion never ceases. They are new every morning. Great is Your faithfulness." For [God's] kindnesses are renewed every morning, as Rashi explains there. It is necessary to have faith in this every day, and particularly on Friday, which is a preparation for Shabbat which is kindness and compassion itself, the "Will of Wills" (Atika Kadisha, a reference to Keter). His kindness to us has been abundant; the truth of God stands forever!

> The words of your father, who encourages himself at all times in all the aforementioned ways and with all that is included in them in all their infinity. May the One Who does great deeds beyond calculation, miracles and wonders without number, be praised! Thus far has His compassion helped me, and His

Letter #251

kindness has not abandoned me. We trust in His Holy Name that He will never forsake us. Writing with tears in my eyes from my great pain and my great joy, and fortifying myself and striving constantly to have joy prevail, and to turn grief and sighing into happiness and joy!

Noson of Breslov

I do not need to tell you that you should read this letter to our true friends — and also to my friend Reb Itze, the son of Reb Avraham Dov. Talk to him for my sake and tell him not to distance himself. If it is difficult for him to travel here, he should at least come to Breslov at a time when I am there, God willing; and at the very least he should stay truly attached to us in his heart at all times. If you can, get together and talk with my friend whom I love as myself, the precious "fruit of the tzaddik." Talk to him alone and show him this letter. Maybe he will glean from it some hints for himself. God knows that I am not motivated by honor, God forbid. I am certainly not worthy of receiving it. It is for his own sake that I am encouraging him. For he surely knows himself that it would be of enormous benefit to him eternally, were he to meet with me at least occasionally. God, as well as his own grandfather, our master, teacher and Rebbe, of blessed memory, undoubtedly desire that he do so. From here on he will do what he deems good. There is always free choice, and barriers do not [really] exist.

The words of his true eternal friend, crying out from the good point in my heart.

Noson, as above

252

With God's help, Wednesday, Chayey Sarah, 5598, Nemirov.

My dear son.

I sent you a long letter with the post on Friday, so I will not tell you any news right now. Just be sure to let me know right away that you received my letter, and answer me regarding everything that was said there. Be certain as well to send me as much money as you can at once. I do not have even a single *prutah* in my house right now and there are many expenses. May God have mercy. My efforts [to be permitted to return to Breslov] are also causing me pain, due to my seemingly endless waiting and longing, as I wrote you (in Letter #251).

But all that I wrote you in that letter also gives me comfort amidst my suffering. For we have nothing to give us life except the holiness of Shabbat on the simplest level, and the holiness of the true tzaddik who is the "Shabbat of all the days" (Zohar III, 144b). He reveals to us and draws down upon us the holiness of Shabbat and the joy of Shabbat. And most important, on Shabbat the splendor of Israel is revealed, how God takes delight in every individual Jew — even the very worst of them — and this provides the vitality and sustenance of the entire week. Thank God, I have much in my heart to say about this too and, if God is with me, I will merit to talk about it, with God's help. Thus far has God's mercy helped me. May He never abandon or forsake me. In His Providence, God sent me the carrier of this letter. "It is good to thank God" for every single thing, good or bad, since everything is really for the best. We know absolutely nothing, for His thoughts are very deep indeed, especially now in the "End of Days." Nonetheless, God always completes the kindness that He does, and He will complete it, eternally.

The words of your father, waiting for salvation to come, as an unearned kindness.

Noson of Breslov

Greetings to all our comrades with a great love.

253

[Publisher's note: This letter was written to a Reb Y. It could be Reb Yitzchak, Reb Noson's son, but more likely it is Reb Itze of Ryrid mentioned below in Letter #254. Reb Noson begins his letter with a quote about Moses, which in Hebrew carries the acrostic of Kislev, the month that was just beginning; see Likutey Moharan II, 7.*]*

With thanks to God, before dawn, Wednesday, Rosh Chodesh Kislev. As "God saw that he [Moses] went aside to look," so may He now look at our poverty and distress in body and soul and quickly save us, 5598.

My dear, learned and illustrious friend, Reb Y., may his light shine.

I received your letter this week. I read it carefully twice over, and I know your pain. Your letter reached me just as I was about to travel here to Breslov. I said to myself, "Why answer you in writing when I will be with you under one roof and can speak to you face to face?" But I arrived here today and, out of my enormous love for you and my desire to work for your benefit, I have undertaken today, before daylight, to study your letter carefully. This is in spite of my tremendous worry and my unutterable distress over the overall situation and all its particulars. May God soon have mercy. For it was the Rebbe's command and holy desire that I give of his true good to you and to every single person, in accordance with that person's desire, his effort and with how much he toils to receive this true, eternal good. So I decided to answer you even from here, because I know that there are many things that cannot be precisely expressed in spoken language. What is more, maybe this letter will generate some hints of true awakening in the rest of our comrades who desire the point of absolute truth. You and those like you already know the essential facts. But I will tell you again — not once, not twice, but times without number.

The truth is indeed as you wrote in your letter, that, thank God, stowed away with me are true cures and Torah prescriptions — remedies, elixirs of life for every person! They are precious, awesome words of incalculable value, replete with advice and cures for the soul and the body and for eternal success for everyone. They simply cannot be described! But all these teachings are also hidden and obscured amidst a great many concealments, as a result of factors both internal and external. For there is layer upon layer of concealment, practically without limit.

If God were not helping me and you, through His awesome pathways and through the holy Rebbe's merit, to uncover, make known and illuminate [these teachings] in the hearts of those people who truly desire the cure of their souls, [it would simply be impossible to accomplish]! And this greatly encourages us. But you must know, that [each person only receives] in accordance with his yearning, his desire and his effort, i.e. how much he pushes and digs with [the words of] his mouth and with his heart to find the water within the holy wells — the wells of fresh, living water that were dug in the days of Avraham and which the Philistines stopped up and filled in with dirt. Afterward our father Yitzchak came back and redug them. He had many fights and arguments over them, because those who opposed him, then called the Philistines, quarreled with him a great deal. He finally dug and found the well of fresh, living water and named it Rechovot (see *Likutey Halakhot, Mikvaot* 1). Yet these wells are still stopped up, and since that time the tzaddikim and prophets of every generation have struggled enormously to dig them out and reveal them.

It is impossible to explain in writing even the glimmer of understanding of this that flashes in my heart. But the tzaddikim in every generation have already accomplished a great deal and they have revealed much to us since that time — particularly since the time of the receiving of the Torah which we merited through the trustworthy shepherd, our teacher Moses, may he rest in peace, and through all the tzaddikim who followed him. They all reached very high spiritual levels and they dug out the wells of fresh, living water to cure the illnesses of the souls of the Children of Israel.

I could not explain to you what took place in every generation and, in any case, there would not be enough time; but each person according to how thoroughly and how sincerely he has studied the holy books, can remotely understand all the miracles and wonders that the tzaddikim did with us in every generation. For the true tzaddik of the generation sustains the entire world during his generation until the very end. About this tzaddik it is said, "'the sun rises and the sun sets' (Ecclesiastes 1:5) —before the sun of the one set, the sun of his successor rose" (Kiddushin 72b). I have already spoken about how, before Shmuel succeeded Eli, the sun had almost set, i.e. the world was nearly devastated and the light extinguished completely. But the prophet Shmuel caused the sun to shine and sustained the world after Eli, the Cohen. So it is in every generation, and in this generation too I saw this phenomenon with my own eyes. For I, poor and destitute man that I am, "grew up among the wise men and rolled in the dust of their feet," and I knew that in our generation the light of the holy Baal Shem Tov, of sainted memory, had just about vanished. But before his sun set, the sun of our master, teacher and Rebbe, of sainted memory, rose. What can I say?! How can I express what I have in my heart about this?

Apparently though, this is all unrelated to any answer to your question and to your bitter cry. But, my son, I know your pain. I know it better than you do. The fact of the matter is that for you and those like you I really have no answer at all. But every individual, to the degree that he searches and looks for the holy wells of fresh, living water that I talked about above, will certainly find [what he needs] in my bag, poor and destitute man that I am, pursued relentlessly from every side. But since I am so persecuted, this bag of mine is full of dirt and rocks and old rags which outsiders put there to hide and cover up the gems of the Rebbe's treasury. Nonetheless, "Great waters cannot extinguish the love and rivers cannot wash it away!" All the darkness and concealment in the world cannot hide the lights of hidden treasuries of life such as these! Something of them has already been revealed in the Rebbe's holy books. But you still need to work very hard at digging after what I, the poor and destitute, have in my possession. But if you work hard you will certainly find it.

This idea is explained in the lesson (*Likutey Moharan* II, 5), "Sound the Shofar-Faith" on the verse, "But, *Af*, my wisdom helped me" (Ecclesiastes 2:9); that is, my wisdom which came with effort, *af*, helped me. It does not require labors which are impossible to bear — only that you "use your mouth and heart" (Deuteronomy 30:14; see *Tzaddik* #295, #441). There is a great deal to say about this too, but it needs to be finished in person. And for this we must work hard and break down barriers, if we are to merit to get together occasionally. At that time, may God look down and see from Heaven, and illumine my eyes and yours to speak what each one of us must say according to his level at that particular time, so that each of us may bind his heart to the good point relating to his heart at that time (as explained in *Likutey Moharan* I, 34).

My dear friend, I never would have considered taking the time to answer you right now. But I know and believe that the fact that I gave you the merit, through God's abundant compassion, of being together with us in Uman this past Rosh HaShanah aroused my heart's love for you both at Rosh HaShanah in Uman and now as well. Thank God, after all my thoughts of confusion and doubt, as I yearned to truly help you (and it seemed to me many times that God forbid, God forbid, all my effort was for naught), I nonetheless fortified myself with the Rebbe's amazing pathways, and worked at this as he wished. Now I look on in wonder as I see that a number of individuals, as a result of my talking to them throughout the year, came [to Uman] for Rosh HaShanah. And you were among them! So I said to myself, "It is worth spending an hour writing you these words. Perhaps I will be able to awaken you." The main thing is for *you* to believe in yourself, at least the way I believe in you, that you can still begin from the present!

I do not have time to go on any longer. Daylight is already here, so this will have to suffice. God's kindness spans the whole day. "God's kindnesses never end and His compassion never ceases. They are renewed every morning." May all these kindnesses shine upon me and upon you, until we merit to truly return to Him, and to spend our days talking about the wonders that God has done with us in our generation, to give life to us today. God's thoughts are from generation to generation. I close.

254

With God's help, Monday night, Shmot, 5598, Nemirov.

Greetings to my dear, beloved son, the learned and distinguished Reb Yitzchak, may his light shine, along with all his lovely children, may they live for many long, good years to come. Amen. May it be His will.

Please receive the letter enclosed here to Reb Itze from Ryrid and send it to Akerman at the address which you know. Make certain to write it in such a way that it will be delivered directly

Letter #254

into his hands and not fall into the possession of outsiders. Although I did not write any secrets there, it is best that it reach him directly. Try to send him this letter at once, as it will greatly encourage him. You know how my letters encourage people, particularly people in places as far away as where he is situated. At the moment I do not know what to write to you, and I have not seen a letter from you since the day you left here.

Thank God, I had seven guests from Breslov with me last Shabbat and among them was Reb Simchah, the son-in-law of the Rav [Reb Aharon, the Rav of Breslov]. Thank God, I spoke many words of truth and the wonders of God, through His amazing salvation. His lovingkindness to me has been abundant, and the truth of God is forever! I am presently preparing to travel to Breslov, but there are many obstacles. As it appears, I will not leave until after this coming Shabbat. May God in His compassion help me to quickly receive a year's entrance visa as I wish. Salvation is in God's hands.

I spoke last Shabbat about how necessary it is to ask God every day to direct us with His good counsel. A person in This World requires very deep advice every day if he is to escape what he must, and grab whatever true, enduring good he can every day. Advice is needed mainly in This World, which is called "the feet." Advice itself is likewise referred to as the "feet," as is in the verse (Exodus 11:8), "the entire people which is *at your feet*" [who follow your advice; Rashi]. I also spoke a lot about what is alluded to in the chapter, "And Yaakov called to his sons" (Genesis 49:1). I talked about the fact that he blessed them with the power and strength of various animals, for instance, the power of a lion, a bull or a wolf. Dan he blessed, "Dan will be a snake on the road" (Genesis 49:17). For all these qualities are required if a person is to prevail in the service of God, through many kinds of advice every day.

And this applies even to the person at a low level of service. If a person does not know how to act, he must simply wait for God's salvation, when He will shine upon him true and perfect advice. At the very least, it is necessary to know that the strategies and advice accepted by the world are nothing but falsehood and lies. For the pollution of the snake, as in "the snake tricked me" (Genesis 3:13), has a grip on this advice. This is the reason that King David, may he rest in peace, began the Book of Psalms, "Happy is the man who does not walk in the advice of the wicked." For there are people who are fairly righteous, and yet their advice is still "the advice of the wicked," because it has not been cleansed of the "pollution of the snake."

I already spoke a great deal about this on Shavuot a few years ago, but last Shabbat I went on to speak about it at greater length. I cannot explain it in writing in this context, but I just mentioned a few words of it to you, because I know your enormous desire to hear words of truth from me. The essential reason behind most of the world's ruined state is that they snatch up their advice too quickly, as in the verse (Job 5:13), "The rash advice of fools is quickly taken." To merit true advice one must wait a long time, as David cried out (Psalms 13:3), "How long must I take counsel in my soul?!" Similarly the verse states (Psalms 106:13), "They quickly forgot His deeds; they did not wait for His advice"; but they should have waited for God's advice in everything that happened to them.

Understand this well, and nonetheless rejoice and be happy that we are worthy at least of knowing this; that the advice and tactics of most people are good for nothing at all. If we have not yet completely attained the true advice by which we will genuinely return to God, at least we know that for this we must wait, and we must pray to God at length every day that He will establish us with good advice and guide us with His counsel, until He looks down from Heaven and sees. Right now though, through God's lovingkindness, we do know about the true advice of "the Torah's 613 pieces of advice," i.e. tzitzit, tefilin, Torah study, prayer and all the holy commandments. Let us rejoice and be happy over all the good points that we grab every day! And let us pray that in the future we will merit perfect counsel and deep advice, as in "deep waters are the counsel in a man's heart" (Proverbs 20:5), until our light will break forth as the morning and our healing will quickly spring forth.

Then the verse will be fulfilled, "He reveals profundities from out of the darkness" (Job 12:22), and we will be able to thank God in accordance with the verse, "I will thank Your Name, for You have performed wonders, advice from afar and perfectly trustworthy" (Isaiah 25:1; see *Likutey Moharan* II, 5:2). Happy are the ears that heard all this! The conclusion of what I have said is that the essential way to perfect counsel is through the holy book, as in "my adversary has had a book written" (Job 31:35, see *Likutey Moharan* I, 61:5). One must therefore be extremely careful to study this holy book every day, and there to seek and search out good, true advice. Then one will merit to study all the holy books which it is necessary to study, such as the Codes and so on. I do not have time to continue any longer.

> The words of your father, waiting to rejoice over you with God's help, when the verse will be fulfilled, "Grow wise, my son, rejoice my heart forever." Greetings to all our comrades with a great love!
>
> *Noson of Breslov*

255

With thanks to God, Monday, Bo, 5598.

The usual greetings. I am ready to make my safe journey to Uman. May God act for the sake of His mercy and direct me on paths of righteousness for His Name's sake. At the moment I have no time to write anything, because I am extremely busy. My friend, the carrier of this letter, is also extremely pressured. As you know, I already answered you beforehand with the letter I sent you before I received any from you. You already know well that all different kinds of events must inevitably overtake a person every day. You need to believe that everything is actually for the good — even all the different distractions and impediments that arise each day.

This is particularly true in these troubled times, in the "End of Days," about which it is said (Deuteronomy 4:30), "Amidst suffering, these things will find you in the 'End of Days,' and you will return to the Lord, Your God." Israel is in terrible straits, both

Letter #255

as a people and each individual Jew. We only have life through God's abundant kindness, as is written (Lamentations 3:18-23), "I said, 'My expectation and my hope in God is lost.' Remember, [God], my bitter destitution and poverty; remember how my soul is bent low. But I said to my heart, 'there is still hope.' God's kindnesses are never-ending and His compassion never ceases. They are new every morning; great is Your faithfulness." I have already spoken about this a great deal, but I still need to talk about it more. For you are still taken by surprise by everything you go through every day and you seek to live in tranquility! I too want this, but who actually has it?! Especially in these times, when "it is a time of trouble for Yaakov; but he will be saved from it." We just have to turn the grief and sighing into joy, that nonetheless we merit all the good points that we grab every day! This is my consolation amidst my destitution.

I do not have time to write any more, but my enormous love for you, along with your great desire, forced me to mention these few words of mine to you. Beyond this you already know. Study them over and over, and literally view them as new every day! Hope to God and He will save you.

> The words of your father, waiting for salvation at all times.
>
> *Noson of Breslov*

Greetings to all our comrades, with great love.

256

With thanks to God, Monday, Tetzaveh, 5598.

Mazal tov to my honored, dear and beloved son, the illustrious and learned Reb Yitzchak, may his light shine, along with all his children, may they live, especially his son, the distinguished groom, David Zvi, may he live.

Reb Eliyahu from Breslov came to me today and gave me the good news that, thank God, the match was made with our friend! If I was a little surprised that you finalized the engagement before I came, I was nonetheless delighted. For in these matters they [the Rabbis] said that it is good to act early (Kiddushin 29b-30a). So now my hands are stretched forth to God Who bestows good upon the guilty, that we will merit to carry through [the connection] completely and propitiously. May it be His will that the match will bring us all *mazal tov*, life, and peace without end. May their young ones go and spread out their branches. May they and their offspring for generations to come all do the will of their Creator, until Israel returns "as doves to their coop." Amen. May it be His will.

Time does not allow me to go on with words of truth right now. You will surely hear from my friend Reb Nachman, may his light shine, a little of what he heard on the way. We will soon be together, with God's help, for it looks as though I will be in Breslov this coming Shabbat and for Purim. May God place in my mouth words of truth that will have a good effect, causing others to constantly fortify themselves anew towards greater holiness and wisdom, and may they lead them to rouse themselves and strengthen themselves anew every moment of every day. For time flies by quickly, and if not now — when? Now we must thank God for the past and petition Him for the future. His kindness to us has been very great, and the truth of God is forever. May He continue in His compassion to bestow further amazing kindnesses, so that we will soon merit to return to Him. Then we will never be ashamed or humiliated, nor will we stumble, forever and ever. Salvation is in God's hands.

The words of your father, praying for you and waiting for salvation at all times.

Noson of Breslov

Greetings to all of our comrades with great love.

257

With thanks to God, Tuesday, Tetzaveh, 5598, Nemirov.

Warm greetings to my learned and distinguished friend, my dear son, Reb Yitzchak, may he live.

Reb Eliyahu from Breslov, who acted as *shadkhan* for you, was here yesterday and he told me the good news about the engagement. I wrote you a letter of congratulations which I sent through him. You have certainly received it. If he has not sent it yet, I have told the carrier of this letter, Reb Shmuel from Breslov, who was the messenger who brought me your letter, to be sure that he sends it through your messenger. So if the letter is still in Breslov, I now repeat my blessing. May God command His blessing to rest upon you and may the connection be an auspicious one for good life and for peace for you and for all of us. May the young ones go forth and may they flourish with the splendor of an olive tree. May we merit to awaken through this and to truly return to God in accordance with all that He has bestowed upon us and in accordance with His great lovingkindness. For He has not dealt with us as our sins would have dictated. His kindness to us has been abundant, and the truth of God is forever!

Concerning the fact that you went ahead and concluded the engagement without my knowledge — I already wrote you there [in the other letter] that from what Reb Eliyahu said, you really had no choice in the matter. This was also the hand of God and it is all certainly for the best. God's deeds are great, and His thoughts are very deep. May the Master of Compassion Who has bestowed such good upon me thus far "never abandon me, even when I am old and gray; until I proclaim Your strength to the generation, and Your might to all who are to come." May God finish everything well for us. It appears that we will soon be getting together through God's salvation, so I will not go on writing now. Besides, I am also busy with the marriage of my stepson, Shmelke, may he live. In fact the messenger who brought your letter came specifically to take care of matters regarding this wedding and I must give him the resplies that he needs right away, so I cannot go on writing to you any more.

> The words of your father, who sees God's wonders and enormous kindness constantly, and who is always waiting for complete salvation.
>
> *Noson of Breslov*

Letter #258

Greetings to all our comrades with a great love.

258

[Publisher's note: This letter refers to the beginning of the fall of Reb Noson's opponents in Breslov.]

With thanks to God, Sunday, Purim, 5598, Breslov.

Happiness and rejoicing for the Jews! And among them my honored son and dear friend, the learned Reb Yitzchak, may he live, along with all his children.

I received your letter just now after the completion of the Megillah reading and I was really delighted. I already wrote you that I received your letter that you sent through a messenger. Your first letter I have yet to receive. You should now know that God is constantly bringing forth new things! Last Friday night your son's father-in-law-to-be had a son and, God willing, the child will enter the Covenant next Shabbat. He therefore came to me requesting and urging me to postpone the *tenaim* [engagement ceremony] until that same Shabbat in order to ease the [financial] burden that the provision of two large meals would cause him. I agreed. I also have my own reasons for feeling that it is better this way anyway, as I will explain to you later. Therefore do not come with your family tomorrow. Rather, God willing, you should just come yourself without delay tomorrow. You can stay here a few hours or a day and afterwards, if you want, you can return home. Then on Friday you should come with your whole family for Shabbat; and Saturday night we will have the engagement celebration together with the celebration meal for the Brit Milah. May God finish everything well. Let us celebrate and rejoice over His salvation!

Now, my son, I will tell you and all our comrades the most amazing news. Last night, after we rejoiced as was fitting (and, thank God, I also danced a great deal on Shabbat day and last night), I went to bed after midnight, but could not sleep. About three hours after midnight a man [named Shneur] who, it is well known, had slandered me to the [non-Jewish] authorities, came to my house. He was weeping profusely, kneeling, bowing down and prostrating himself. At first he sent his teacher to me, our friend Reb Yitzchak HaCohen, the son of Reb Yudel, who got me up and told me that this man was already downstairs and was crying before the *tzaddeket* Adil, may she live. The man's wife had grown extremely weak, to the point of death and, as it turned out, she passed away at that very hour. Then he and his teenage son came up to my upper room. As soon as he entered he fell at my feet and began kissing them with such force that I can still feel it in my feet. He did this many, many times, falling at my feet and kissing them a great deal. Crying, he requested forgiveness from me with tears rolling down his cheeks and saying, "I have sinned! I was responsible for all the informing! What can I do! Forgive me!" He gave me two silver rubles as a redemption and cried that he had no more to give. He promised that if he could rectify the damage he had done, he would certainly do so, and that he would work for my benefit with all his might. He said that I can even come here [to Breslov] today. It is impossible to describe everything.

Come and see the works of God! So may all the *mitnagdim* merit to appease me to their eternal benefit! The ways of God are very, very pleasant indeed! How great are God's deeds; His thoughts are very deep! Rejoice, my brothers and friends, over God's salvation! Thus far has His compassion and kindness helped us. May He continue to show us His kindness many, many times over and to grant us His salvation — all through the power of the holy elder, the greatest of all kindnesses! Rejoice in God and in His holy tzaddikim; especially now, on Purim, the time of joy for everyone! Purim is here! Purim is here! I do not have time to continue. I have not yet begun to fulfill the mitzvah of getting drunk on Purim. May I perform it properly and rejoice as I should, until we merit to fulfill "they upheld and accepted" anew in our days!

Noson of Breslov

259

With thanks to God, Sunday, Tzav, 5598, Nemirov.

Greetings to my dear, learned son, Reb Yitzchak, may his light shine.

I arrived home safely on Thursday night from Vinnitsa and Brahilov. I did not speak at all with your in-law, as I left Breslov before he reached home. Regarding the gift for your son, may he live: if he gives it, he gives it; and if not, do not be upset about it in the least. I have already said many times that there is no good in This World that is not mixed with some pain or deficiency. This is the reason that the world is full of so much suffering, grief and want for every person at all times, every moment of every hour of every single day. It is only that the troubles vary radically from person to person. They change drastically for each individual, at various times, from one day to the next and from one period [of time] to another. It is all included in what Kohelet wrote (Ecclesiastes 3:1-9), "For every thing there is a season," and he enumerated twenty-eight seasons — fourteen good and fourteen bad. Then he concluded, "What advantage does the toiler gain for all his labor?" There is no solution but to flee to the toil of Torah.

If I have already spoken about this a great deal, it is nonetheless necessary to repeat it daily. The vicissitudes that come upon every person, down to the smallest details of his life, are many indeed. You see for yourself! A quarter of a year ago it never occurred to you that your son might be receiving beautiful gifts for Pesach! He did not have a new hat either! But now God has helped you and he has become engaged, which certainly constitutes a great salvation for you. How many parents are waiting to have their children engaged! How much incalculable anxiety and yearning do people have over this! But after God has helped you attain this, and after your son has already received the beautiful gift of the hat, now you are waiting expectantly for [more] beautiful presents?! Even if you were not particular about this yourself, you still yearn for it because of what your wife and your son want, and because of other people's respect. If he sends you a present though, then you will need to think about sending him at least some small present in return, and this would also be difficult for you right now.

See now, understand and grow wise: there is nowhere to

flee but to God and the Torah. The main thing is to talk to God about everything. For when a person does this, even someone who has sunk to wherever he has, he can still bind everything, even the most mundane matters, to God. He can think at every moment about what each thing will mean in the end. Our days are like a passing shadow. Not long ago, in the days of my youth, they also sent me engagement gifts. But my youth has passed in the wink of an eye and all that has happened to me during my life has passed. In the same way, the time of everyone in the world will pass like the wink of an eye, and nothing will remain except what each person grabbed for himself for the eternal goal. "Vanity of vanities, says Kohelet, vanity of vanities. All is vanity." Now, my son, be happy that at least we are able to talk about this and to incline our will toward the eternal goal; and especially be happy that we rely every moment, at all times, on the great power of the holy elder! This is our consolation! This is our salvation! This is our hope and our joy forever and ever! *Ashreinu!* Happy are we!

> The words of your father, waiting for salvation.
> May God help us to rejoice appropriately in the joy
> of the approaching holy festival. Let us be happy
> and rejoice in His salvation!
>
> *Noson of Breslov*

Greetings to all our comrades with a great and mighty love! Pay very, very close attention to these words of mine. This is no irrelevant point — it is your life forever! Be sure to send me a letter through the deliverer of this letter and extend my greetings to my dear, distinguished friend, "fruit of the tzaddik," [Reb Nachman Chayales, Rebbe Nachman's grandson,] may his light shine. Tell him that he should hear from Reb David the delights and delicacies that fill his uncle's office [a reference to some government office]. Still Reb David does not even know one thousandth of what is happening there. This too ought to serve as a lesson for him to return to the ways of his holy, awesome ancestors and to think about his eternal purpose. I will simply go ahead and fulfill my obligation of reminding him each time. For I am obliged to serve his holy ancestors and to carry out their holy will, and they truly wish to draw their holy seed close to the absolute truth. Free will always exists though. May God, in His compassion, help him so that from now on at least we should merit to get together, for his benefit in This World and the Next, forever and ever. Amen. May it be His will.

Noson, as above

260

With thanks to God, Thursday night, Erev Shabbat-Tzav

I prepared the [enclosed] letter on Sunday after midday, and I intended to send it through Reb Zev from here (this refers to the preceding letter, #259). He was delayed though and did not travel then, and afterwards he set out without my knowledge. Your letter came to me through the post after I had written that letter, and then I saw the wonders of God. For when I was writing my letter I never intended to send greetings to my friend Reb Nachman and to remind him to get together with me. But by

Letter #260

the hand of God this matter occurred to me just as I was finishing. I always believe that, when something like this happens, it is always for a reason. Surely, [I thought,] Reb Nachman must have had some stirring or yearning in this direction, and this in turn awakened me to think about the matter. Afterwards, when your letter arrived with greetings from him full of love and eagerness [to see me], the news that he wishes to be here on Shabbat Chol HaMoed, was very precious to me indeed. For I saw the miraculously great power of holy desires and yearnings and how they are able to effect an awakening at a distance of many miles, even in This World; and how much greater is the effect on high, when "an arousal from below creates an arousal up above!" (Zohar I, p.235, 244). There is much to say about this and you should tell Reb Nachman what I wrote. May God fortify his heart to bring his good desire from potential to actual. God willing, when he is here, I will say to him face to face the words that God puts in my mouth for our eternal benefit.

Now, my son, fortify yourself mightily to rejoice in the joy of the approaching holy festival! May you merit to be among "all those who speak at length about the exodus from Egypt." For, thank God, we have a great deal to relate and to give thanks for regarding all the miracles and wonders that God is constantly doing for us. "In every generation each person is obligated to see himself as if he [himself] left Egypt" (Pesachim 116). And the same applies to every year, especially for us, the most persecuted of people. If God had not been with us... But we truly rely on God's great lovingkindness that He will never abandon or forsake us — not in our livelihoods, not in our flight from those who hate and persecute us for no reason and, most important, not in our wish to truly draw close to Him, so that we will never be ashamed. There is a great deal to say, but there is not enough time. The main thing is that you should be happy that you were in Uman for Rosh HaShanah on a number of occasions, and that we hope to be at Rosh HaShanah [every year, in Uman] throughout our lives. At present this is all that comforts me. My whole direction right now is to give everyone who listens to my words the merit of being at the holy burial place of our master, teacher and Rebbe, of blessed memory, at Rosh HaShanah, throughout their lives. They will undoubtedly be grateful to me forever. Let us be happy and rejoice over this forever, especially on Shabbat and Yom Tov! Let joy in God be our strength!

261

With thanks to God, Friday, Erev Shabbat-Shemini, 5598.

Greetings to my dear, learned son, Reb Yitzchak, may his light shine.

You should know that I came here to Breslov yesterday, and it appears that I will stay here until Monday or Tuesday. May God always lead me on the path of truth. On the last day of Yom Tov I received your letter of the first day of Chol HaMoed through the post, and I was delighted. I cannot write much at the moment, because it is before the Morning Prayers and I have practically nothing to write with. If the honored Reb Nachman, may his light shine, grandson of our master, teacher and Rebbe, of sainted memory, wants to come here after Shabbat, that would be wonderful. If he wishes he can travel together with me to Vinnitsa, as I am seriously considering going there. But he should hurry to get here on Sunday, or Monday at the latest. Just let me know through the merchants if he or you or any of our comrades are coming.

May God rejoice our hearts with His salvation and may we merit to welcome Shabbat in great joy, as we should. May we merit to begin learning *Pirkei Avot* anew and to feel in our hearts the loveliness of the instruction and holy practices that the tzaddikim hid there in their profoundly deep words. How many new things, both concealed and revealed, are taking place every day! How great are God's deeds and the unprecedented wonders that He performs every day! We can vaguely discern a tiny fraction of them from afar, and beyond this we have to believe what I have said on the verse, "They are new every morning; great is Your faithfulness." These words too must be new every day! Then a person will awaken himself to see God's action and handiwork which are renewed every day by miracles that are totally new! All this for lowly man, all the days that he lives upon the earth. How great are God's works! His thoughts are very deep!

The words of your father, waiting expectantly for complete salvation.

Noson of Breslov

Loving greetings to all our comrades; in particular to my dear friend, the illustrious "fruit of the tzaddik," Reb Nachman, grandson of the crown of our heads, of sainted memory, and to all his family. Greetings and abundant salvation.

262

With God's help, Sunday, Behaalotekha, 5598, Uman.

My son and beloved friend.

I received all your letters before Shavuot. On Erev Shavuot close to evening I received your letter in which you write that you should be included among the souls who are possessed with a strong desire to draw close to God. I also received a letter from you this morning. "No good desire is ever lost" and everything is written and recorded on high in one's favor. If only you had been here with us in body too! "How good and pleasant it is for brothers to sit together!" But your enormous, intense desire and yearning and your great longing are also very much to your credit. Do not be sad about the past. Just petition God for the future that through His enormous compassion I will be able to return safely to my home in Breslov. Then perhaps we will be able to get together there many times a year and speak about the miraculous truth of the Rebbe's holy, original Torah teachings which bring a person to good action, the Torah teachings which I merited [to receive] through God's consummately amazing and awesome favors! What can we give back to God?!

Right now I am extremely busy [preparing] to set off immediately on my safe journey, so I have absolutely no time. But my love for you compelled me to write you these few words. God

Letter #263

willing, when I return from my trip, I will write you more, with God's help. You will hear everything from our comrades. You will also receive the tune that was composed just now on the holy Yom Tov to the words "How good and pleasant it is for brothers to sit together!" To my mind this is one of God's amazing kindnesses, and it too is included in the Rebbe's holy teachings, as you will hear from the deliverer of this letter. I am tremendously inspired by this. "How good and pleasant it is for brothers to sit together!"

> The words of your father, waiting to rejoice over you for many long, good years in This World and the Next, forever.
>
> *Noson of Breslov*

Greetings to my friend Reb Yaakov, may his light shine. How I felt for you that you were unable to be counted among us on this holy festival, the time of the Giving of the Torah! From now on may we merit to get together frequently, so that we may merit to choose our paths wisely and to enjoy a good end eternally. Amen. May it be His will.

263

With God's help, Tuesday, Korach, 5598, Kremenchug.

Warm greetings to my beloved, learned son, Reb Yitzchak, may his light shine.

I was here for last Shabbat and I do not know myself when I will set out for home. I have no time at all right now. I am only writing you about my whereabouts and what I am doing out of my love for you and your desire for my letters. May God in His compassion lead me safely on the way of truth, both in the worldly and in the spiritual. May He guide me on paths of righteousness for the sake of His Name. There is not enough time to write you words of truth, inspiration and encouragement.

Up to here I wrote in Kremenchug, but the letter was held up for a number of reasons and was never sent from there. I stayed in Krakov last Shabbat and, thank God, we spoke much of God's wonders. Specifically, I told the story of the Fifth Day (*Rabbi Nachman's Stories*, #13, pp.398-410). How great are God's deeds! I cannot express all that is in my heart though, especially not in this context. Time is very short as the time for the Morning Prayers has arrived. I was amazed that I did not find a letter of yours when I arrived in Tcherin yesterday. Today is Wednesday, [Torah reading] Chukat, and I am sending you this letter from here. I was stunned when I got here yesterday and did not find a letter from you. I do not know what to think. May God help so that everything will be for the best and we will merit to understand His ways and the wonders and awesome deeds that He performs every hour of every day. May they provide us with hints on how to draw close to Him at all times.

I have absolutely no time to go on; indeed I considered not even sending a letter. Only your love and your strong desire forced me to write at least these few words. Rejoice, my son and all my friends, in every single good point of Jewish holiness that we have! Yesterday I went over the lesson *Azamra!* (*Likutey Moharan* I, 282) with someone and I literally saw it as if for the first time! May God allow us to apply this lesson every day, constantly. It is just incredible. These things are the hand of God! How great are God's deeds and all that He has wondrously wrought for us! What can I say?! Fortify yourselves anew with the utmost determination every day, each one [of you] wherever you may be. For all of our vitality and subsistence is drawn from each individual movement and each individual point by which we draw ourselves on each occasion away from bad in the direction of good. Every Jew, no matter what he is like, draws all his vitality and subsistence from this. In the end we will all return to God through this! I cannot elaborate on this in this context.

> The words of your father, yearning constantly for the eternal goal, for us, for our children and for all of Israel forever.
>
> Noson of Breslov

264

Warm greetings to my dear, learned son, Reb Yitzchak, may his light shine.

I arrived here in Uman just now, close to midday. Thank God, I am alive and well. I did not find the honored Reb Naftali at home as he had stepped out for a little while, and when I entered his house, I found your letter on the table. I was overjoyed! The postman is presently in a great hurry, so it is impossible for me to continue at all or to answer your question. Thank God, it seems to me that the letter which I wrote to you from

Tcherin, before I received your letter with its bitter cry, contains more than enough to give you new inspiration. Even though the words there are old, they are *really* old. For they are the words of the Ancient of days which, in the most incredible way, are fresh and new at every moment for a person who truly wants to receive them. Listen carefully, my son. Understand well what I am writing you. The lesson *Azamra!* is no insignificant matter; nor are the holy gestures which I have told you many times accompanied the Rebbe's statement that we need to apply this lesson [zealously]. Study it over and over! It is your life forever!

It appears that I will set out for home, God willing, after Shabbat. May God guide me on paths of righteousness for the sake of His Name.

The words of your father, writing hurriedly.

Noson of Breslov

265

With God's help, Wednesday, Matot-Masai, 5598, Breslov.

Greetings to my honored, dear and beloved son, my dear friend, the learned and distinguished Reb Yitzchak, may his light shine.

I arrived here last night and I am prepared to make my safe journey home today. I was just writing you now when I received your letter. I was delighted. I cannot continue right now as I am extremely busy. God willing, when we meet, we will speak together about the kindness and miracles that God has done with us, overall and in every detail. If our mouths were filled with song as the sea, [it would still be impossible to thank Him enough]. So may He continue with His kindness in just the same way. May He never ever forsake us, until we merit in this life to return to Him quickly and completely. Let it be soon! I am just too pressured and I cannot continue.

The words of your father, writing hurriedly.

Noson of Breslov

Warm greetings to all our comrades with a great love.

266

With God's help, Monday, Ekev, 5598, Nemirov.

Warm greetings to my dear son whom I love as myself, the learned and illustrious Reb Yitzchak, may he live.

You have already heard from Reb Nachman and Reb David what has been happening recently regarding my return to Breslov. I still wait longingly for God's salvation, for it appears that the affair is nearly finished, with God's help. We still need salvation and great mercy for God to bring the matter to a most favorable conclusion. It is all in God's hands. I cannot go into the details in this context and, for the time being, I am still here. Most likely I will be in Breslov next Shabbat, though I am still unsure about this.

To relate to you God's greatness and miracles — particularly the miracles and kindnesses that I see and believe are born anew every day through the most enormous and awesome wonders — would just be too much for my mouth to express or my pen to write. "If all the seas were ink and all the marshes quills; if all the people in the world were scribes and all the tongues in the world sang praises," [it would still not be enough]! And while the imagery [of this phraseology] is old and is written in the holy poetry, it is new for me every day, through God's kindness. The fact that I merit to genuinely believe this is also a result of God's miracles and kindness. And it is all because of the tiny glimmer of God's kindnesses, wonders and amazing deeds which I perceive through the awesome, original Torah teachings I merited to see and to hear from the Rebbe's holy mouth! How great are Your deeds God; Your thoughts are very deep! My sole consolation in the midst of my destitution is that I remember on each occasion how he said, "God is very great and people know absolutely nothing of it. Things are taking place in the world and people know nothing about them at all" (see *Rabbi Nachman's Wisdom* pp. 106-7, #3).

How can I express to you, my dear son, the glimmer of understanding that I have in my heart about this? To my way of thinking, all of you could inspire yourselves now with this and with all the awesome, new teachings that we saw and heard. I do not know with whom this letter will be sent, since I am sending it to my son and friend Reb Shachneh, may his light shine, in Breslov; therefore I cannot expound any further. Only because of my love for you and your desire for my letters did I write you what I did. Most likely we will soon be together and then we will speak face to face whatever God puts into our mouths. God willing, when I arrive in Breslov, I will be sure to

Letter #267

inform you about my situation. Loving greetings to all our comrades. I do not have time to write any more.

> The words of your father, with loving greetings for your learned person; praying for you, and for all of you, and waiting to see you in joy.
>
> *Noson of Breslov*

267

With God's help, Wednesday, Teitzei, 5598.

Greetings to my dear, beloved and learned son, Reb Yitzchak, may his light shine.

You are receiving a letter for Reb Yosi, the son of Reb Lipa, in Odessa. The letter is urgent, so be sure to send it right away. I am encouraging him to come [to Uman] for Rosh HaShanah; and when another soul is added to the holy gathering and the number of "houses" is thereby multiplied, it is also a great favor for all of us (*Likutey Moharan* II, 8:6). The Master of Compassion Who has so abundantly bestowed His kindness upon us by allowing us to taste awesome, original Torah teachings such as these, the likes of which have never before been heard, will finish the building that He has begun. May the number of inhabitants continue to grow until He gathers in all the stones of holiness which have spilled out into the streets. This also alludes to the damage which results from blemishing the Holy Covenant and to its rectification through this [the continual growth of the number of inhabitants], as you will understand for yourself. I am too pressured to write any more, since I want to leave today for Uman for the approaching holy and awesome Rosh Ha-Shanah.

The words of your father, waiting to see you, along with all our comrades, in Uman for Rosh Ha-Shanah. May the Master of Compassion grant that we be written and sealed for good, long lives and for peace.

Noson of Breslov

Greetings to all our comrades with a great love.

I do not need to tell you how terribly and deeply pained I am by the weakness of our friend, Reb Nachman, may his light shine. May God have compassion on him and on us and speedily send him a complete recovery. Be certain to send me a letter immediately with the first post to Uman, and let me know the good news about his condition. May you quickly give me good news! Amen. May it be His will.

I have received all your letters and they themselves contain the response to your question. At the moment I have no time to go on and write you an answer. Salvation is in God's hands. May He correct everything in His great compassion and mercy. Amen. May it be His will.

268

With God's help, Wednesday night, Tavo, 5598, Uman.

To my dear son, Reb Yitzchak, may his light shine. Peace and all good.

I saw your brief letter which was enclosed in the letter from Reb Nachman, may his light shine. You really uplifted me with the news that, thank God, Reb Nachman is beginning to recover his strength. May God finish and give him a complete recovery. I am pained though that you did not tell me about his little son. At the moment I have nothing to report to you. "It is good to thank God" that I merited to be here half-way through the month [of Elul]. Thank God, many of our comrades were here, and Reb Efraim, the son of Reb Naftali, may he live, has already come for Rosh HaShanah. I am eagerly waiting to see you alive and well, and to see all our comrades coming amidst rejoicing, so that you may gain eternal good. I am comforted in my destitution by the fact that you will certainly bear me infinite and eternal gratitude that I enabled you to have this merit, which includes everything and is impossible to describe. I am too pressured to write any more. I wrote you these words out of my love for you and because of your desire for my letters.

The words of your father, praying for you.

Noson of Breslov

Letters from 5599 (1838-9)

The year in review

The red tape which caused his exile to Nemirov, combined with the efforts of his enemies, thwarted Reb Noson's efforts during most of the previous year to obtain the required residency papers and permission to return to live in Breslov. Permission was only granted at the beginning of 5599 (October 1839), between Yom Kippur and Sukkot. Upon his return, the saga of the "Years of Oppression" ended. We have therefore included in this volume the first few letters of 5599.

269

With God's help, Erev Shabbat-Erev Yom Kippur, 5599, Breslov.

May the light of God's lovingkindness shine upon you as the light of the morning, to fortify and bring joy to your heart, my dear son and friend, to reproach those who opppose you and to strengthen your heart not to look at them all. Do not look behind you and in the course of time they will go away by themselves.

My dear, precious son! You and your friends, our comrades, who hold on to the point of truth and look every day at the eternal goal, still do not yet have the slightest inkling of what is taking place in the world, not overall, and not on the individual level, with every single person. If you knew a thousandth of it, you would be so very joyful all your days that all the thorns and thistles, which constantly oppress and trouble each one of you in his own particular way, would of their own accord, just leave you alone! What can I say?! What can I say?! His kindness to us has been abundant, and the truth of God stands forever!

Enclosed is a letter for our friend, Reb Yaakov, but it applies to you as well. Similarly, this letter [to you] also applies to him and to all who desire the real truth. The time for the Morning Prayers of Erev Yom Kippur 5599 has arrived. Now, my son, you will understand the enormity of my love for you, and my desire to do good for you and to tell you unshakable words of truth. For I have taken out time for you at so hurried an hour as this, between the mitigation of the strict judgments by the *kaparot* and the Morning Prayers; in such a rush on such a busy day, when all Israel experiences both excitement and apprehension at the approach of the fearsome and awesome day that comes but once a year. I shed tears as I write and think about your enormous pain. And my pain is thousands, indeed tens of thousands of times greater than yours. For I have to hear and to listen to all the different and varied bitter cries of each and every one of you, cries which rise up to the Heavens. In spite of all this, I rejoice and am happy over the kindness which He has bestowed upon us so very, very abundantly. Who can utter God's mighty deeds? Thank God, I constantly see God's kindnesses and wonders amidst the sweep of my pain. For the measure of good is greater.

You should know, my son, that, thank God, I have a beautiful, fine, *kosher* Cyprian [Greek] *etrog*, of the choicest kind. You should be sure to buy a new *lulav* and *hadasim* for me. May God help to effect our plea of *Selach Na*, "Please forgive!" this holy Yom Kippur, so that we may merit a good and holy Chanukah, which is the concept of the dedication of the Holy Temple. May we draw holy understanding upon ourselves, so that we will know at every moment at all times that the Lord is God! And may we banish the spirit of foolishness from our midst, by drawing His Godliness upon us no matter what, at all times. The whole world is full of His glory and His Rulership extends to all places!

If I have done nothing but inform you that a person must never, ever despair, it would be enough. You should know that this is the real truth for every person in every time; and if the whole world knew it and genuinely believed it, the world would have already attained complete rectification. Salvation is in God's hands, so that with the years everyone will know this, as well as everything else that I heard. But it is good to thank God that we know about this, and more and more and more! With what can we come before God?! "The hidden things are in the hands of the Lord, our God, and what is revealed is ours and our children's — forever" (Deuteronomy 29:28). I have a great deal to say about this now through God's salvation, but it is impossible to relate it in this context. Besides, there is no time. With God's help, there will be another opportunity.

The words of your father, praying for you, and for all of you.

Noson of Breslov

Greetings to all our comrades with a great love; in particular to my friend, Reb Nachman, may his light shine, from Heissen. I am greatly pained by his sufferings. May God in His kindness sweeten and nullify all the strict judgments from him and from all Israel. Amen. May it be His will.

270

With God's help, Erev Shabbat-Erev Yom Kippur, 5599, Breslov.

A good, long life and peace to my dear, learned and distinguished friend, Reb Yaakov, may his light shine. May God bestow good upon him and his family, and seal them for good in This World and the Next, eternally. Amen. May it be His will.

I received your letter yesterday shortly after my arrival home from Uman, and I read it very closely. While I am greatly pained by your sadness, which is extremely harmful both physically and spiritually, I nonetheless thank God that up to now His compassion has helped us beyond all calculation. It is also one of His wondrous, enormous exhibitions of compassion that at least you are crying out over the pain of your sadness. It is not possible for me to answer you properly right now, because it is close to the Morning Prayers. It is a great kindness from above that I am writing you these words now. Perhaps you will seriously try to carry out the words of our master, teacher and Rebbe to turn all the grief and sighing into joy, about which I have already spoken with you a great deal (see *Likutey Moharan* II, 23).

But there is still a tremendous amount to be said, if you are to genuinely understand how to fulfill this: to fortify yourself to turn everything into joy with the fact that His kindness to us has been so great that we know the real truth! And this truth is that nothing will remain of a person but the few good points that he grabs from This World; This World which passes in the wink of an eye and which is full of toil, pain, grief and bitterness of innumerable kinds and varieties for every person. There is no life except for the relief that God in His compassion gives us within the suffering — and He helps us constantly every day to grab good points of Torah [study], and commandments which every Jew merits to fulfill every day. The truth is that all the people in the world are only alive because of this, but most of them do not understand about their lives and suffer pain over a world which is not theirs. They never think to encourage themselves with the true, eternal good that God allows them in the midst of their bitter toil.

Letter #270

What can we give back to God for all the good He has bestowed upon us, that we merited to know a little about life — that there is no good or vitality except Torah, prayer and good deeds! If indeed we know that we do not fulfill our obligations, and not even a half, a third or a quarter of them — would that we only refrain from doing wrong, God forbid! — nonetheless, He provided us with the treatment in advance, to strengthen us, fortify us and give us life through our good points in the way that I just mentioned! While I have already spoken about this a great deal, you still need me to tell you to review it a thousand times every single day! For these words are our life and the length of our days, for us and for our descendants in This World and the Next forever.

As regards the fright you are experiencing over your efforts — fortify yourself mightily and put you trust in God. As He has helped you thus far, so He will finish for you and rescue you. Your enemies will see and be ashamed, and you will celebrate and rejoice over God's salvation and miraculous kindnesses! Just strengthen yourself determinedly to walk on the path of truth that the Rebbe taught us, to set aside some time every day to express yourself frankly to God and afterwards to fortify yourself with all your strength to be happy all day. Study a lot every day and pray with concentration. Force all your thoughts into the words of the prayers your mouth is pronouncing before the Searcher of Hearts, and bind your thoughts to what you are saying with a mighty, tight bond so that you think about the meaning of the words as you say them. While I know how much the Evil One arrays himself against this, you will at least grab a small part of the prayers through the effort that you expend in carrying out these words. In addition, the effort itself which a person expends in order to concentrate on his prayers, even if he does not succeed, is very valuable. These attempts are made into sacrificial offerings, as in "for You we are killed all day long," as explained in the Rebbe's holy books (*Likutey Moharan* II, 46; *Rabbi Nachman's Wisdom* #12).

Due to the demands of Erev Yom Kippur it is impossible to expound further. But out of my great love for you I snatched the time for your sake to write you my words which can strengthen you very much. God will conclude the seal [of our fate on Yom Kippur] for true life, for us and all Israel. Amen. May it be His will.

The words of your true, eternal friend.

Noson of Breslov

[Editor's note: This will serve as a record that after this Yom Kippur, salvation arrived in the form of an order from the governor allowing our master and teacher (Reb Noson) of blessed memory, to return to the city of Breslov. "It is good to give thanks to God."]

Appendix A

Biographical sketches

Biographical sketches

To enable the reader to keep track of the many people mentioned in this work, we provide short biographical sketches of those who played a more prominent role in the life of Reb Noson.

Details of the life of Rebbe Nachman can be found in *Until The Mashiach, The Life of Rebbe Nachman*, by Rabbi Aryeh Kaplan. A short sketch is also available in *Rabbi Nachman's Wisdom*, Appendix A, and in *Crossing the Narrow Bridge*, Appendix C. Full details of Reb Noson's life can be found in *Through Fire and Water, The Life of Reb Noson of Breslov*, by Chaim Kramer. A short description is provided in *Eternally Yours*, Volume 1. See also "Biographical Sketches" in *Through Fire and Water*, pp.689-708.

* * *

Adil, eldest daughter of Rebbe Nachman (1787-1864). Adil was married in 1800 to Reb Yoska the son of Rabbi Avraham Ber of Chmelnik, a leading chassidic master at that time. She suffered terribly from several miscarriages and the Rebbe finally promised her children. She had a son, Reb Avraham Ber (q.v.), and a daughter, Rivkah Miriam, who married her cousin, Reb Simchah Barukh, son of Sarah (q.v.), and Reb Yitzchak Isaac. Widowed in the mid 1820s, Adil remarried in 1831 her brother-in-law, Reb Yitzchak Isaac, Sarah's widower, after Sarah's sudden passing in childbirth in Kremenchug, where she had moved. After Reb Yitzchak Isaac's sudden passing in 1833, she returned to Breslov. She was very supportive of Reb Noson. A match was proposed between Adil and the Savraner in 1827, which Reb Noson advised her against. This contributed to the fomenting of the enmity of the Savraner against Reb Noson.

Aharon b'Reb Moshe Goldstein, Rabbi, the Rav of Breslov (1775-1845). As a young man Reb Aharon was already a noted halakhic authority, and even served as a rav in Kherson, where his father was rabbi, during his father's lifetime. Rebbe Nachman said of him that he went to his *chuppah* with a "clean garment" (i.e. he was pure). Rebbe Nachman thought so highly of Reb Aharon that he invoked his ancestral merits in order that Reb Aharon should be rav in Breslov. He and Reb Naftali were chosen as the two witnesses of Rebbe Nachman's promise to save anyone who goes to his *tsion*, gives charity and recites the Ten Psalms of the *Tikkun HaKlali* (see *Rabbi Nachman's Wisdom* #141). See *Until The Mashiach*, Appendix F.

Avraham Ber b'Reb Yoske, Reb (d.1860s). Rebbe Nachman's grandson through his daughter, Adil, Reb Avraham Ber married Miriam Raitze (q.v.), Moshe Chenkes' daughter, but divorced her at the onset of the Years of Oppression. He later married the daughter of Reb Ber (q.v.), one of Rebbe Nachman's earlier followers from Tcherin. Reb Ber was very wealthy and Reb Avraham Ber entered the family business and prospered even more. (The Breslover community in the Tcherin-Kremenchug-Medvedevka triangle was quite wealthy and well-established and was very supportive of the projects initiated by Reb Noson.) Reb Avraham Ber was noted for his great piety and acts of charity.

Avraham Weinberg of Uman, Reb. A friend and follower of Reb Noson, he had a great deal of influence with the government and supported Reb Noson and the Breslover Chassidim during the Years of Oppression. His governmental influence helped protect the *kloyz* after hooligans began damaging it on Purim in 5595. His son was Reb Shmuel Weinberg of Breslov (q.v.).

Barukh Dayan (d.1838). One of Reb Noson's major opponents and slanderers during the Years of Oppression.

Barukh b'Reb Shlomo of Brahilov, Reb. Reb Noson's son-in-law (Chanah Tsirel's husband) was known as a brilliant scholar.

Ber Otkoptchik, Reb. This appears to be Reb Ber (Dov) of Tcherin, who was one of Rebbe Nachman's earliest followers, even before Reb

Noson became close to the Rebbe. After marrying in Dashev, Reb Ber returned to Medvedevka and became a disciple of the Rebbe. He later introduced Reb Yudel (q.v.) and Reb Shmuel Isaac (q.v.), who lived in Dashev, to Breslover Chassidut. After Reb Avraham Ber's (q.v.) divorce, he married Reb Ber's daughter. Reb Ber was a very successful businessman and was very supportive of Reb Noson. As immersed as he was in commerce, his awe of God was legendary. Rebbe Nachman told Reb Ber to give a *chomesh* (20%) of his income to charity (as opposed to *maaser*, 10%). Reb Ber said, "With my *chomesh*, I have nothing to fear from the Heavenly Tribunal."

Chaim Pais. His father, Avraham Pais, was among Rebbe Nachman's welcoming committee when he first came to Breslov. A partner of Moshe Chenkes, he died in 1834 intestate. The ensuing problems were a major factor behind Reb Noson's advice to Moshe Chenkes to write a will, which resulted in the violence of the Years of Oppression. Avraham Pais' son, Chaim, became a major opponent of Reb Noson and made many attempts to harm him.

Chanah Tsirel (b.1817?) was Reb Noson's only daughter. She was married around 1831 to Reb Nachman, the son of Reb Zvi Aryeh of Breslov, but divorced shortly afterwards. Her second marriage was to Reb Barukh of Brahilov. Her daughter was Esther Shaindel [Shaintzay], named after her mother. She had other children but their names are not known.

Dishel (or Dishle). Reb Noson's second wife, whom he married in November, 1826. She was the mother of Reb Noson's two youngest children, Reb Nachman and Reb Yosef Yonah. She also had two children from her first marriage: a daughter, Chanah, who married Reb Noson's son, Reb David Zvi (q.v.), and a younger son, Reb Shmuel Shmelke (q.v.).

David Zvi, Reb (b.1819?). Son of Reb Noson, Reb David Zvi, who was a hunchback, suffered immensely during his life. He married his stepsister, Chanah (Dishel's daughter) in the summer of 1835, just prior to Reb Noson's imprisonment during the Years of Oppression. Having the impoverished Reb Noson as both father and father-in-law, Reb David Zvi lived a life of poverty. His only son died as a young child and his wife died a few months later in 1844. Reb David Zvi himself passed away about ten years later.

Efraim b'Reb Naftali Weinberg, Reb (1800?-1883). Son of Reb Naftali (q.v.). Although Reb Naftali was himself one of Rebbe Nachman's closest followers and had a following in his own right, he sent Reb Efraim to study Breslover Chassidut from Reb Noson, whose close follower he became. He spent much time with him, and later wrote two books patterned after his mentor's works. The first is *Likutey Even*, following the style of *Likutey Halakhot* in explaining the Codes in the light of Rebbe Nachman's teachings. The second is *Tefilot HaBoker*, a volume of prayers based on Reb Noson's teachings. Reb Efraim was very modest and published both volumes anonymously. Reb Efraim moved to Kremenchug, where he was a successful jewelry merchant, and an even greater devotee of God. He was often found engaged in hitbodedut and crying in his booths at jewelry fairs held in various cities. He was wealthy, supported Reb Noson's projects and assisted him whenever he came to the Kremenchug area. Reb Efraim was a very close friend of Reb Noson's son, Reb Yitzchak (q.v.), and both were held in high esteem by Reb Noson.

Elki. Second wife of Moshe Chenkes (q.v.). She was the sister of the Rav of Tomoshpiel, who was a follower of Reb Moshe Zvi of Savran (q.v.). Elki's brother was remiss in his duties at the brit of Moshe Chenkes' son (c. 1819-1820), which caused a Breslover Chassid to intervene on the infant's behalf. The Rav, rather than attributing this to his incompetence, viewed it as an insult and began sowing the seeds of the Savraner's hatred towards Reb Noson and the Breslover Chassidim. As a brother to Elki, he used every opportunity to degrade and slander Reb Noson and was ultimately successful, turning Elki from a family friend of Reb Noson into a most formidable enemy. Her influence caused Moshe Chenkes to turn against Reb Noson.

Esther Shaindel. Daughter of Rabbi David Zvi Orbach (q.v.) and Reb Noson's first wife. She was born around 1781, and married Reb Noson in the summer of 1793. Mother of Reb Shachneh, Reb Yitzchak, Chanah Tsirel and Reb David Zvi, she died in September 1826.

Feivel, Reb was a follower of Reb Noson who habitually said, *"Ashreinu!"* Though ridiculed by some of his neighbors, Reb Feivel's persistence in saying *"Ashreinu!"* brought him great joy and happiness throughout his darkest moments.

Hirsh Ber was a leading *maskil* ("enlightened") who lived in Uman. He was befriended by Rebbe Nachman before the Rebbe passed away in 1810 and remained a friend to Reb Noson in the ensuing years. He knew the Czar and was very influential with the authorities. During the Years of Oppression, he offered to intervene with the authorities on Reb Noson's behalf saying, "Within 24 hours there won't be a remnant of your opponents left within the Russian borders." Reb Noson replied, "First of all, this would only exacerbate the enmity. Secondly, and foremost, my reliance is upon prayer."

Leibel, son-in-law of Reb Reuven, Reb. He was a very close follower of Reb Noson and stayed with him through the difficult Years of Oppression. Reb Leibel moved to the Holy Land some time after Reb Noson passed away and lived in Tiberias.

Miriam Raitze. Daughter of Moshe Chenkes and Elki (q.v.). Born through Reb Noson's efforts to have Moshe divorce his first (barren) wife, she later turned against Reb Noson with a fury.

Mordekhai Shpielband b'Reb Shmuel of Tulchin, Reb. The son of Reb Shmuel of Teplik (q.v.), Reb Mordekhai lived in Tulchin. He was a very dear friend of Reb Yitzchak and a close follower of Reb Noson. He introduced Reb Yaakov of Tulchin (q.v.) to Breslover Chassidut. He was tortured in Tulchin by the opponents of the Breslover Chassidim but refused to submit to them and curse Reb Noson.

Moshe Chenkes (d.1838). Moshe Chenkes lived in Sherevitz, a small village adjacent to Breslov. He was one of the trio of community

354 / *Eternally yours*

leaders who welcomed Rebbe Nachman to Breslov in 1802. Rebbe Nachman blessed him and his business ventures, and he became extremely wealthy and influential, and a close follower of the Rebbe. He had no children from his first wife and, after the Rebbe's passing, Reb Noson told him that the Rebbe had said, "If Moshe divorces, he will have children." Moshe finally agreed. His second wife, Elki (q.v.), was sister of the Rav of Tomoshpiel. They had two children. Later, the Rav of Tomoshpiel incited Elki against Reb Noson and eventually drew Moshe Chenkes into the fracas. Moshe thus turned from being a strong supporter of Reb Noson into a most formidable enemy.

Moshe Fishel Landau was a doctor and a leading *maskil* from Uman. He, like Hirsh Ber (q.v.), was befriended by Rebbe Nachman and remained a friend of Reb Noson. During the Years of Oppression he also wanted to help Reb Noson and even visited Breslov to calm down Reb Noson's opponents. As Reb Noson wrote in his letter, "Moshe Landau is a thorn in their eyes." Had Reb Noson permitted, he would have destroyed Reb Noson's enemies.

Moshe Zvi of Savran, Rabbi (1779?-1838). A disciple of both Rabbi Levi Yitzchak of Berdichov and Rabbi Borukh of Medzeboz, he served for a while as rav in Berdichov before assuming a position in Savran. As one of the few leading chassidic masters in the Ukraine in the early 19th century, his following numbered in the thousands. His opposition to the Breslover Chassidim is chronicled in our text. His wife passed away when he was forty-four years old and he never remarried. Reb Noson said that his remaining a widower was a major contributing factor to his opposition to Rebbe Nachman's teachings and the Breslover Chassidim. Interestingly, his son, Rabbi Shimon Shlomo (d.1848), befriended the Breslover Chassidim.

Nachman Chayales, b'Reb Zalman, Reb (1817?-d.1889). Rebbe Nachman's grandson, the son of the Rebbe's daughter Chayah. His father, Reb Zalman b'Reb Yaakov Yosef of Zlatipolia, died shortly after he was born, and his mother remarried. Therefore, he is known by his mother's name, Reb Nachman (the son of) Chayah's. He married the granddaughter of Rabbi Shlomo of Karlin and moved to Tulchin where he became a very close friend of Reb Yitzchak (q.v.).

Nachman, Reb. Reb Noson's fifth child, he was born in the late summer of 1827. He was married in the summer of 1844 in Lipovec. He had two children, a son, Reb Noson of Dimitrivka, who moved to Eretz Yisrael and is buried on the Mount of Olives, and a daughter, who married Reb Mordekhai Shochet of Breslov.

Nachman, Reb of Heissen. He was also known as Reb Nachman (Chazan) of Tulchin (1814-1884). Reb Nachman's grandfather was a follower of Rebbe Nachman. Born shortly after the Rebbe passed away, Reb Nachman was named after the Rebbe. Orphaned as a very young child, he grew up in his uncle's house in Heissen, where he met Reb Noson on the latter's pilgrimage to the Holy Land in 1822 (see *Through Fire and Water*, Chapter 27). Reb Noson made such a deep impression upon him that the young Nachman decided to attach himself to Reb Noson. He indeed became Reb Noson's most intimate follower, and eventually the leader of the Breslov movement. Reb Nachman was the *chazan* (prayer leader) for *mussaf* at the Breslover *kibutz* in Uman on Rosh HaShanah, and hence the family name Chazan. He prayed with such intensity that those assembled felt he was "standing on air" during the service. His great fervor was matched by his modesty. Despite the fact that he was leader of the Breslover Chassidim at that time, Reb Nachman did not consider it beneath his dignity to serve others. Immediately after praying the daily prayers with great devotion, he would take the water buckets to draw water for the synagogue.

Reb Nachman published the first volume of his mentor's *Likutey Halakhot* while Reb Noson was still alive. Later, he edited and published the remaining seven volumes. His first wife passed away not long after they married and around 1830 Reb Nachman remarried and moved to Tulchin where he lived for eighteen years. He is therefore mentioned in these letters as Reb Nachman of Heissen and in later letters will be seen as Reb Nachman of Tulchin. After Reb

Noson's passing, he moved to Breslov in order to continue Reb Noson's work. After eighteen years in Breslov, Reb Nachman moved to Uman, where he lived for another eighteen years, serving as *shamash* (attendant) of the Breslover *kloyz* there. This last move caused the focus of Breslover Chassidut as a whole to shift to Uman. Reb Nachman's son was Reb Avraham Chazan, author of the *Biur HaLikutim*, an important profound work explaining the *Likutey Moharan*.

Naftali Hertz b'Reb Yehudah Weinberg, Reb (1780-1860). Reb Noson's childhood and closest friend, he became a follower of Rebbe Nachman at the same time as Reb Noson, just before Rosh HaShanah, 1802. He and Reb Aharon the Rav (q.v.) were chosen as the two witnesses of Rebbe Nachman's promise to save anyone who goes to his *tsion*, gives charity and recites the Ten Psalms of the *Tikkun HaKlali*. Rebbe Nachman once said, "Only two people really know anything of me, Reb Noson, and Reb Naftali a little." Rebbe Nachman told Reb Naftali to say words of Torah at the Third Meal (attended by souls requiring rectification) in a private room.

Sarah, second daughter of Rebbe Nachman (1790-1831). Sorke, as she was known, was married to Reb Yitzchak Isaac, son of Reb Leib Dubrovner. Reb Leib was extremely wealthy and paid a handsome dowry. The wedding took place in Medvedevka and the couple moved to Kremenchug. Rebbe Nachman praised her greatly, alluding to her having *ruach hakodesh* (divine inspiration). Though comfortable in the monetary sense, her life was a difficult one as she suffered several illnesses during her short lifetime. She had three sons: Reb Yisrael, Reb Simchah Barukh and Reb Efraim, who was left an orphan at birth. She also had one daughter, Feiga Sashia.

Shachneh, Reb (b.1802) was Reb Noson's eldest child. He married in 1817 and was very instrumental in helping Reb Noson print the Rebbe's works in Reb Noson's "underground" press. He was the first to print the *Tikkun HaKlali* with Reb Noson's prayer. Reb Shachneh had three sons and one daughter. His sons' names were: Reb

Nachman, Reb Naftali Hertz and Reb David Zvi. His second son, Reb Naftali Hertz (1843-1903), married Devorah, the daughter of the Tcheriner Rav, and their son was Reb Avraham Sternhartz (1862-1955), a leading Breslover Chassid of recent times.

Shimshon, Reb (d.1870?). As a young man, Reb Shimshon was drawn to Breslover Chassidut. His father opposed this and sought ways to keep Reb Shimshon from going to Reb Noson. One Shabbat afternoon, his father took away Reb Shimshon's clothing. Reb Shimshon, whose heart burned with an incredible thirst for Reb Noson's teachings, found some old, torn clothing, put them on and left. When he arrived at Reb Noson's *bet midrash*, he felt embarrassed at his appearance. Reb Noson encouraged him for his self-sacrifice and said to him, "It will come to use." After Reb Shimshon passed away, he appeared in a dream to Reb Avraham Ber (q.v.) and told him that Reb Noson helped him pass through *Nahar Dinur* ("the River of Fire") and brought him into *Gan Eden*.

Reb Shimshon subsequently moved to Tulchin and became a businessman. He was a very close friend of Reb Noson's son, Reb Yitzchak (q.v.). Reb Shimshon was childless for many years and Reb Noson kept exhorting him to pray and give charity and saying he *would* have children. Eventually, Reb Shimshon had two sons: Reb Yehudah Eliezer and Reb Yisrael Mendel, and two daughters, both of whom married grandchildren of Reb Noson. One was married to Reb Michel, Reb Yitzchak's son, and the other to Reb Shachneh's son, Reb Naftali Hertz (a second marriage for him). Reb Yisrael Mendel married the Rebbe's great-granddaughter, the granddaughter of Sarah, through her son Reb Efraim.

Their child was Reb Shimshon Barski (1873-1935) who was one of the leading Breslover Chassidim in Uman during the early part of the twentieth century and who wrote the *Likutey Eitzot in Yiddish*. This important work is a commentary on the *Likutey Eitzot* that Reb Noson authored. Reb Shimshon Barski understood that the "Collected Advice" in Reb Noson's version was too concise for the coming generations. He therefore took Reb Noson's work and rewrote it in Yiddish, elaborating on most points and giving the work a deeper, yet more easily understood, approach. By writing in the vernacular, he was able to reach a much wider readership. His work was lauded by the Breslover Chassidim in Poland, where the Yiddish language publication found a very wide audience. Breslover Chassidim are fond of saying that one should never cease to pray for one's needs. One need only look at the "fruits" of Reb Shimshon's prayers to see the incredible dividends that can be attained!

Shmuel Isaac of Dashev, Reb (1765-1827). Reb Shmuel Isaac, together with his very close friend, Reb Yudel (q.v.), became a follower of Rebbe Nachman while the Rebbe lived in Medvedevka. Reb Shmuel Isaac's devotions were legendary, and he once said, "If I were to recite the *Shema* today with the same feelings as I had yesterday, I would no longer have any reason to live!" He was extremely strong physically, and Rebbe Nachman told him that during *hitbodedut* he should speak to each of his limbs in turn explaining to it the vanity of the material world. When he complained to the Rebbe that his limbs were not "listening," Rebbe Nachman said, "They will!" Eventually Reb Shmuel Isaac reached a level where, if someone so much as mentioned the lusts of this world, he felt faint. His rift with Reb Noson was the first major split among leading Breslover Chassidim but fortunately it was contained. Rebbe Nachman transmitted to Reb Shmuel Isaac the ability to rectify certain souls.

Shmuel Shmelke, Reb. Reb Noson's stepson and Dishel's son. He was orphaned very young and was only around 4 years old when his mother married Reb Noson in 1826. He was married in the winter of 1838.

Shmuel Weinberg of Breslov, Reb. A very close friend and follower of Reb Noson, he had some influence with the government and stood by Reb Noson whenever possible during the Years of Oppression. His father was Reb Avraham Weinberg of Uman (q.v.).

Shneur of Breslov. Fluent in Russian, he hosted the State Investigator and influenced his decision to banish Reb Noson from Breslov in the summer of 5595 (1835). On Purim, 5598 (1838), realizing his family's suffering was due to his deeds, he asked Reb Noson's forgiveness.

Yaakov of Tulchin, Reb. A friend of Reb Mordekhai b'Reb Shmuel (q.v.), he became a Breslover Chassid and traveled to Reb Noson. His family at first was supportive of him but later they became opponents of the Breslover Chassidim. He suffered immeasurably but persevered and remained a Breslover Chassid.

Yitzchak, Reb (1808-1871) was Reb Noson's second son. He was married at age fifteen into a family in Cherkassy, but divorced about two years later. After his second marriage, to Chanah, he lived in Tulchin (about nine miles from Breslov). Reb Yitzchak was held in high esteem in the community, and the local authorities entrusted him with the responsible position of manager of the post office (which in those days also served as a government bank). *Alim LiTerufah*, Reb Noson's collected letters, is largely made up of his letters to Reb Yitzchak. Reb Noson said, "I had no time to write all the letters I wrote to my son! They were written as a result of Reb Yitzchak's burning desire to hear words of encouragement." Reb Yitzchak wanted to move to the Holy Land, but Reb Noson told him not to do so until he was sixty years old. Reb Yitzchak moved there in the summer of 1868, when he turned sixty. He died a few years later in Safed, and is buried next to Rabbi Yosef Karo, author of the *Shulchan Arukh*. Reb Yitzchak had three children: a daughter (b.1827) and two sons, Reb David Zvi and Reb Michel. After Reb Yitzchak moved to Eretz Yisrael, his sons took over the management of the Tulchin post office. Reb Michel was known to some of the Breslover Chassidim of the past generation, who testified to his extensive knowledge of the Talmud and *Shulchan Arukh* as well as other works.

From Reb Noson's constant encouragement and exhortations, one might receive the impression that Reb Yitzchak was not a very diligent devotee to God. However, this is a wrong assumption. Reb

Yitzchak was a very great tzaddik in his own right. As most Breslover Chassidim, he always saw room for growth and tried exceedingly hard to achieve greater devotions. This was the main thrust of his letters. And, as we have seen, Reb Noson did not allow any self-recriminations. He kept up his constant admonition, knowing full well his son's ambitions and capabilities, always showing him the proper drive and restraint to attain higher levels. Because Reb Yitzchak honored and respected his father so dearly, he was extremely careful to preserve whatever letters were written to him, providing us with this masterpiece, *Alim LiTerufah*, "The Collected Letters of Reb Noson."

Yosef Yonah, Reb (1829?-1889). Reb Noson's youngest son, he was known for his simplicity and the fervor of his devotions. Reb Noson passed away before he married. Reb Yosef Yonah married his niece Esther Shaindel, daughter of his sister Chanah Tsirel (c. 1846).

Yudel of Dashev, Reb (1757?-1838). Older than Rebbe Nachman by some fifteen years, Reb Yudel was an accomplished kabbalist even before he met Rebbe Nachman. Originally from Dashev, he moved to Medvedevka after becoming the Rebbe's follower, and served there for a while as rav. Rebbe Nachman transmitted to Reb Yudel the ability to mitigate decrees through a *pidyon* (redemption). He was very close to Reb Noson, and excommunicated Reb Noson's adversaries during the Years of Oppression.

* * *

Appendix B

Rebbe Nachman's Lessons

Rebbe Nachman's Lessons

When Reb Noson wrote to his followers, he took it for granted that they were familiar with the Rebbe's teachings and made just passing references to an idea he wanted to set forth. To enable the reader to better understand Reb Noson's references, we present here a short review of those Lessons.

The Rebbe once said, "Each Lesson can be applied to the entire Bible and Oral Law (Talmud, Midrash, Zohar and the Kabbalah)" (*Rabbi Nachman's Wisdom* #201). One who is even a little familiar with Reb Noson's *Likutey Halakhot* is already aware of this! Thus, these summaries are very concise and the reader should be aware that there is far, far more to each Lesson than might appear on these pages. We have brought only those areas of discussion applicable to Reb Noson's letters.

* * *

Rabbi Nachman's Stories

Rebbe Nachman told many stories but his best known are those collected in the *Sipurey Ma'asiot*, Rabbi Nachman's Stories. In "The Seven Beggars," two young children, a boy and a girl, are lost in the forest. Each day they cry for sustenance and a different beggar brings them their needs. There are Seven Beggars: the Blind Beggar, the Deaf Beggar, the Stammerer, the Crooked Neck, the Hunchback, the Handless Beggar and the Footless Beggar. After each encounter, the children wondered how these Beggars got around (e.g. how could a Blind Beggar see?). After meeting the Seven Beggars, they leave the forest, grow up together and marry. On each day of the *sheva berakhot*, the seven days of the wedding celebrations, a different Beggar appears and explains his story: who he is, what he is and what he does.

Likutey Moharan I, 4

The sins we commit are "etched upon our bones." Confession of one's sins before a true tzaddik has the power to remove all trace of the sins and bring complete atonement and spiritual healing. Seeing the tzaddikim, giving charity to them and confessing before them, one can attain a level of *bitul*, surrender and self-transcendence, before God. Then one becomes "merged" with God, the Infinite, and can know that everything that happens to one is for the best.

Likutey Moharan I, 6

A person must seek humility. He can achieve this by remaining silent for God's sake (not because of his own inability to retort) when embarrassed, thereby minimizing his own honor, while at the same time honoring God. This brings a person to repentance. One of the reasons for this is that a person cannot immediately enter into holiness. He must be very patient and wait until he can enter the gates of holiness. Then, by repenting, one attains the level of (Ezekiel 1:26), "The Man who sits upon the throne." This "man" is alluded to in the Hebrew letter *aleph* which contains an upper point, a lower point and a center (diagonal) line. The upper point corresponds to the very great tzaddik who illumines his followers (the lower point) with perceptions of Godliness. The line represents the channel (pipeline) through which these perceptions flow. The upper and lower points correspond to very great levels of awareness of God. These levels are known as the "ascent," "there You are" — always seemingly far off and encouraging one to strive to even greater heights. Yet, at the same time, one must never fall from the lowest of levels, for "here You are." This is the level of "descent." For God is everywhere and can always be found if one but looks for Him. This is the idea of the month of Elul, the month of repentance.

Likutey Moharan I, 9

One's main life-force is attained through prayer. However, one's prayers should be with truth, absolute truth. One must always seek the truth and never let go of it, even when one's mind is clouded with extraneous thoughts. Truth is light, God's light. This truth then breaks through all the "clouds" and will illumine one's words during the prayers. Rebbe Nachman said that, "The wise and intelligent should pray his entire life that he merit to utter even one word with absolute truth before God." See below, Lesson I, 112.

Likutey Moharan I, 10

Nothing enhances God's glory as much as when people who were previously very distant from Him draw near — whether Jews who become penitents or gentiles who convert. The greater the distance from God, the more His glory must spread in order to be recognized by those so far from Him. But pride keeps the person from drawing close to the tzaddikim who can teach him how to serve God.

Likutey Moharan I, 14

God's honor is elevated when those distant from Him draw close to Him.

This can be accomplished through Torah study and humility. Then the person causes an awakening of the souls. But, in order to draw close, one must also shed one's "soiled garments," i.e. the blemishes caused by one's sins. These "soiled garments" create obstacles which further distance a person from God. When obstacles are overcome, a person begins to attain Awe of God, which rectifies his blemishes. He attains completeness, wholeness, the concept of peace.

Likutey Moharan I, 21

To attain perceptions of Godliness, one must sanctify one's Seven Candles. These are the seven apertures of the head — two eyes, two ears, two nostrils and the mouth. Then a person is ready to receive an influx of Godliness. But to attain even higher levels, one must cry out and pray in order to "give birth" to these newer, greater perceptions. It is especially propitious to cry out for these new perceptions in Elul.

Likutey Moharan I, 23

There is a countenance of holiness, of joy and life, and a countenance of idolatry, melancholy and death. One who seeks truth and faith merits joy and life. An example of this is one who is satisfied with his lot and knows that God provides for his needs through Divine Providence. He is content, joyous and appreciates life. One who doesn't have faith that God provides, tastes bitterness in all his endeavors. Even when a person is successful, his avarice is never sated. He always lusts for more and more. He is full of sadness and melancholy. This is not life, it is death. One cannot attain faith and truth except by guarding the Covenant [of Abraham, i.e. sexual purity]. Falling into the lust for money signifies that one has also fallen into other lusts and immorality. One can rectify this through the tzaddik, who always guards the Covenant. This tzaddik is likened to salt, which is also called the covenant. Salt is used both to preserve and as a condiment. Thus, were it not for the salt (the tzaddik) one could not bear the bitterness of This World. For attachment to the tzaddik brings a person to morality, guards him from avarice and brings him contentment in life.

Likutey Moharan I, 27

True peace is preceded by bitterness, which is why healing — accomplished by bringing all the body's elements into harmony — necessitates the use of bitter herbs and medicines. The bitterness necessary to heal the spiritual maladies caused by sin may be so great that the individual, weakened as he is by sins, cannot bear it. But God in His mercy knows this, and only sends the person as much bitterness as he can endure in order to be healed.

Likutey Moharan I, 30

One cannot attain perceptions of Godliness except through a series of channels which bring this great wisdom from the upper levels down to the lower ones. These "channels" are the mitzvot. The more a person performs the mitzvot, the greater is his attainment of perceptions of God. It takes a very special teacher to be able to break down these great perceptions into smaller "packages" for the student to receive. The greater the teacher, the greater his ability to do this. Thus, in Egypt, when the Jews were on a very low level, they required a teacher no less than Moses himself to enclothe a perception of God to them. Therefore, we must accept rebuke from the tzaddikim. They suffer greatly on our behalf, especially through their efforts to elevate us. This is especially so during prayers. Prayer is called *TeHiLaH*, like the word *TaHaLaH* (confusion). Our prayers are full of confusion, which disturbs the tzaddikim who work to elevate our prayers. Thus, we must accept rebuke from them.

Likutey Moharan I, 33

God can be found everywhere, even in places which seem most devoid of Godliness. The same applies to the different times we go through in life: we can find God in all situations. A person who begins to control his evil inclination is no longer deceived by outward appearances or fooled by his lower instincts. This person can always find God.

Likutey Moharan I, 34

The main "ruling power" that is found in the tzaddik is the ability to arouse a person's heart to serve God. Each person has an ever-changing "point" within himself, which is why people's moods and ideas are constantly changing. The main goal of the person should be to illumine the "point" that is applicable to him *at that moment* (for there is only the present and one should not concentrate on "what was" or "what will be"). The way to illumine this "point" is by the "three daily conversations." One should speak to God. Everything that happens to one, or whatever one desires, all one's feelings, should be put forth in the form of a prayer to God. (This practice is known as *hitbodedut* and is discussed at length in *Outpouring of the Soul, Crossing the Narrow Bridge* and *Under the Table.*) The second conversation is with one's friend. It is necessary to maintain a friendship and to converse so that each person can benefit from the other's positive points. This is dialogue, where people exchange views and, from the other's perception, can find something positive with which he too can now come closer to God. (This does not mean conceding to another just to maintain contact. It means a full exchange of views and values, where each person remains *himself* yet shares with another.) The third daily conversation is speaking to the tzaddik, personified by one's teacher or mentor, for the tzaddik reflects the "points" of all the Jews. With these three conversations, one can develop one's "own individual point" to perfection.

Likutey Moharan I, 48

Holy speech creates a "sukkah," a protective covering around a person. Unworthy speech creates a false sense of security for a person. This causes evil to ascend to power and conceals truth from the world. It also distances people from the Holy Land. Conversely, speaking words of Torah, prayer and holiness protects a person from conflict, is beneficial for children and enables one to attain the holiness of the Land of Israel.

Likutey Moharan I, 51

Falsehood is detrimental to one's sight. A single item can seem like two items when viewed from a distance, or a large object is seen as a small one. This is falsehood. But the truth is only one, denoting clarity. When one wants to merge with the "One," the One God, one must beware of falsehood and speak only truth.

Likutey Moharan I, 54

A person must guard his memory. He must never forget that there is another world beyond this one, the World to Come. As soon as he rises, he should immediately attach his mind to the future and not forget that this world is temporary. A person must also strive to increase his own knowledge and awareness of God. He can accomplish this by looking for God in his daily affairs, even in the mundane. For God can be found everywhere. But a person must realize that looking for God in the mundane can be dangerous, for he might sink into the mire of materialism. Thus, a person must seek out God to the best of his ability. One who can will make lofty rectifications according to his level. Those who cannot readily make rectifications still accomplish great *tikkunim* by some deeds and mitzvot performed daily: sleep, tzitzit, tefilin, Torah study, reciting the *Shema*, prayer and business. Forgetting the Ultimate Goal is like death. To protect one's memory from falling into this death, one must guard oneself from the "evil eye." The evil eye can be translated as jealousy, as when one casts a jealous eye upon another's success. There are other similar examples, and it is insufficient merely to guard against the evil eye. One must also guard against the power of imagination, which often leads to errors in judgment. One might *observe* another doing something but will only *imagine* the reason for it, wrongly passing judgment on the other's deed or intent. One who guards himself against speaking (or hearing) slander, will be protected from a false power of imagination. Conversely, one should use one's power of imagination to originate Torah ideas, which are predicated upon a knowledge of the Codes. If they are within the acceptable boundaries of Torah, these *chidushey Torah* (original Torah ideas) bring with them bounty. On the other hand, if they are not Torah-oriented, they stall the descent of bounty and it is more difficult to obtain a livelihood. Joy also helps maintain and guard one's memory. This is alluded to in the mitzvah of Chanukah, which is performed with oil. For oil corresponds to knowledge — knowledge of God.

Likutey Moharan I, 60

There are pathways of Torah which are inaccessible except through great wealth. To obtain this great wealth, one must attain "Length of Days," long life. This can be achieved by increasing one's knowledge of God daily. That is, every day begins with a constriction. One must face numerous obstacles before starting the day. It seems very difficult to accomplish the devotions one sets out upon when one first begins. But, as the day wears on, one begins to attain one's goals, adding and increasing one's devotion to God. Through Awe of God, one can merit to increase one's days as we read in (Proverbs 10:27), "the fear of God *adds* life," for one grows spiritually. There exist many types of false grace. Some people act falsely whether in their eating, drinking or even speaking with others. They put on an act of being charming and delightful. A person who has fallen victim to lust will be taken in and fooled by these false acts. And immorality ultimately leads to poverty, the opposite of the great wealth necessary to attain the pathways of Torah. (We can now see the necessity of Awe of God to protect oneself from sin.) To perfect Awe, one must attain awe in its three aspects: fear of God, of one's teacher (the tzaddik) and of one's parents. Then one merits wealth. Awe is revealed when barren women give birth. To cause barren women to give birth involves awakening people from their slumber. There are people who seemingly serve God, yet they are asleep. Their devotions are without full concentration and their minds are asleep. Through sleep, one cannot bring about conception or birth (see text). To awaken the people, one needs to tell stories. That is, a blind person cannot be exposed to direct light immediately after an operation to restore his sight, for fear of damaging the eyes further. He must be exposed little by little to light. So too, one who has been distant from God cannot be exposed to the direct light of Torah. This light must be garbed in stories [e.g. aggadic sections of the Talmud and the stories of the Midrash]. Those whose slumber is not very deep can be awakened with "current" stories. Those whose spiritual slumber is very deep cannot be aroused except through the "Stories of the Ancient of Days" (the long life, the exalted pathways of Torah).

In the summer of 1806, Rebbe Nachman told the first of his famous stories, "The Lost Princess." Shortly afterwards, on Rosh HaShanah of 5567 (September, 1806), he gave this Lesson which explains why he began telling stories.

Likutey Moharan I, 61

Faith in tzaddikim clarifies one's mind. Tainting one's faith in the tzaddikim blemishes the mind, causing excesses within one's thought process. When this occurs, one can never attain clear advice. There are false leaders who are called "rabbis." Nonetheless, since they cannot lead even themselves, they are certainly unworthy of being leaders in the Jewish community. Ordaining these "rabbis" causes a weakening of Jewish writings [i.e. studies] and even leads to the banishment of Jews from their dwellings. But strife against a person causes him to arouse himself to greater levels of faith. Thus, though strife has terrible implications, one can ascend through strife to greater levels of faith: in God, in the true tzaddikim and even in one's own goodness.

This lesson, given in 1807, was referring to the edict of the "Jewish Pale of Settlement." Nevertheless, it predicted the mass migrations of the Jews which took place in the last century and a half, and are still taking place today, due to the ascent of the "leaders" of the haskalah (enlightenment) in Rebbe Nachman's time.

Likutey Moharan I, 66

The letters of the Hebrew alphabet are like bodies without souls. They require "life." This "life" is contained in the vowel points. The letters, when enunciated properly, attain life and begin "moving" in the direction the vowels indicate. The "vowels" are created by one's desires; that is, a person's desires to attain a certain devotion in serving God. At present, he does not feel the "life" within this devotion, but he can attain it through perfected speech. Proper "punctuation" assists a person in his attempt to attain his goal. He can then proceed with his devotions. Thus, good desires assist him to attain his goals. However, there are barriers to be broken down first. The reason for the barriers is to test a person in order to see whether he truly desires to serve God. If he does, then he will make every attempt possible to overcome all barriers that are placed before him. The greater one's goal, the greater one's barriers, and the greater the effort required to break them down. A great deal of effort, yearning and longing are required in order to overcome the opposition and barriers to good, to Torah and mitzvot, to God. But when one does overcome these obstacles (*MeNIoT*), all the barriers that were faced are turned into pleasantness (*NeIMoT*). Thus, breaking down barriers is accomplished by enunciating one's desires and is an absolute necessity for entering the realm of holiness.

Likutey Moharan I, 75

Strife is a result of one's unpurified bloodstream (*damim*, blood in Hebrew, also connotes strife). To purify one's blood, one must speak words of holiness.

Likutey Moharan I, 84

Every day has its own good that a person must seek. But each day also arrives with a barrier to the good contained within it. One's good desires can break down these barriers so that one can attain good on a daily basis.

Likutey Moharan I, 112

This Lesson is similar in many ways to Lesson 9 mentioned above. It is explained in detail in Tsohar (Light) by Avraham Greenbaum, published by the Breslov Research Institute.

Likutey Moharan I, 122

There is an evil characteristic known as Victory. This characteristic never allows a person to admit the truth. He must always prevail in his arguments and viewpoints. Even if he sees the truth of the other side, he will never admit it. He will fight hard to prove his point.

Likutey Moharan I, 165

A person should be thankful even when bad things are happening to him. For, according to the person's sinful deeds, his punishment should be far worse than he is receiving. Thus, even in "bad," God is acting benevolently towards him.

See also above, Lesson 27.

Likutey Moharan I, 192

A word of pure truth is far greater than words of incomplete truth. Thus, the words spoken by a true tzaddik, even on the mundane, are more precious than words spoken by another tzaddik, who is not a true tzaddik. For that is a blended truth.

Likutey Moharan I, 195

There is suffering in This World. Yet, in *every* suffering, there is an "expansion." That is, a person must hope to God that the suffering will eventually cease, but even in the suffering itself, one can find some reason for relief. By examining the "not so terrible" or "it could have been worse" aspects of the suffering one is enduring, one finds salvation. This way, a person can always find God.

Likutey Moharan I, 250

All miracles are rooted in the Future Redemption, when God's Divine Providence will be revealed for all to see. Everything will then be miraculous. This is because everyone will then be filled with the Knowledge of God. Suffering now is because of a lack of this Knowledge. The crying and shedding of tears before God by a person in anguish will cause the Knowledge of God, the Divine Providence, to shine upon him even in the present.

Likutey Moharan I, 272

"Today! If you listen to His voice" (Psalms 95:7). A person should only look at the *present* day. If he sees too much, if he sees that there is so much to accomplish, he won't be able to bear the burden. But a person can always carry a burden for one day. Therefore, think only of today, of the present, of the now!

Likutey Moharan I, 282

This Lesson is known in Breslov circles as *Azamra!* (I will sing). It speaks about the importance of *always* finding good in others and of seeking one's own good points. This way, a person always has a source from which he can draw joy and happiness. A person who finds positive points within himself can always rise above the low points in his life.

This is one of Rebbe Nachman's most important and oft-quoted Lessons, and is the only one to carry an advisory for a person to remember it constantly. It is explained in detail in Azamra! *by Avraham Greenbaum, published by the Breslov Research Institute.*

Likutey Moharan II, Foreword

"Abraham was one" (Ezekiel 33:24). That is, when it came to serving God, Abraham viewed himself as an individual in the world. He did not worry about the obstacles placed before him by family, friends or opponents. He looked only towards God, to serve Him in the proper manner.

Likutey Moharan II, 2

Chanukah is a time of thanksgiving. Thanksgiving itself is the concept of the World to Come, when sin (and want) will be eradicated and there will be only praise of God and an ever-increasing knowledge of Him. Studying the Codes is a similar concept (for one reaches a conclusion as to what one must do and doubts are eradicated). Praising God and studying the Codes assist a person against suffering and are beneficial for childbirth. This is because new perceptions of Godliness are similar in concept to a birth, a new child. When a person merits to praise God properly, he merits the "three aspects of truth." His prayers are said with truth. His Torah is received from a true Torah scholar who will lead him on the correct path and to a proper match (marriage, partnerships and so on). This truth will then illumine the "four parts of speech." The four parts consist of: "Speech of charity" (words of kindness); "Speech of repentance" (to speak before God in prayer); "Speech of those close to the authorities" (to nullify evil governmental decrees and effect acts of kindness and benefit for the Jews); "Speech of leadership" (the true leaders of the Jews, e.g. Moses, David, Mashiach). One who attains perfected speech, as outlined in this Lesson, can control nature. Giving charity to support true Torah scholars is very precious because it allows them to study Torah and clarify the Codes, revealing a great measure of kindness in the world.

Likutey Moharan II, 7

Only one who has true mercy can be a leader of the Jews. Mercy is principally necessary to remove the Jews from sin, for the Jewish soul, at its root, is very distant from sin. A tzaddik who has such mercy constantly attempts to teach people about God, so that they become "people of knowledge"; otherwise, without knowledge, they are like animals who only look human. It is incumbent upon everyone to spread his knowledge in this world (knowledge that leads to a revelation of God). This applies even after a person passes away. That is, he must leave behind children and students who will continue to pass on the paths of knowledge that he revealed in order to save Jews from sin. Even just by speaking to a friend about God makes the recipient of these words a kind of student, so that every person, by speaking words of the Awe of God with his friends, can leave behind "his knowledge." Speaking to a friend about God allows the person to acquire an even greater perception of God, for it allows him to attain in This World the Exalted *Makifin* (the Transcendental Intellect) which will be revealed only in the future. This is possible for each person according to his level. There is a tzaddik, however, who attains this on the loftiest of levels. This tzaddik must comprise two areas of expertise in teaching. He must show the *darei ma'alah* (the dwellers on high: righteous and learned people, the aspect of a son, of Rabbi Eliezer) that, as much as they think they have attained, there are much higher levels of Godliness to be attained, so that they haven't even really begun to truly perceive God. On the other hand, this tzaddik must be able to show the *darei matah* (the dwellers below: those distant from God, the aspect of a student, of Rabbi Yehoshua), that God is Ever-Present, no matter where they are, no matter how low they have sunk. This tzaddik must know how to speak with each and every person and also when to remain silent. There are times when the tzaddik cannot teach openly, he can only allude to his teachings with hints — an aspect of hand signals. These hints are the pathways through which bounty is transferred to the world. When a person merits to understand these hints, he can attain such a lofty level of desire during his eating that he can ascend beyond corporeality.

We have seen that the main effort is to release Jews from sin and that each person will merit Chanukah in accordance with how much forgiveness, *Selach Na*, he effects, for Chanukah corresponds to the Holy Temple which itself corresponds to Holy Knowledge.

Likutey Moharan II, 8

Though rebuke is a very great mitzvah, not everyone is qualified to offer it. When giving rebuke, one must arouse a good "smell" in the recipient, who then awakens to serve God. This is spiritual food and strengthens the soul. Improper rebuke, on the other hand, can cause the recipient to regress further, resulting in the weakening of his soul. Rebuke requires a pure voice, a voice that corresponds to the voice which will sing the Song of the Future. Excessive eating and drinking strengthen the body and its desires, but weaken the soul. This reduces the power of smell through which one can differentiate between a good and bad odor (of rebuke). One's mind has three sections. These are likened to three curtains which can protect a person from immorality. They can help a person flee from folly, from evil desires. One must strengthen one's intellect in order to counter folly. In the main, prayer is dependent upon pure knowledge. Pure knowledge is true mercy. But a person might use his intellect to sin, thereby blemishing mercy. He might think it clever to pursue wealth and other physical desires, having compassion on the body but ruining the soul. This is not mercy or pity but cruelty. And, when one errs in this manner, the Other Side draws its nourishment from knowledge, from one's intellect, and desires to swallow one's prayers. Then a tzaddik who knows how to pray with judgment and effect mercy must pray in order to rescue the prayers which were swallowed up. The prayer gets "stuck in the throat" of the Other Side which must vomit forth all the prayers and holiness it has swallowed until then. People then recognize God and honor Him, and many become converts or penitents. This progressively enlarges the "building of holiness," creating an atmosphere of prophecy, and brings forth the Song of the Future, which will be played on a harp of Seventy-Two Strings. It brings forgiveness, great joy Above, and healing to the ill. Faith is spread out in the world, leading to the Divine Providence of the Future when all will be miraculous.

Likutey Moharan II, 23

When a person is joyous, his sorrows usually wait by the side. A person should "grab" his sorrows and bring them into his happiness, turning his anguish into joy.

Likutey Moharan II, 24

It is a very great mitzvah to be happy at all times. Joy has great healing power and can effect a cure. One should always strive for joy. There may be times when the only way to attain joy is through acts of silliness. If so, then go ahead and engage in silliness, for joy is extremely important.

Likutey Moharan II, 25

Hitbodedut, private secluded prayer, is greater than any other devotion. It is also very great to "turn Torah into prayer." That is, after studying, a person should pray to God to help him fulfill what he just studied in the best manner possible.

Likutey Moharan II, 46

The main obstacles a person faces are those of the mind; doubts, confusion and so on keep a person from his best performance. One should know, however, that God never sends an obstacle that one cannot overcome. One must be strong in one's desire for spirituality and be willing to endure hardship for it. Then the obstacles will be easily overcome.

Likutey Moharan II, 48

A person must be very stubborn in his devotions to God. That is, he must never be willing to "let it go" if he finds himself faltering. He must strengthen himself again and again and eventually he will succeed in serving God. Rebbe Nachman concluded, "A person in this world must cross a very narrow bridge. The main thing is not to be afraid!"

Likutey Moharan II, 49-54

These Lessons provide short, concise and pertinent advice about how a person's thoughts are constantly trying to overwhelm him and how he can learn to control his thoughts, just as easily as one controls a horse by the reins.

Likutey Moharan II, 61

Time is within the concept of limited knowledge. One with an expanded knowledge realizes that time is extremely short and actually doesn't even exist. For example, one can experience in a fifteen-minute dream (constricted consciousness) a lifetime of seventy years. Upon awakening (expanded consciousness), one realizes that the dream lasted only fifteen minutes. So too, when one attains Expanded Consciousness, one realizes that a lifetime of seventy years, as we measure it, is less than a moment of Eternity.

Likutey Moharan II, 62

Blemishing faith causes one to travel. But if when traveling the Jew remains attached to God, his travel is a rectification for blemished faith. Then (Genesis 43:14), "God will *give you* compassion." That is, there are difficulties that people must endure, for God knows that ultimately this will be beneficial to a person. But he must still suffer. By rectifying faith, God places the compassion in a person's hands, so that we, as human beings, will dispense compassion sympathetically.

Likutey Moharan II, 67

The true tzaddik is the beauty and grace of all Israel. He is the "head of the household" of the entire world. When his name becomes well-known, God's honor is revealed (for he reveals Godliness in the world). Whoever attaches himself to this tzaddik has his eyes "opened." He sees his shortcomings and can correct them. Conversely, when the tzaddik's name is concealed, God's honor is similarly concealed. This leads to an increase in the number of false leaders and to destructive fires. The true tzaddik is a light to his generation. False leaders are likened to a burning fire which consumes. One should rise at *chatzot* and lament over the Holy Temple. The Temple also corresponds to the beauty of the world. This will bring forth true beauty from its concealment.

Likutey Moharan II, 77

Every person has to experience some type of suffering each day. The greater one's *daat* (knowledge), the greater one's experience of suffering. Eating with holiness and fear of Heaven "sweetens" this suffering and contains it. Eating in holiness results in a person ascending to the level of a human being, as opposed to descending to the level of an animal (which also eats).

Likutey Moharan II, 78

Life is drawn from the Torah as in (Deuteronomy 30:20), "For it is your life." But no-one, not even a tzaddik or Torah scholar, can be engaged in Torah twenty-four hours a day. He has bodily needs to attend to. And what about those who are businessmen or simple people or those very distant from Torah? Or the gentile nations? From where do they draw life? The answer is from God's treasure of unearned gifts. Prior to the Revelation at Sinai, God sustained the world by His lovingkindness alone, from this treasury. This corresponds to the Concealed Torah, the Hidden Torah. The tzaddik who ascends to such a high level can draw sustenance from this treasury of unearned gifts, from the Concealed Torah that sustains the world even when the Torah is not available. Though for a moment the tzaddik engages in the mundane, he has earned reward from the treasure of unearned gifts and can draw from it "treasures" — life. The tzaddik then draws from this treasury and passes on life to those who are not engaged in Torah. The closer one draws to the tzaddik, the greater one's ability to draw from this great treasure. Thus, even one who has fallen to the lowest depths can draw life, if he attaches himself to the great tzaddik. There is always hope. But one must act with simplicity, without any sophistication whatsoever. One must seek high and low for this tzaddik in order to draw close to him. Concluding the Lesson, Rebbe Nachman said, "*Gevalt!* Never give up!"

Likutey Moharan II, 82

People experience *k'seder* and *shelo k'seder* (order and disorder) in their daily lives. Order stems from a closeness to God, disorder from a distance from God. Arrogance distances a person from God. Thus, when a person experiences disorder, he should know that it stems from his haughtiness. When things go awry, one should draw closer to God.

* * *